Informed Societies

Informed Societies

Why information literacy matters for citizenship, participation and democracy

Edited by Stéphane Goldstein

Published by Facet Publishing
c/o British Library, 96 Euston Road, London NW1 2DB
www.facetpublishing.co.uk

Facet Publishing is wholly owned by CILIP: the Library and Information Association.

British Library Cataloguing in Publication Data
A catalogue record for this book is available from the British Library.

ISBN 978–1–78330–422–6 (paperback)
ISBN 978–1–78330–391–5 (hardback)
ISBN 978–1–78330–392–2 (e-book)

First published 2020

Typeset from author's files in 11/14 Elegant Garamond and Myriad Pro by Flagholme Publishing Services
Printed and made in Great Britain by CPI Group (UK) Ltd, Croydon, CR0 4YY.

Contents

Figures and tables

Figures

Tables

Notes on the authors

Andrea Baer

Dr Andrea Baer is a Public Service Librarian at Rowan University in New Jersey (USA). At the time of writing this chapter, she was an Instructional Services Librarian at the University of West Georgia (Georgia, USA). She holds a PhD in comparative literature from the University of Washington and a Masters in Information Sciences from the University of Tennessee. Andrea's work in libraries and education is informed by her prior teaching experience in writing and literature and by her interests in writing studies, critical pedagogy and reflective practice. She is the author of *Information Literacy and Writing Studies in Conversation* (2016) and the co-editor of the book *Libraries Promoting Reflective Dialogue in Times of Political Polarization* (2019).

Jamie Barker

Dr Jamie Barker is Senior Lecturer in Sport and Exercise Psychology at Loughborough University, UK, and has an international research profile in applied (sport and performance) psychology based around intervention effectiveness (including applied research methods), group dynamics and resilience. Dr Barker has authored over 60 scholarly publications, including 45 peer-reviewed papers, 12 book chapters, and four books. His scholarly activity has been facilitated by involvement in international and national collaborative research initiatives. He has received approximately £210,000 of external funding and more than £250,000 of internal funding for PhD research. As a consultant Dr Barker has experience working in business and professional sport; for example, he has acted as a consultant for Sony Europe, Sony Mobile, Impact International, the Football Association, the England and Wales Cricket Board,

Nottinghamshire County Cricket Club and Great Britain Rowing. Dr Barker was the sport psychologist to the Great Britain Cerebral Palsy Football team at the Rio 2016 Paralympics.

John Crawford

Over the course of a long career John Crawford has specialised in library and information history and in performance measurement and evaluation in library and information services and information literacy. He has authored two books on performance measurement and evaluation in library and information services and written all but two chapters of a book on information literacy. He has authored some 100 refereed academic journal articles and other papers and conference proceedings. From 2002 onwards he specialised in information literacy and went on to direct the first national information literacy project in the British Isles, the Scottish Information Literacy Project, which was copied in Wales and influenced developments in Ireland. He was the first chair of the online community of practice The Right Information, Information Skills for a 21st Century Scotland, which succeeded it after his retirement in 2009. Since then he has been active in information literacy advocacy and also serves as chair of Leadhills Heritage Trust. He is a former trustee of CILIP: the Library and Information Association, having served as chairman of various committees. He has recently been awarded an Honorary Fellowship by CILIP.

Stéphane Goldstein

Stéphane Goldstein is Executive Director of InformAll, a research and policy consultancy that specialises in information and digital literacy and which he founded in 2015. He is an established researcher and research manager, having published reports and articles on information literacy and other themes relating to the information and data environment. He has produced material for organisations in the information world including CILIP, SCONUL and Knowledge Exchange. He is familiar particularly with qualitative research methodologies, including interviews, coding and analysis. He set up InformAll with the aim of helping to develop evidence-based awareness of the importance and relevance of information literacy, having previously worked at the Research Information Network, where he undertook and supported projects addressing open access, open science, the role of libraries in supporting research and research data management, as well as information literacy. He is an RSA Fellow, a member of CILIP: the Library and Information Association and the Advocacy and Outreach Officer on CILIP's Information Literacy Group.

Alton Grizzle

Dr Alton Grizzle is a happily married husband, father and Christian. He works at the UNESCO HQ in Paris as Programme Specialist in Communication and Information. He manages UNESCO's global actions on media and information literacy (MIL) and is a focal point on gender and media. He has written on the topic of MIL and presented at various conferences and meetings around the world. He has diverse education and experience in the fields of education, management, information systems and media and communication. He has conceptualised and spearheaded many projects and co-authored and edited books relating to MIL, gender and media, media development and communication for development. Prior to joining UNESCO, he was an educator/principal at secondary school and adult vocational training levels of the education systems in Jamaica for ten years. He holds a Diploma in secondary education from Mico University College, a BSc in Management and Economics from the University of the West Indies (UWI), an MSc in Computer-based Management Information Systems from the UWI, an MA in Media and Communication from the University of Leicester, UK, and a PhD from the Autonomous University of Barcelona – under the supervision of Professor José Manuel Perez Tornero – where he carried out research on citizens' response to MIL competencies.

Maureen Henninger

Maureen Henninger was in the forefront of research and practice in the digital environment, and specifically with the advent of the internet, published and consulted widely on digital literacy for industry, government and non-government organisations, both in Australia and internationally, and has been a guest speaker at many conferences within the information, medical, biotechnology and education professions. As an information professional she has worked with government and international organisations to deliver digital literacy and projects for the preservation of information artefacts in many Asian and Pacific countries. In her academic career, her research, curriculum and teaching has been in the field of digital literacy, and more recently, data literacy, particularly in the journalistic field, and she is currently an academic in digital information management at the University of Technology Sydney. Her longstanding interest in political science and democratic processes led to her current research and publishing that has focused broadly on the information and digital literacy requirements for accessing government information and datasets. Her current concern is with governmental mechanisms and practices that enable or constrain democratic processes and active citizenship.

Lisa Janicke Hinchliffe

Lisa Janicke Hinchliffe is Professor/Co-ordinator for Information Literacy Services and Instruction in the University Library at the University of Illinois at Urbana-Champaign and an affiliate faculty member in the University's School of Information Sciences. Lisa is the chair of the IFLA Information Literacy Section, a member of the UNESCO GAPMIL-North American Chapter Steering Committee, and served as the 2010–2011 President of the Association of College and Research Libraries (ACRL). Lisa has also served on various committees and groups in the American Library Association (ALA), Illinois Library Association, Association of Research Libraries, National Information Standards Organization and LOEX. Lisa has presented and published widely on information literacy, teaching and learning, the value of libraries, library assessment, programme evaluation, organisational innovation and scholarly communications and publishing. She is an internationally sought-after speaker and has conducted workshops and training on five continents. Lisa received the 2017 Larry Romans Mentorship Award from the Government Documents Roundtable and the Gay, Lesbian, Bisexual, and Transgender Roundtable in ALA. Lisa was the recipient of the 2015 ACRL Instruction Section (IS) Miriam Dudley Instruction Librarian Award as well as the 2009 ACRL Special Presidential Recognition Award for Information Literacy Immersion Program. Lisa received her Master of Education in Educational Psychology and Master of Library and Information Science degrees from the University of Illinois at Urbana-Champaign.

Glynnis Johnson

Glynnis Johnson is currently Principal Librarian (Commerce and the Centre for Higher Education Development) at the University of Cape Town Libraries. Previous positions held include Information Services Librarian in the Humanities Division and Information Services Librarian in the Knowledge Commons. Glynnis holds a Bachelor of Social Sciences (1996–8), Honours in Social Anthropology (1999), Postgraduate Diploma in Library and Information Studies (2011) and a Masters in Library and Information Studies cum laude (2013–16), all from the University of Cape Town. Her professional interests include knowledge, skills, competencies and competency indexes for academic librarians; professional development and training; new trends in librarianship; and undergraduate and postgraduate student experience – especially in the African context and global south context.

Bill Johnston

Bill Johnston is an Honorary Research Fellow in the School of Psychological Sciences and Health at the University of Strathclyde. Before retiring in 2010 Bill was Senior Lecturer and Assistant Director at Strathclyde's Centre for Academic Practice and Learning Enhancement. His academic interests include: information literacy; strategic academic development; the First Year Experience at university; and curriculum and course design. He has taught, researched and published, and continues to be academically active, in these areas and also in the field of lifelong learning. At an earlier stage in his career Bill was a professional librarian and worked in both public and academic library settings. He is the author of numerous refereed journal articles and the following monographs: *The First Year at University: teaching students in transition* (2010); co-author, with Anthony Anderson, of *From Information Literacy to Social Epistemology: insights from psychology* (2016); and Johnson, B., MacNeil, S. and Smyth, K., *Conceptualising the Digital University: the intersection of policy, pedagogy and practice* (2019).

Jesús Lau

A leader and spokesperson for information literacy, Dr Jesús Lau currently is a Professor at Universidad Veracruzana, the fourth largest public university in Mexico, and currently on sabbatical leave with a National Council of Science and Technology grant. He holds a Law Degree from Universidad Autónoma de Sinaloa, Mexico; a Master's Degree in Library Science from University of Denver, CO; and a PhD in Information Science from the University of Sheffield, UK. He is the author of more than 200 papers and articles and 20 monographs, including the IFLA Information Literacy Guidelines (translated into 12 languages); the IFLA InfoLit Marketing Manual, and co-author of the Mexican Info-Skills Standards for Higher Education; he is also author/researcher of UNESCO Media and Information Literacy (MIL) Global Assessment Framework, among other UNESCO MIL publications. He is the recipient of numerous awards recognising his professional contributions, such as Librarian of the Year by the Border Regional Library Association (USA); FIL-Guadalajara Librarian of the Year; IFLA Medal – Netherlands; John Cotton Dana award by the Special Libraries Association (USA); Ibero-American Education Excellence Award by EduAction Conference; INFO 2014 Award (Cuba); and the Global MIL Award by UNESCO, United Nations Alliance of Civilizations, and Global Alliance Partnerships for Media and Information Literacy, among other awards.

Stephan Lewandowsky

Professor Stephan Lewandowsky is a cognitive scientist at the University of Bristol, UK. He was an Australian Professorial Fellow from 2007 to 2012, and was awarded a Discovery Outstanding Researcher Award from the Australian Research Council in 2011. He held a Revesz Visiting Professorship at the University of Amsterdam in 2012, and received a Wolfson Research Merit Fellowship from the Royal Society upon moving to the UK in 2013. He was appointed a Fellow of the Academy of Social Science and a Fellow of the Association of Psychological Science in 2017. In 2016, he was appointed a Fellow of the Committee for Skeptical Inquiry for his commitment to science, rational inquiry and public education. His research examines people's memory, decision making, and knowledge structures, with a particular emphasis on how people update information in memory. His most recent research interests examine the potential conflict between human cognition and the physics of the global climate, which has led him into research in climate science and climate modelling. As a result of his work in climate science he was appointed Visiting Scientist at the CSIRO Oceans & Atmosphere Laboratory in Hobart, Tasmania, in August 2017. He has published more than 200 scholarly articles, chapters, and books, including numerous papers on how people respond to corrections of misinformation and what variables determine people's acceptance of scientific findings.

Zanele Majebe

Zanele Majebe is currently in the position of Junior Librarian at the University of Cape Town (UCT) Libraries (2018). She has also worked at FAMSA as a Librarian Intern (2017). Zanele holds a Bachelor of Arts Degree in Communications (University of the Western Cape 2003) and a Postgraduate Diploma in Library and Information Studies (UCT 2017). Her professional interests include bibliometrics, open access, information literacy and language literacies, especially aspects around translanguaging (pedagogy of supporting multilingualism) and facilitating multilingual instruction.

Konstantina Martzoukou

Dr Konstantina Martzoukou is Teaching Excellence Fellow and Course Leader for the MSc Information & Library Studies and MSc Information Management programme at Robert Gordon University, Aberdeen, Scotland. She is also a Senior Fellow of the Higher Education Academy in the UK. Her research work encompasses a number of interrelated areas, including information-seeking behaviour and information and digital literacy, with an emphasis on the everyday life context. Konstantina has been co-editor of *Trends in Music Information Seeking, Behavior, and Retrieval for Creativity* (IGI Global), addressing the cognitive, affective, behavioural, and contextual factors associated with human information seeking, retrieval and creativity in the context of music. Her recent research work has included an exploration of the information literacy experiences and the socio-cultural adaptation of Syrian new Scots. Konstantina is currently a member of the Editorial Advisory Committee of *Library Management Journal* and in 2017 she was editor of a special issue on 'The future role of librarians'. Since 2018, she has been Co-judge of the Librarians Information Literacy Annual Conference (LILAC) Information Literacy Award in the UK. She is a regular peer reviewer (e.g. ESRC and the Irish Research Council) and member of the Conference Programme Committee of the European Conference on Information Literacy (ECIL) and the Higher Education Advances (HEAd) conference (Valencia, Spain).

Matthew Pointon

Dr Matthew Pointon is Senior Lecturer within the Department of Computer Information Sciences at Northumbria University, UK and currently delivers a range of modules in the area of the human-computer interface (HCI) on undergraduate and postgraduate programmes. Prior to this Matthew was a programme leader for a number of degree programmes within computing, information science and creative media. Matthew has also worked as a consultant liaising with instructional designers, developing materials and implementing new pedagogies with a focus on information standards and accessibility conforming to equality and inclusion policies. As the lead academic Matthew worked with the University Enterprise team designing the HCI/UX laboratory: this lab supports enterprise and consultancy within the department and university and is used as a base to support regional industries. In 2017 Matthew completed his Professional Doctorate, which has supported his research profile. He has continued his engagement with industry and created new collaborative research opportunities within the information sciences (IS), HCI and information retrieval (IR) fields.

Gianfranco Polizzi

Gianfranco Polizzi is a PhD researcher in the Department of Media and Communications at the London School of Economics and Political Science.

His academic interests range from media literacy, citizenship and education to participation and democratic theory. Funded by the Economic and Social Research Council, Gianfranco's doctoral research looks at the intersection of digital literacy and civic and political engagement among digital experts and activists and individuals involved in politics in the UK. His interest in digital literacy encompasses a focus not only on education and the learning of how to be literate in the digital age, but also on the civic and political opportunities that digital literacy entails for citizens of all ages. In this respect, Gianfranco is interested in the phenomenon of misinformation and in the practical policy implications inherent in the promotion of digital literacy in the context of education, civic and political engagement and democracy.

Reggie Raju

Reggie Raju is the Deputy Director at the University of Cape Town Libraries. He has been in academic libraries for more than 30 years. He holds a PhD in Library and Information Science and is the author of several publications in peer-reviewed national and international journals and chapters in books. His research focus is on research librarianship with an emphasis on open access. He has also been invited to national and international forums to engage on the issue within his focus areas. He has served on the Executive of the professional body in South Africa and is currently a member of the Academic and Research Libraries Standing Committee of IFLA, co-convener of the Library Publishing special interest group, Chair of SPARC Africa and a Fellow of the Library Publishing Coalition. He is currently on the editorial management team of the *South African Journal of Libraries and Information Science* and the editorial board of the *Journal of Librarianship and Scholarly Communication*.

Martin Turner

Dr Martin Turner is Associate Professor of Psychology at Staffordshire University. Martin's work centres on the psychophysiology of stress, emotion management using cognitive-behavioural approaches (rational emotive behaviour therapy, REBT), and the transference of research to practice through consultancy. Martin is a Registered Sport and Exercise Psychologist with the British Psychological Society (BPS) Chartered and Health Care Professions Council (HCPC), a Chartered and British Association for Sport and Exercise Sciences (BASES) Accredited Sport and Exercise Scientist, a certified European Psychologist (EuroPsy) with the European Federation of Psychologists' Associations (EFPA), and an Associate Fellow of the BPS. Martin has published over 40 peer-reviewed papers, over ten book chapters and three books, frequently speaks at conferences and delivers CPD workshops in the use of REBT in performance settings. Martin has received national and international awards for his research, winning the 2013 BPS Division of Sport and Exercise Psychology (DSEP) PhD Award, and more recently the 2018 Albert Ellis Award for Research. Currently he is Chair of the BPS West Midlands Branch, and leads the Research Working Groups initiative as part of the BPS DSEP committee.

Geoff Walton

Dr Geoff Walton is Senior Lecturer in the Department of Languages, Information and Communications at Manchester Metropolitan University, UK. He is Programme Leader for the MA in Library & Information Management. Geoff has authored over 100 scholarly publications, including 16 peer-reviewed journal articles, over 50 peer-reviewed conference papers, six books and 12 book chapters. He is currently working on three funded projects: the CILIP Information Literacy Group (ILG)-funded project Information Discernment and Psychophysiological Well-Being in Response to Misinformed Stigmatisation: another CILIP ILG-funded project Investigating the Information Literacy of Scotland's Teenagers to Inform Teaching Practice: and an ERDF-funded project to create an e-learning portal for Jeff Gosling Hand-Controls, the leading UK manufacturer of adaptive engineering for domestic motor vehicles. Geoff has also recently completed a British Academy-funded project with Dr Ali Pickard and the late Professor Mark Hepworth. His main research interests are information literacy, information behaviour, technology-enhanced learning, data literacy and public libraries.

Andrew Whitworth

Dr Andrew Whitworth is Director of Teaching and Learning Strategy at the Manchester Institute of Education, University of Manchester, UK. He is the author of two monographs on information and digital literacy: *Information Obesity* (2009) and *Radical Information Literacy* (2014). A third, provisionally entitled *Information, Mapping and Power* is in preparation and due to be published by Facet Publishing in 2020. He was keynote speaker at the European Conference on Information Literacy in 2017. His research is principally concerned with how groups of learners negotiate collective information practices.

Andrew Wilkinson

Andrew Wilkinson BSc, PGDip, MSc is a PhD student at Loughborough University, UK, currently researching the subject of challenge and threat states in elite performance settings. Andrew holds a Master of Science degree in Sport and Exercise Psychology and has worked on multiple research projects concerning the topics of resilience, challenge and threat, rational emotive behaviour therapy (REBT) and information literacy. His main interests and expertise include the investigation of psychophysiological responses to stress, and the implications for performance and well-being.

Hilary Yerbury

Hilary Yerbury has a longstanding interest in the relationships between information and civil society. Her background in European social and political cultures, information management and development studies has given her a broad-based approach to the use of information in everyday decision making and in social change. She has extensive experience in working with young people on development issues, especially online, and with grassroots organisations on social impact. More recently, she has brought an information studies perspective to the exploration of human rights activism and of the role of local NGOs from small nations at risk from climate change in knowledge creation and dissemination. Her concern for the relationship between libraries and democracy has marked her professional life. After a number of years as an academic in librarianship and information studies at the University of Technology Sydney and a member of its Cosmopolitan Civil Societies Research Centre, she is now a Visiting Scholar in the School of Communication at the University of Technology Sydney.

Foreword

Lisa Janicke Hinchliffe

To say that this book is timely is an understatement.

Whether one is at the moment reflecting on Brexit, considering elections in Brazil or the USA, tracking developments related to academic freedom in Hungary, monitoring the development of censored search engines in China, to name but a few cases, one cannot but consider how information, information literacy (or lack thereof), and information technology has and continues to shape these social and political developments.

As those who study and teach information literacy, we are confronted with the dual reality that our work is urgently needed and that our past practices may not be sufficient for the kinds of challenges we are currently facing. The authors in this book have provided us with the gift of the opportunity to see our work through various lenses in order to confront the demands of contemporary global society and the context that networked technology has created for global civic engagement.

From my vantage point as the current Chair of the Information Literacy Section of the International Federation for Library Association and Institutions (IFLA), I am keenly aware of the importance of information literacy for all peoples. Information literacy enables people and communities to identify issues, make decisions, solve problems, and pursue future visions in all aspects of life. As the 2011 *IFLA Media and Information Literacy Recommendations* states:

> Media and Information Literacy is a basic human right in an increasingly digital, interdependent, and global world, and promotes greater social inclusion. It can bridge the gap between the information rich and the information poor. . . Media and Information Literacy is closely related to

Lifelong Learning. Lifelong Learning enables individuals, communities, and nations to attain their goals and to take advantage of emerging opportunities in the evolving global environment for the shared benefit of all individuals, not just a few.

This inspiring statement of the pursuit of equity and collective good continues on:

We urge governments and intergovernmental organizations as well as private institutions and organizations to pursue policies and programs that advocate for and promote Media and Information Literacy and Lifelong Learning for all. In so doing, they will provide the vital foundation for fulfilling the goals of the United Nations Millennium Declaration and the World Summit on the Information Society.

With subsequent adoption of the United Nations 2030 Agenda for Sustainable Development and its Sustainable Development Goals, the centrality and importance of media and information literacy to civic participation and engagement as well as educational attainment, equality and social justice is increasingly apparent. Individual countries cannot achieve these global goals except by working co-operatively and enabling collaborative efforts across political, social, national and sector boundaries.

In her book *Informed Learning*, Christine Bruce observed that 'we cannot learn without using information' (Bruce, 2008, viii). I would observe the parallel that we cannot participate civically and democratically without using information. But, I would also add that there is nothing inherent in information that demands it be used in pursuit of the common good. As we have seen, the digital age has brought about not a democratising of access to information and channels for communication but also the weaponisation of information in order to mislead, disrupt, oppress, and even destroy.

Information literacy practices must include not only the skills and mindsets that enable one to seek out and use information but also those that enable one to question information. This questioning must be inherently sceptical but not cynical, so that it remains in the service of discernment, reflection, enlightenment, and deliberative dialogue aimed at creating just and inclusive societies. In other words, civic engagement and democratic participation demand critical information literacy practices that enable one to interrogate how information structures, systems, and technologies encode power and privilege in order to reveal injustices which can be collectively organised around and remedied through action and policymaking.

Some have despaired of the various challenges to democracy and civic engagement that we can observe in today's contemporary world. For me, my own daily work is a source of hope and resilience. College students hunger for change in the world and tenaciously seek out and demand truth and justice of their communities. Library school students embrace their role and identity as information literacy educators and the vision of the library as fostering inclusive and equitable communities.

It is our challenge to make the potential for digital democracy a reality. The vision of what is possible sends us forth as information literacy researchers, teachers, and learners.

References

Bruce, C. (2008) *Informed Learning*, Association of College & Research Libraries.
IFLA (2011) IFLA *Media and Information Literacy Recommendations*,
    www.ifla.org/publications/ifla-media-and-information-literacy-recommendations.

Introduction

Stéphane Goldstein

This book is for anyone who cares for informed participation in society. It is for any reader, anywhere in the world, who suspects or recognises that inclusive societies function best when their members have the means, capability and confidence to make the most out of the information that they encounter on a daily basis. In this sense, it deals with the capacity of human beings to achieve genuine autonomy. The book is for individuals who feel that engaged citizenship thrives on informed, evidence-based views of the world. It is for anyone interested in reinforcing, reinvigorating and deepening democracy in the face of the dangers represented by misinformation and attempts to deceive – whatever the nature and the source of the deception. But at the same time, the book is absolutely not intended as an arcane treatise for experts, and although it is written with academic rigour, it is accessible, engaging and deliberately provocative. And whilst recognising many worries, difficulties and obstacles, it is ultimately optimistic about the ways that a well-informed citizenry can underpin healthy, lively democratic systems. Such is the gist of informed societies.

So, in the light of this, why information literacy, and how does it fit in?

It was in 1974 that Paul Zurkowski first explicitly suggested the concept of information literacy (Zurkowski, 1974). He framed this simply as the abilities to use information tools to mould information solutions that address the problems of individuals. Although this view was set out in the pre-internet age, 45 years on, the inference remains valid: information literacy is a means of helping people to address their information needs, which are as varied as the life experiences and aspirations of individuals. This variety reflects many if not all aspects of people's lives: in education, in work, in leisure, in creativity, in well-being, in addressing financial and material needs. And one further, crucial part of this variety is the relationship with an important aspect of human endeavour: people's ability to function and take part in society, to contribute to shaping its rules and conventions, to take advantage of the opportunities for participation that democracy entails and, just as significantly, to create new opportunities for engagement and participation.

The rationale for the book is therefore that information literacy is an important determinant for being an informed member of society, either as an individual or as part of a community. Moving on from Zurkowski, more recent definitions of information literacy frame the concept as a human right that helps to promote social inclusion (UNESCO/NFIL/IFLA, 2005) and as a means of empowering citizens to develop informed views and to engage fully with society (CILIP, 2018). In a world saturated with readily available information – online especially, but also in print and oral – an ability to make sense of it is vital in order to make sense more broadly about the world. Moreover, given that the quality, the reliability and the veracity of information varies hugely, information literacy is also about developing the capacity and confidence to make judgements about information, to adopt healthily critical approaches towards it, to understand its purpose, its provenance and the way that it is mediated. And on that basis, to challenge it and offer alternative narratives – on the understanding that these too are founded on rational, well-informed discourse. Encouraging and nurturing such a discerning approach to information has become particularly important, and urgent too, in the light of the dangers represented by online misinformation, disinformation, 'fake news', 'post-truth' and information behaviours that fall prey to political and commercial manipulation – these dangers are discussed throughout the book. As Lisa Janicke Hinchliffe suggests in the Foreword, the book thus has the added merit of being highly timely and topical.

However, in spite of its power as a concept, information literacy isn't widely recognised as a term outside the realms of the information professions and of information science. It is unusual for it to feature explicitly in public discourse – Barack Obama's Proclamation on information literacy, at the time when he was US President, is a relatively rare exception (White House, 2009). More often, it is the closely related concepts of digital literacy (sometimes also presented as digital skills) and media literacy that attract attention and are better recognised by policymakers, politicians and civil society. In reality, however they are termed, these different literacies overlap considerably and to some extent are used indistinguishably. Thus for instance, the UK Parliament's Interim Report on disinformation (House of Commons, 2018) carried important recommendations aimed at promoting among the public a more discerning and critical approach to online information – but the report placed this under the heading of digital literacy rather than information literacy. In its own report on tackling disinformation, the European Commission recognises the importance of developing critical thinking and good personal practices for discourse online (European Commission, 2018), and places that under the joint heading of media and information literacy (MIL) – reflecting UNESCO's global approach that also frames the issue around MIL, as described in Chapter 5 of this book. An earlier European Commission report placed the gathering, processing, understanding and critical evaluation of information in the context of digital competence (Ferrari, 2013).

We can therefore say that information literacy is subsumed into other literacies and competencies. It is implicit in public discourse, its essential characteristics are increasingly recognised. One of the purposes of this book is to highlight the societal importance of information literacy, to encourage its further recognition and give it its due place, by making reference to it very explicitly as a vital factor in the functioning of a healthy, inclusive, participatory society.

It follows that the book is in essence political. Indeed, it deliberately seeks to situate information literacy in the political realm and to demonstrate the political implications of information literacy. If politics is defined as 'the activity through which people make, preserve and amend the general rules under which they live' (Hague and Harrop, 2013), then there is a correlation with the sort of empowerment suggested by the CILIP definition outlined above. The premise of the book is based on this correlation: effective democratic participation in society – the act of politics in its broadest sense – is underpinned by people's ability to reach informed views; while the very essence of a judicious and discerning information behaviour forms part of the process through which individuals and groups can behave politically.

In charting this correlation, the book follows a narrative that starts with an examination of political theory and principles, inasmuch as these relate to information literacy. This is covered by the first two chapters, which look at concepts such as democratic theory, models of democracy, power and authority. The narrative then shifts to the interface between psychology, politics and information literacy, with two chapters delving into how information behaviour is affected respectively by intellectual empathy towards the beliefs of others, and by a propensity to believe misinformation. The following chapters move on to the more applied realm of the international and national policy environments (it being understood that relevant policies are largely the product of political will and circumstances), at the global level and in case studies in the northern and southern hemispheres. And the final chapters describe how information literacy, in very practical ways, can foster participation and engagement in four particular contexts: among young people, through the action of libraries, among vulnerable communities (as exemplified by refugees) and among older people. It should be no surprise that education – in schools, universities and elsewhere – runs as a thread throughout the narrative.

It follows that the book encompasses a variety of perspectives, addressing information literacy from multiple angles, beyond just the viewpoint of information professionals. The contributing authors thus reflect different disciplinary backgrounds, roles and countries of origin, as explained in the following paragraphs. An originality of the book is that it allows for varied voices and opinions to reflect on the societal and political importance of information literacy. The tone and styles of the chapters differ, reflecting a multiplicity of authors' positions, whether didactic, instructive, advocating, personal or reflective; but they all feed into a narrative that recognises information literacy as an engine of change and improvement.

The book starts with an examination of political and democratic theory, and how this relates to discourses on the ability of individuals to evaluate online information, and to develop reflexivity about the digital environment in which information circulates. In Chapter 1, Gianfranco Polizzi sets out the relationship between information literacy, media literacy, critical digital literacy and political literacy, and how this is important for democracy and for engagement in civic and political life – not least in the context of confronting misinformation (which is further addressed in some detail also in Chapters 4 and 8). On that basis, he examines how different theoretical models of democracy define the way that citizens participate in democratic processes – and by extension, how an ability to evaluate information may contribute to such types of participation. The relevance of different models or traditions of democracy is picked up again, albeit from more particular perspectives, in Chapter 7, which considers political philosophy and culture in South Africa; and in Chapter 9, which relates democratic models to the approaches and practices of academic and public librarians.

Whereas Chapter 1 adopts a macro approach, using the broad lens of the political-democratic framework, Andrew Whitworth's Chapter 2 is focused on micro-politics, termed as the relations of power, authority and inequality that stem from everyday language and discourse. Here, the suggestion is that discerning approaches to information can enable individuals and communities to build on their own diverse perspectives, reflecting their identities and world-views, to make informed and meaningful political judgements and thereby to counter and challenge power, authority and prevailing hegemony. So information literacy may here be seen not just as an aid to participation in society, but also as an enabler of personal and social emancipation. Later in the book, Chapter 11 builds on this view in the particular context of older members of society.

In Chapter 3, Andrea Baer develops the notion of belief and identity and sets out an approach to information literacy that stresses the significance of personal beliefs and social identity to information behaviour. In this view, information literacy is not just about achieving a perception of objectivity and neutrality regarding information: it encourages self-awareness and, on that basis, promotes critical engagement. And, crucially, it can help foster intellectual empathy, an ability to consider the viewpoints, experiences and reasoning of others and to appreciate how social identity and social difference may influence beliefs. This provides a more rounded and solid ground for democratic dialogue and civic engagement.

Further developing the psychological angle touched upon above, in Chapter 4 Stephan Lewandowsky reflects on the political and psychological consequences of the 'post-truth' world (taken up also in Chapter 9). The question here is what the cognitive sciences can contribute to addressing the highly topical and very political challenge of misinformation – an insidious problem that contributes to undermine the democratic process. There is much evidence to suggest that, once acquired, misinformation is difficult to debunk and dislodge from the minds of individuals. There are ways of countering this, and the chapter proposes that 'inoculating' or 'prebunking' people against misinformation, before it is presented, is an appropriate strategy. But such solutions are unlikely to be effective on their own, and a multidisciplinary approach – notably including technological solutions – is needed to confront the scale of the challenge. And ultimately, this needs to be associated with political mobilisation and public activism.

The next three chapters move beyond the sphere of theory, culture and human behaviour to examine the international and national public policy environments that bear on information literacy; the principles that underpin the relevant policies; and the practices that stem from such policies. In Chapter 5, Jesús Lau and Alton Grizzle consider the evolution of media and information literacy (MIL), as defined by UNESCO – which, as the UN's cultural and educational agency, is the global body that has taken the lead in this area. UNESCO sees MIL as an enhancer of human rights, and the chapter charts the ways in which over the years the agency, and a variety of global initiatives associated with it, has refined and promoted the concept of MIL; and the ways in which, over time, the concepts of information literacy and media literacy have tended to converge.

Chapters 6 and 7 then look at information literacy policy through the prism of some national case studies. In Chapter 6, John Crawford examines the broad challenges associated with scoping national information literacy activities, policies and strategies; he then describes how these challenges have been addressed through the contrasting experiences of three European countries/regions: Scotland, Wales and Francophone Belgium. The development of workable frameworks and the relationship between information literacy initiatives and other areas of public policy are notable features of these experiences, and the chapter concludes that information literacy activity and policy making are a process – and often a somewhat drawn out one – and not a single, time-limited event. Chapter 7 provides a contrasting view, with Reggie Raju, Glynnis Johnson and Zanele Majebe arguing that information literacy provides the basis for lifelong learning and therefore plays a significant role in helping to nurture a fledgling democracy in the global south. The chapter draws from experiences in South Africa and places information literacy in the context of human rights (reflecting UNESCO's view); of the government's constitutional obligation to foster an inclusive, cohesive, equitable society; and of the humanism encapsulated in South Africa – and, to an extent, in Africa more broadly – by the Ubuntu philosophy. Further context is provided by the South African school education landscape, the respective roles played by school and public libraries and the difficulties associated with the introduction of a new school curriculum. And, as the chapter points out, there are particular and severe challenges in a country that suffers from low literacy rates and the iniquitous continuing legacy of apartheid.

As suggested above, the final four chapters seek to demonstrate how information literacy can foster participation and engagement in four different contexts, each of which relates to particular communities. In Chapter 8, Geoff Walton and his colleagues explore how young people aged 16–24, mostly in school and university undergraduate settings, make judgements about the information that they encounter. The chapter recognises the importance of young people being information-savvy, not only to enable them to take part in civic, democratic society, but also for the sake of their physical and mental well-being. It addresses the levels of trust towards information (and thereby touches on some of the questions around misinformation addressed in Chapter 4); how young people make judgements about information; and, concretely, how they can be helped to develop a discerning approach to information.

In Chapter 9, Hilary Yerbury and Maureen Henninger pick on the important part that libraries and librarians have traditionally played in the provision of information to support democracy and democratic processes. But in a world where there is less concern with creating a consensus of knowledge, and where there is a shift from a regime of truth to one of 'post-truth', libraries – which tend to operate in institutional regimes of truth – face challenges in the way that they provide their offer, including their information literacy offer. The chapter explores how university libraries and public libraries serve their respective users in ways that are both similar and different, the differences being accounted for by the contrasting ways that each of these two sectors conceptualises democracy.

Chapter 10, by Konstantina Martzoukou, focuses on how the building of information capabilities contributes to support vulnerable communities. The chapter draws on work undertaken in Scotland with the integration of recently arrived refugees from Syria – individuals and families scarred by conflict. It examines their information needs, their habitual and adaptive information literacy practices and the barriers and enablers they encountered within their new socio-cultural setting. Looking at the practical implications, the chapter examines the ways in which public libraries in particular help refugees gradually build capacity for active contribution to their new host society, thereby fostering civic participation and inclusion.

And finally, in Chapter 11, Bill Johnston looks at how information literacy helps to create civic possibilities to meet the needs and issues of an ageing population. Older people have particular needs, stemming from their retirement from the workforce and related to the support structures that they draw upon in later life. But this dependency does not mean that seniors should play a passive role simply as recipients of services and retirement income – or even worse, that they should accept the prejudiced perception that they are a burden on society. They can and should counter ageist narratives by being civically engaged and active – and information literacy can play an important role in helping them to develop the sort of knowledge that is most appropriate for this stage in their lifecourse. Thus information-literate ageing and civic participation go hand in hand.

The book's broad sweep should thus provide a rounded picture of the relevance of information literacy to citizenship, participation and democracy. It is hoped, too, that the different perspectives and frames that it covers will provoke reflection on why an information-literate population is an important asset in contemporary society, across the globe. Of course, the book cannot address every single social, cultural or political circumstance in which information literacy might apply. But perhaps it will provide a basis for asking questions relating to other thematic and geographical areas, or about how the evidence base might be further developed.

Nurturing an informed society should not be regarded as a marginal issue, nor should it be treated as an endeavour of secondary importance in national and international policy environments. Whether information literacy is recognised explicitly or implicitly, awareness of its vital contribution to society needs to continue growing. This book should help in that process.

References

CILIP (2018) *CILIP Definition of Information Literacy 2018*, CILIP: the Library and Information Association, https://infolit.org.uk/ILdefinitionCILIP2018.pdf.

European Commission (2018) *A Multi-dimensional Approach to Disinformation*, report of the independent high level group on fake news and online disinformation, Directorate-General for Communication Networks, Content and Technology, https://ec.europa.eu/digital-single-market/en/news/final-report-high-level-expert-group-fake-news-and-online-disinformation.

Ferrari, A. (2013) *DIGCOMP: a framework for developing and understanding digital competence in Europe*, European Commission Joint Research Centre, http://ftp.jrc.es/EURdoc/JRC83167.pdf.

Hague, R. and Harrop, M. (2013) *Comparative Government and Politics: an introduction*, rev. edn, Macmillan Education.

House of Commons (2018) *Disinformation and 'Fake News': interim report*, Digital, Media and Sports Committee, Fifth Report of Session 2017–19, 24 July 2018, https://publications.parliament.uk/pa/cm201719/cmselect/cmcumeds/363/363.pdf.

UNESCO/NFIL/IFLA (2005) Beacons of the Information Society: the Alexandria Proclamation on Information Literacy and Lifelong Learning, High-Level Colloquium on Information Literacy and Lifelong Learning, Bibliotheca Alexandrina, Alexandria, Egypt, 6–9 November, www.ifla.org/publications/beacons-of-the-information-society-the-alexandria-proclamation-on-information-literacy.

White House (2009) Presidential Proclamation National Information Literacy Awareness Month, 1 October, https://obamawhitehouse.archives.gov/the-press-office/presidential-proclamation-national-information-literacy-awareness-month.

Zurkowski, P. G. (1974) The Information Service Environment Relationships and Priorities. Related Paper No. 5, National Commission on Libraries and Information Science, November, https://eric.ed.gov/?id=ED100391.

1

Information literacy in the digital age: why critical digital literacy matters for democracy

Gianfranco Polizzi

Introduction

There is growing concern that Western liberal democracy has been undermined over the decades by citizens' participation deficit in institutional politics and distrust of institutions and the media. More recently, in the context of Brexit and the 2016 US Presidential election, there have also been concerns about misinformation undermining citizens' engagement in civic and political life. Inasmuch as civic and political engagement is highly mediated by the internet – at least in the West (e.g. Europe and North America) – this chapter explores the relevance of information literacy to democracy by looking at its interrelation with 'critical digital literacy', approached here as a set of critical abilities, knowledge and interpretations necessary for engaging with information in the digital age. After unpacking how the internet facilitates democracy while remaining subject to structural constraints, this chapter discusses what has been achieved by media research on critical digital literacy and civic and political engagement. It then draws on political research and democratic theory to discuss how the knowledge and abilities required by citizens to engage civically and politically vary, depending on how we understand democracy.

This chapter addresses gaps within media research, political science and democratic theory. It is argued that critical digital literacy can be a useful concept for democratic practice in line with different normative models of democracy, provided it is not just reduced to the ability to evaluate information in relation to trustworthiness, bias and representation. In order to contribute to the active participation of well-informed and critically autonomous citizens in democracy in the digital age, critical digital literacy needs to include knowledge about the digital environment where information circulates. It needs to incorporate an understanding of how the internet operates socio-economically along with its potentials and constraints for democracy, politics and civic and political participation.

Information literacy and critical digital literacy

The concept of information literacy transcends traditional and digital media, as it refers to the ability to access, 'identify, locate, evaluate, organise and effectively create, use and communicate information' (Information Literacy Meeting of Experts, 2003, 1). In an age where information is highly mediated by digital media, the boundary between information literacy and terms such as media literacy is blurred (Livingstone, van Couvering and Thumim, 2008). As captured by UNESCO's adoption of media and information literacy (MIL), 'the 21st century digital environment is deeply affecting the meaning and use of media and information' (UNESCO, 2014, 1). As a result, media literacy, traditionally emphasising the critical understanding and creation of media texts, has come to be used as an umbrella term referring to a variety of literacies, including information, media, digital, multimodal and network literacies (Livingstone et al., 2013).

Digital literacy may be understood as a variant of media literacy, one that is specifically about digital media and the internet. It can be interpreted as twofold: while functional digital literacy refers to the practical skills and understanding necessary for engaging online, critical digital literacy should be approached as more than just the ability to evaluate online information. Insofar as the internet offers both opportunities and constraints for democracy and civic and political participation, critical digital literacy needs to include users' understanding of socio-economic issues underpinning how information is accessed, used and produced in the digital age (Buckingham et al., 2005; Buckingham, 2007). It needs to incorporate political economy reflections on how advertising and ownership, for instance, shape how online content is consumed and created, and with what implications. Ultimately, users should understand how using the internet has the potential to affect democracy and civic and political participation (Fry, 2014). It follows that critical digital literacy should be approached as an ensemble of critical abilities, knowledge and interpretations that are essential in the context of democratic participation and social inclusion in the digital age (Trültzsch-Wijnen, Murru and Papaionnou, 2017).

In order to address why critical digital literacy should be conceived in this way and why it matters for democracy, the next section of this chapter reflects on the potentials and constraints that the internet presents for democratic participation. A section follows on what has been achieved, and with what limitations, by media research on critical digital literacy and civic and political engagement. Within this section links are established with the literature on information literacy and librarianship. Insights from political research are then presented to elucidate how the knowledge and competences that citizens need to engage civically and politically vary on the basis of how we understand democracy. Finally, a discussion on critical digital literacy and democracy follows, showing the complexities of how the former can facilitate the latter. It is argued that a crucial dimension of citizens' knowledge and competences required to engage in democracy in the digital age needs to intersect with critical digital literacy. Relatedly, it is emphasised that the ability to evaluate online information in synergy with knowledge about the broader digital environment can benefit democracy and its different normative models. More specifically, critical digital literacy has the potential to do so by contributing to the civic and political engagement of informed, critically autonomous and active citizens in ways that are mediated by the internet.

The internet and democratic participation

The notion of democratic participation entails not just the activities that citizens perform to influence decision making, but also a psychological dimension (Schonfeld, 1975). Thus, what citizens do to engage in civic and political life may not necessarily influence politics but may be an expression of what matters to them. Such an understanding of democratic participation resonates with the notion of civic and political engagement, which includes citizens' subjectivity about their practices (Dahlgren, 2003). Crucial to institutional and non-institutional civic and political engagement may be activities, both online and offline, which range from using government websites and seeking, sharing and commenting on civic and political content, to signing a petition, using alternative media and participating in a demonstration (Dutton, Blank and Groselj, 2013; Theocharis, 2015; van Laer and van Aelst, 2010).

Western liberal democracy operates through representative institutions and under principles of individual liberty and equality. For decades, it has been affected by a decline in citizens' participation in electoral politics and their alienation as a result of their inability to influence the political process (Coleman, 2013). In an age where nation-states are challenged in dealing with social inequalities by supranational politics and global capital flows, liberal democracy and public communication in the West have been undermined by citizens' distrust of institutions' and traditional media's ability to represent their concerns (Dahlgren, 2004; Coleman and Blumler, 2009). But while the representative character of Western political institutions has dwindled, we 'have evidence of alternative' practices of resistance and activism 'outside the parliamentarian context' (Dahlgren, 2004, ix). In addition, the advent of the internet has been accompanied by hopes about its potential to revitalise democracy by facilitating both institutional and non-institutional civic and political participation. Because of its interactive features allowing users to consume, share and produce content, the internet has been championed for its potential to decentralise politics, allow marginalised groups to engage civically and politically, foster an online public sphere and facilitate a deliberative democracy where citizens participate in decision making (Benkler, 2006; Coleman and Blumler, 2009; Martin, 2015). Furthermore, the internet has been celebrated for strengthening civil society and non-institutional politics by contributing, for example, to better-organised activism and the creation and consolidation of communities and collective identities (Cammaerts, 2015; Garrett, 2006).

However, as a technology that is embedded in power structures, the internet is far from having just a positive potential. Central to an ecosystem characterised by online content, usage and technical features as well as ownership, governance and socio-economic processes (van Dijck, 2013, 28), the internet presents structural constraints. With just a few corporations such as Facebook enjoying most online traffic (Freedman, 2012), the internet reinforces ideological extremism because of how its algorithms amplify and feed users with popular content that generates strong reactions (Vaidhyanathan, 2018). Given the internet's implications for privacy and security, issues of surveillance are also typical of the digital age. Insofar as user-generated content is shared with advertising companies by corporations such as Google and Facebook, the internet contributes to both commercial and government surveillance, as such corporations often work closely with governments (Fuchs, 2010; McChesney, 2013). Online content, furthermore, is fragmented and polarised (Sunstein, 2007). And as the fake news phenomenon demonstrates, it is also subject to issues of trustworthiness, bias and (mis)representation, issues that undermine democracy and its reliance on a well-informed citizenry (Garrett, 2006; Oxley, 2012).

Critical digital literacy and civic and political engagement within media studies

Not inherently democratising or undemocratic, the internet offers opportunities for reinvigorating democracy by contributing to institutional and non-institutional engagement in civic and political life. However, as it also poses challenges, citizens need to engage with information in the digital age in ways that involve an understanding of its civic and political potentials and limitations. Conceived as incorporating knowledge about the digital environment, critical digital literacy can encourage civic and political engagement and contribute to democracy. To reflect on how it may be expected to do so, it is worth drawing on what has been achieved in media studies, highlighting the gaps within different traditions.

Given media studies' interdisciplinary nature, approaches to media literacy have drawn on, and overlapped with, traditions ranging from social psychology, cultural studies, critical pedagogy, information science and the New Literacy Studies, which see literacy in socio-cultural terms, rather than just as an individual, cognitive phenomenon. These traditions have generally focused on education and young people rather than adults. But such a focus does not necessarily lie in opposition to civic and political engagement. A few studies implementing quantitative methodologies widely adopted in social psychology have measured the extent to which critical analytical skills and knowledge about traditional media in the context of media education correlate with civic and political engagement. They have argued that the ability to analyse and evaluate traditional news media is associated with civic engagement online (Martens and Hobbs, 2015). Appreciation of knowledge about news production and bias in the news corresponds to higher levels of civic engagement online and offline (Hobbs et al., 2013). Knowledge about mass media structures correlates with the intention to participate in media activism (Duran et al., 2008). And the ability to evaluate the trustworthiness of websites is associated with political engagement online and 'higher levels of online exposure to diverse perspectives' (Kahne, Lee and Feezell, 2012, 19).

Another strand of research that has looked at critical literacy and civic and political engagement in the context of education has taken inspiration from critical pedagogy and cultural studies. A major emphasis of this strand lies not only in the ability of internet users to critically evaluate media content, but also in their ability to express their voices by producing alternative media, re-writing media content subject to prejudice, bias and misrepresentation (Kellner and

Share, 2007). While this strand has remained focused on students' learning practices, to a less extent it has also underpinned work on social movements and activists' engagement with alternative media (Feria-Galicia, 2011). Critical pedagogy prescribes a teaching approach that encourages students' critical reflections against dominant representations together with political action (Freire, 2005; Luke and Freedboy, 1997). A limitation of this approach is that it has often assumed a relationship between critical literacy and political engagement. Drawing on critical theory, it has perpetuated the idea of social action as necessarily critical of dominant ideologies.

In an age where politics is increasingly polarised, it is essential to differentiate between, on the one hand, the questioning of media representations with a view to empowerment and on the other, misinformation propagated, for instance, by far-right ideologies questioning media credibility (Mihailidis and Viotty, 2017). Nevertheless, we also need to recognise that the potential of critical digital literacy to debunk misrepresentation and misinformation is not exclusively at the service of progressive and liberal ideologies. Critical pedagogy has overlooked the extent to which the questioning of dominant representations can be aligned with conservative politics and, problematically, with extreme ideologies disregarding evidence with the objective of delegitimising the political process. Such ideologies entail a risk of succumbing to a post-truth society where emotions, personal beliefs and distrust in expertise prevail over respect for evidence (Nichols, 2017). Restrictively, critical pedagogy has left little room for more comprehensive interpretations of civic and political engagement as institutional/non-institutional and ideologically multifaceted. In addition, it has encouraged citizens' critique against dominant representations while only sporadically emphasising the importance of understanding media structures and the broader digital environment where information circulates (Pangrazio, 2016, 164).

With the advent of digital media, the overlap between information literacy and media literacy has signalled the convergence of information science and media studies (Livingstone, van Couvering and Thumim, 2008). As with media scholars, information scientists and librarianship scholars have drawn on critical pedagogy to approach critical information literacy as the ability to question power and authority in ways that facilitate social justice (Correia, 2002; Elmborg, 2006; Jacobs and Berg, 2011). The new definition of information literacy adopted by CILIP (2018) resonates with such an approach in the way that it recognises the relevance of information literacy to citizenship. From such a perspective, librarianship has been interpreted as inherently promoting democratic values such as intellectual freedom and access to knowledge (Gregory and Higgins,

2013). However, only on occasion has critical information literacy been approached as including the questioning of 'the social, political, economic, and corporate systems [. . . underpinning] information production, dissemination, access, and consumption' (Gregory and Higgins, 2013, 4; Cope, 2010). In a similar vein, few media scholars have drawn on critical pedagogy to approach critical digital literacy as incorporating an understanding of the internet as embedded in power structures, in relation to production/consumption processes and its democratising potentials and structural constraints (Buckingham, 2007; Fry, 2014). Unlike critical digital literacy, however, most definitions of information literacy do not explicitly incorporate knowledge about the internet. They do not address 'the now pervasive online environments' where information circulates in the digital age (Mackey and Jacobson, 2011, 63).

The New Literacy Studies represent another tradition that is relevant to media studies. Approaching different literacies as embedded in the social context, this tradition has explored young people's ability to engage with multimodal content that integrates different media texts (Bulfin and North, 2007; Hull and Katz, 2006; Jewitt, 2008). Nevertheless, it has not always focused on their ability to evaluate content or their understanding of the digital landscape (Pangrazio, 2016, 167). Furthermore, it has placed little emphasis on civic and political engagement. Exceptionally, a few studies have addressed young people's civic engagement with multimedia content within online communities as facilitating the development and sharing of critical reflections on socio-political matters, personal storytelling, blogging and transnational identities resisting dominant representations (McGinnis, Goodstein-Stolzenberg and Saliani, 2007). But only a few have explored young people's understanding of the internet's potential to facilitate, for instance, both surveillance and storytelling (e.g. Shresthova, 2016).

The different traditions relevant to media studies, which have been discussed above, have rarely transcended a focus on education and young people to look at adults' digital literacy in the context of their civic and political practices. Relatedly, they have overlooked how understanding the digital environment may be relevant to civic and political engagement. By contrast, digital divide research has investigated the extent to which users' attitudes and dispositions towards the internet facilitate their online engagement (Durndell and Haag, 2002; Eynon and Geniets, 2016; Hakkarainen, 2012; Reisdorf and Groselj, 2017). However, having predominantly looked at the functional aspects of digital literacy, this strand of research has retained an individualistic focus neglecting users' civic and political practices and understanding of the socio-political dimension of the internet. A few media studies on social movements, instead, have explored activists' interpretations of traditional and digital media. They have argued that awareness of the internet's potentials and limitations can facilitate a pragmatic approach to using it for political purposes (Barassi, 2015; McCurdy, 2010, 2011; Treré, 2015). But these studies have made no reference to media literacy theory.

Another limitation within media studies is that although it has been emphasised that critical digital literacy can benefit democracy by contributing to well-informed, critical and empowered citizens, the notion of democracy has been approached rather monolithically by neglecting the different ways in which it can be understood. Some have argued that critical analytical skills and the ability to produce alternative media against dominant representations can facilitate a radical, pluralistic democracy, one that 'depends on a citizenry that embraces multiple perspectives', resulting in more participatory, 'democratic self-expression, and social progress' (Kellner and Share, 2007, 14, 17; Mihailidis and Thevenin, 2013). It has also been suggested that 'it is vital for citizens of a pluralistic democracy . . . to develop . . . competencies [such as] reading or watching the news . . . commenting on an online news story, contributing to an online community network . . . evaluating the quality of information [. . . and] sharing ideas and deliberating' (Hobbs, 2010, xi). The problem, however, is that media research has provided a limited understanding of how critical digital literacy can benefit civic and political engagement in ways that incorporate knowledge about the digital environment. Furthermore, what has remained obscure is how critical digital literacy can do so depending on how we conceive of democracy. In order to address these questions, it is worth drawing on political research and democratic theory.

Citizens' knowledge and competences in democracy: insights from political research

Political education studies have argued that 'to be engaged in democracy, there must be political literacy, the absence of which would make the prospect of meaningful social justice in society less likely' (Lund and Carr, 2008, 13). Political literacy revolves around factual knowledge of history, the political system, political and community groups, government, politicians and civic and political affairs. It also includes the ability to participate in politics, influence decision making and engage with communities. Ultimately, resonating with information literacy and critical literacy, it may be understood as entailing informed judgements based on critical thinking and 'respect for truth and reasoning' (Lund and Carr, 2008, 14; Davies and Hogarth, 2004; Giroux, 2017).

Within political theory, Robert Dahl (2006, 52) has argued not only that citizens need to know how to use resources such as time and money, but also that democracy depends on 'equal opportunities' to develop 'enlightened understanding[s]' and the ability to 'seek out independent information' (Dahl, 1998, 37–8; 2006, 12).

While the concept of political literacy overlaps with information literacy and critical literacy, political science and political communication studies, lying at the intersection of political research and media studies, have *de facto* focused on political knowledge as 'the primary indicator of citizen competence' (Rapeli, 2014, 2). Referring to factual and objective knowledge, the concept of political knowledge lacks a subjective dimension concerned, for instance, with 'whether . . . information is perceived to be correct or not' (Rapeli, 2014, 11). Except for a few studies (e.g. Bennett, Wells and Rank, 2009), political research has overlooked whether citizens are able to evaluate information. Instead, it has emphasised that citizens should have factual knowledge of the political system, the government, its rules and values, and how institutions operate (Barber, 1969, 38; Neuman, 1986, 196; Weissberg, 1974, 71). They should understand socio-political contexts and voting procedures (Downs, 1957, 215). And they should be familiar with domestic and international affairs, politicians, parties, key policies, relevant history, socio-economic conditions and political alignments (Dahl, 1992, 46; Delli Carpini and Keeter, 1993, 1182–3; 1996, 14; Neuman, 1986, 186).

What political research has overlooked is whether and to what extent citizens' required knowledge is underpinned by the ability to evaluate information in relation, for instance, to bias, prejudice and trustworthiness. Furthermore, while we live in an age where civic and political life is highly mediated by the internet, political research (similarly to media research, as suggested earlier in this chapter) has placed little emphasis on citizens' knowledge and interpretations of how the internet operates as a technology embedded in power structures. It has neglected that citizens should understand the civic and political opportunities and constraints that characterise the digital environment where information circulates. A few political scientists have measured the extent to which citizens' perceptions of internet-based electronic surveillance predict online political activity (Best and Krueger, 2008; Krueger, 2005). But they have made no reference to media literacy theory. In short, what has remained silent in political research is that a crucial layer of citizens' civic competence and required knowledge in the digital age should intersect with critical digital literacy.

Despite such a lacuna, recent work in political theory has offered insights into the interrelation of citizens' knowledge and democratic participation, which is relevant for addressing why critical digital literacy matters for democracy in the digital age. The notion of democracy entails both a descriptive and normative connotation. At the descriptive level, countries in the West are equipped with a system whereby citizens delegate representative power to institutions and politicians through elections. This system goes under the name of liberal democracy, operating under principles of political and economic individual liberty and equality. At the normative level, however, democracy may be understood in ways that build on or transcend the representative character of liberal democracy (Held, 2006). Drawing on democratic theory, Rapeli (2014) has employed Held's description of modern, 20th-century forms of democracy as a frame to theorise that citizens' political knowledge and participation in democracy vary depending on whether the latter is conceived in competitive elitist, pluralistic, participatory or deliberative terms (Rapeli, 2014, 69–74). Such an approach may not be exhaustive, since an understanding of democracy as predominantly dependent on the legal system was deliberately put aside. But it is a step towards refining our understanding of what citizens should know to participate civically and politically, in line with four 'models which are generally considered the main types of modern democracy' (Rapeli, 2014, 78):

1   The **competitive elitist** normative model prescribes liberal democracy as relying entirely on a 'political elite capable of making necessary legislative and administrative decisions' (Held, 2006, 157; Rapeli, 2014, 70). It revolves around citizens' political knowledge of competing parties and their electoral participation.

2   A **pluralistic** vision of democracy assumes that 'power is contested by numerous groups' and emphasises the role of factions seeking political influence (e.g. state, pressure groups, corporations, international organisations) (Dahl, 1982, 5; Held, 2006, 173). Intended as a 'polyarchy', a pluralistic democracy requires citizens' knowledge of politics, policies, electoral competition and political groups. It implies that citizens 'engage in politics in . . . other way[s] than just by voting', as exemplified by their involvement in civil society (Rapeli, 2014, 71).

3   The **participatory** democratic variant advocates 'direct participation of citizens in the regulation of the key institutions of society, including the workplace and local community' (Held, 2006, 215). It emphasises the importance of a well-informed and knowledgeable citizenry that actively participates in decision making (Rapeli, 2014, 71; Held, 2006, 215).

4   Finally, **deliberative** democracy implies that it is 'public deliberation of free

and equal citizens [. . .that] legitimate[s] political decision making'
(Bohman, 1998, 401). It requires a knowledgeable citizenry which, capable
of rational argumentation, participates through deliberation in the public
sphere (Held, 2006, 253; Rapeli, 2014, 72).

Democracy's normative variants present different limitations. While the
competitive model is *per se* elitist, reducing citizens to spectators of the political
process (Held, 2006, 153), a participatory democratic vision is subject to
problems of time and size. It requires citizens to commit time to participate in
civic and political life. And it barely transcends the level of towns and cities to
apply to more complex systems such as nation-states with large populations and
numerous political actors (Dahl, 2006, 118). As a result, participatory
democracy is generally *de facto* approximated as local government-led initiatives
such as neighbourhood committees, public forums and participatory budgeting
– initiatives that make governance more legitimate and interactive but not
necessarily direct (Rosanvallon, 2011, 203–5). Deliberative democracy is
constrained by issues of exclusion intrinsic to expecting citizens to deliberate in
rational terms, lacking an affective dimension. It also assumes too easily
citizens' equal access to deliberation, relying too enthusiastically on the
internet's deliberative potential to facilitate their participation in decision
making (Held, 2006, 238). Finally, the pluralistic model neglects systematic
imbalances in the distribution of power as public policies are generally skewed
towards the interests of more influential, resourceful groups. In addition, it falls
short of recognising that not all groups engaging in democracy are equally
listened to by those in powerful positions (Held, 2006, 165).

Drawing on democratic theory allows us to nuance how we understand what
citizens should know with a view to social inclusion and democratic
participation. What stands out from Rapeli's (2014) approach is that more
knowledge is required as citizens' participation increases, depending on whether
democracy is assumed to be competitive elitist, pluralistic, participatory or
deliberative. As citizens' engagement in civic and political life increases, civic and
political knowledge becomes more essential, not just for legitimising power
through voting, but also for expressing individual and collective interests, holding
politicians and policies accountable, resisting dominant ideologies, calling for
greater socio-economic and political equality, and ultimately contributing to
decision and policy making (Rapeli, 2014, 19, 26–7). With respect to the role that
information and communication technologies play in mediating politics and civic
and political engagement, Rapeli (2014, 5) acknowledges that 'in order to

understand how democracy functions or fails to function, it will become particularly important to understand how political information is produced, managed, presented, received, utilized and recalled'.

To date, however, no links have been established between media literacy theory and how knowledge and participation vary in democracy. Dahl (1982, 144) has emphasised that citizens' required knowledge and competences have become more abstract and complex within the nation-states, as opposed to 'knowledge of . . . the common interest' within smaller contexts enhanced by 'direct experiences and perceptions'. Such an argument implies that what citizens need to know and reflect on to engage in civic and political life can change over time. From this perspective, in an age that is highly mediated by digital technologies, it seems fair to suggest that critical digital literacy should be understood as a set of abilities, knowledge and values that are indispensable for participating in democracy.

Critical digital literacy and democracy

Critical digital literacy does not just involve the ability to critically evaluate information, which is central to the notion of information literacy. Inasmuch as digital media are not neutral but embedded within wider power structures, a critical reading of different traditions relevant to media studies allows us to revisit how we approach critical digital literacy. It enables us to conceive of it as incorporating knowledge and values about the internet in relation to how it operates socio-economically, and how its democratising potentials and structural constraints characterise the digital environment where information circulates. Different strands of research, inspired for instance by social psychology, critical pedagogy or the New Literacy Studies, have offered limited insights into how critical digital literacy facilitates civic and political engagement. These strands have generally explored critical digital literacy in the context of education, overlooking adults' civic and political practices. Conceptually, they have largely approached critical digital literacy as the ability to question online content and dominant ideologies, without necessarily incorporating knowledge about the internet and its civic and political potentials and limitations (Pangrazio, 2016, 164, 167). In addition, critical digital literacy has been interpreted as intrinsic to political engagement that is ideologically critical, as with research inspired by critical pedagogy. Alternatively, in the case of the New Literacy Studies, it has often been explored by privileging a focus on internet users' creativity over their critical reflections (Pangrazio, 2016, 167).

Research inspired by social psychology has emphasised that appreciation of knowledge about bias in the news and the ability to evaluate information correlate with civic and political engagement online and exposure to diverse political opinions (Hobbs et al., 2013; Kahne, Lee and Feezell, 2012; Martens and Hobbs, 2015). Additionally, research aligned with the New Literacy Studies has pointed out that networked engagement within online communities can facilitate the development and sharing of critical debate. And it can contribute to the formation of identities that resist dominant media representations through blogging and storytelling (McGinnis, Goodstein-Stolzenberg and Saliani, 2007; Shresthova, 2016). Insofar as critical digital literacy is essential for debunking online misinformation and misinterpretation, research inspired by critical pedagogy has argued that citizens can resist dominant representations by creating alternative media to express their voices (Kellner and Share, 2007). However, we need to recognise that the questioning of dominant representations can serve different political agendas (Mihailidis and Viotty, 2017) – which is why respect for expertise is crucial for countering extreme ideologies that disregard evidence (Nichols, 2017). While these conclusions suggest that critical digital literacy can benefit democracy by contributing to civic and political engagement, critical digital literacy has often been approached restrictively within media studies. And the notion of democracy has also been employed rather monolithically by overlooking that it can be understood in different ways.

The concept of political literacy has been addressed in political education studies as overlapping with information literacy and critical literacy (Lund and Carr, 2008, 13–14). Political research, however, has predominantly employed the notion of factual and objective political knowledge as an indicator of civic competence (Rapeli, 2014, 2). In order to participate in democracy, citizens are expected to have knowledge, for instance, of the political system, how the government works, politicians, policies and civic and political affairs. Depending on how we conceive of democracy, recent research has argued that as citizens are expected to engage more actively in civic and political life, their political knowledge is also expected to increase (Rapeli, 2014). Restrictively, however, this model fails to refer to critical digital literacy as a crucial dimension of citizens' required knowledge and competences in the digital age.

It is only when combining a media studies perspective with insights from political research and democratic theory that we can better understand why critical digital literacy matters for civic and political engagement and democracy, depending on how the latter is normatively understood. It is reasonable to imagine that as citizens' engagement in civic and political life increases in ways that are mediated by the internet, it becomes more essential for them to have not only political knowledge, but also critical digital literacy. From a competitive elitist perspective revolving around citizens' electoral obligations, it may be supposed that gathering online information – for example, on competing parties, politicians and public affairs – is enhanced by the ability to evaluate content in relation to bias and trustworthiness. And it is also enhanced by knowledge and critical interpretations of the internet, how information is generated online, the role of targeted advertising and what it means for privacy, along with the internet's potentials and limitations for journalism and for navigating civic and political content.

While such a range of abilities, knowledge and interpretations is central not just to a competitive elitist vision of democracy but also to every other model of democracy, questioning online information in synergy with knowledge about the digital environment is crucial for engaging from a pluralistic perspective in ways that go beyond voting and seeking information. From such a perspective, citizens need to be able to evaluate content transcending institutional and electoral politics. They need to be able to engage with alternative media and content produced by activists and different publics, including those that are marginalised from dominant communications (Downey and Fenton, 2003). They need to do so in ways that do not delegitimise respect for evidence and expertise. In addition, citizens need to understand how the internet operates socio-economically, along with its civic and political potentials and limitations. Critically understanding the internet's potential for civil society and activism may be useful for interacting within online community settings, engaging in voluntarism, producing alternative media challenging dominant ideologies as well as organising, and seeking and sharing information about, demonstrations and other forms of public protest. In this respect, media research on social movements has emphasised the importance of understanding the opportunities and constraints of the internet in the context of non-institutional engagement in politics (Barassi, 2015; McCurdy, 2010, 2011; Treré, 2015).

A participatory democratic perspective entails that citizens should not just be aware of how they may participate in decision making – for example, via referenda, public forums or multi-stakeholder initiatives bringing civil society actors together to propose legislation. Inasmuch as citizens' political literacy needs to intersect with critical digital literacy, they should also know what potentials and constraints the internet presents for participating in decision making, reflecting on issues of access and security affecting the possibility of gathering information, exchanging opinions or collaboratively preparing a policy document. Finally, exemplifying a specific form of participatory democracy, the deliberative model revolves around citizens' deliberative practices, generally promoted through government-led online initiatives. These practices may be enhanced not just by the ability to evaluate information, but also by knowledge about the internet's potentials and limitations for deliberation. Citizens, for instance, should understand the internet's potential to facilitate connectivity and marginalised groups' participation in the public sphere as well as government surveillance and how algorithms affect online visibility, reinforcing polarisation and ideological extremism (Blumler and Coleman, 2010; Hindman, 2009; Martin, 2015; McChesney, 2013; Vaidhyanathan, 2018).

For now, the proposition that critical digital literacy can benefit democracy in different ways, depending on how we conceive of democracy, remains theoretical. What needs to follow is empirical research. It may be fruitful to explore civic and political practices ranging in institutional/non-institutional character, mapping out their interrelation with critical digital literacy and different democratic paradigms. Alternatively, a case study methodology may be advisable, based on case studies exemplifying different democratic variants. Regardless of these options, critical digital literacy should be approached not only as the ability to evaluate information online, but also knowledge about the internet in relation to socio-economic issues, its democratising potentials and structural constraints. Combining a media studies perspective on critical digital literacy with insights from political research and democratic theory invites future media research to investigate how the notion of democracy may be employed in relation to critical digital literacy. In addition, it invites political research to acknowledge that a crucial dimension of the knowledge and competences that citizens require in order to participate in democracy in the digital age should intersect with critical digital literacy.

Conclusions

This chapter has explored why critical digital literacy matters for democracy and civic and political engagement. For decades, Western liberal democracy has been undermined by citizens' distrust in politics, traditional media and institutions' inability to represent citizens, and ultimately, citizens' lack of participation in electoral politics. However, not only have non-institutional forms of participation emerged, but the advent of the internet has also been accompanied by hopes about its potential to contribute to both institutional and non-institutional politics. The internet has been praised, for instance, for diversifying political content, allowing marginalised groups to participate in civic and political life, and facilitating resistance and activism. Nevertheless, as it is embedded in power structures, it also contributes to surveillance and ideological extremism affecting civic and political participation. Among other issues, it also contributes to misinformation and misrepresentation, which undermine democracy and its reliance on a well-informed citizenry.

While information literacy revolves around the ability to access, locate and evaluate information, critical digital literacy should be approached as being about evaluating online content in relation to bias, prejudice and trustworthiness. It should also incorporate knowledge about internet-related socio-economic issues concerning, for instance, how ownership and advertising shape online information. Ultimately, critical digital literacy should be about understanding the internet's democratising potentials and structural constraints. Different traditions relevant to media studies have largely neglected the importance of conceiving critical digital literacy in this way. What we know from these traditions is that the ability to evaluate online information corresponds to higher civic and political engagement and exposure to political content. Critically interpreting media representations is crucial to producing alternative content challenging dominant ideologies. Networked engagement within online communities facilitates the construction and sharing of critical reflections on socio-political matters. Furthermore, despite overlooking media literacy theory, media research on social movements has emphasised that understanding the potentials and limitations of the digital environment is essential for engaging in resistance and activism. Not only has the contribution of media studies remained limited as to how critical digital literacy, as approached here, can benefit democracy and civic and political engagement, but the notion of democracy has also been employed rather monolithically by neglecting the different meanings that it can have. What has remained obscure is how critical digital literacy can benefit civic and political engagement depending on how we understand democracy.

This chapter has argued that a media studies perspective, enriched with insights from political and democratic theory, can help us gain a more nuanced understanding of why critical digital literacy matters for democracy in the digital age. Political education studies have approached political literacy as overlapping with information literacy and critical literacy. But political research has *de facto* focused on citizens' factual and political knowledge as an indicator of civic competence. Even though we live in an age that is highly mediated by digital technologies, political research has paid little attention to the idea that citizens' required knowledge and competences depend on their critical digital literacy.

Recent work in political theory has explored how citizens' political knowledge and participation vary on the basis of whether democracy is normatively assumed as competitive elitist, pluralistic, participatory or deliberative. While this work does not account for critical digital literacy, this chapter has suggested that it can help us understand how critical digital literacy can benefit democracy. What stands out is that as citizens' civic and political engagement increases in ways that are digitally mediated, not only does their political knowledge become more essential, but so also does their critical digital literacy.

By drawing on media studies in synergy with political and democratic theory, this chapter has argued that critical digital literacy can benefit democracy in different yet not mutually exclusive ways aligned with different democratic variants. From a competitive elitist democracy perspective, critical digital literacy can benefit citizens' electoral engagement by allowing them to critically evaluate online content as well as understand how information circulates, and with what implications, in the digital age. While the ability to evaluate online information is essential under each democratic variant, in a democracy conceived as pluralistic, critical digital literacy is crucial for evaluating content transcending institutional and electoral politics. In addition, knowledge about how the internet operates socio-economically, along with its democratising potentials and structural constraints, is particularly relevant in the context of civil society, community engagement, alternative media, resistance and activism. From a participatory democracy perspective, citizens should also understand the internet's potentials and limitations for participating in decision making, in relation, for instance, to issues of access and security affecting government-led participatory initiatives. Finally, in a democracy conceived as deliberative, citizens should be particularly aware of the internet's potentials and constraints for connectivity and participation in the public sphere, and also in relation to government surveillance and issues of exclusion.

By drawing on media studies and political research, this chapter has offered an interpretation of how critical digital literacy can benefit different democratic variants. Not only is critical digital literacy indispensable for citizens' engagement in democracy in the digital age, but it can also facilitate civic and political engagement, in whichever way democracy is conceived.

Acknowledgements

This work was supported by the Economic and Social Research Council (grant number ES/J500070/1). Many thanks to Sonia Livingstone and Nick Couldry for their comments on an earlier version of this chapter.

References

Barassi, V. (2015) Social Media, Immediacy and the Time for Democracy: critical reflections on social media as 'temporalizing practices'. In Dencik, L. and Leistert, O. (eds) *Critical Perspectives on Social Media and Protest: between control and emancipation*, Rowman & Littlefield International, 73–88.

Barber, J. D. (1969) *Citizen Politics: an introduction to political behaviour*, Markham.

Benkler, Y. (2006) *The Wealth of Networks: how social production transforms markets and freedom*, Yale University Press.

Bennett, W. L., Wells, C. and Rank, A. (2009) Young Citizens and Civic Learning: two paradigms of citizenship in the digital age, *Citizenship Studies*, 13 (2), 105–20, doi:10.1080/13621020902731116.

Best, S. J. and Krueger, B. S. (2008) Political Conflict and Public Perceptions of Government Surveillance on the Internet: an experiment of online search terms, *Journal of Information Technology & Politics*, 5 (2), 191–212, doi:10.1080/19331680802294479.

Blumler, J. G. and Coleman, S. (2010) Political Communication in Freefall: the British case – and others?, *International Journal of Press/Politics*, 15 (2), 139–54, doi:10.1177/1940161210362263.

Bohman, J. (1998) The Coming of Age of Deliberative Democracy, *Journal of Political Philosophy*, 6 (4), 400–25, doi:10.1111/1467–9760.00061.

Buckingham, D. (2007) Digital Media Literacies: rethinking media education in the age of the internet, *Research in Comparative and International Education*, 2 (1), 43–55, doi:10.2304/rcie.2007.2.1.43.

Buckingham, D., Banaji, S., Burn, A., Carr, D., Cranmer, S. and Willett, R. (2005) *The Media Literacy of Children and Young People: a review of the research literature on behalf of Ofcom*, Ofcom, http://discovery.ucl.ac.uk/10000145.

Bulfin, S. and North, S. (2007) Negotiating Digital Literacy Practices across School and Home: case studies of young people in Australia, *Language and Education*, 21 (3), 247–63, doi:10.2167/le750.0.

Cammaerts, B. (2015) Social Media and Activism. In Mansell, R. and Ang, P. H. (eds) *The International Encyclopedia of Digital Communication and Society*, Wiley-Blackwell, 1027–34.

CILIP (2018) *CILIP Definition of Information Literacy 2018*, CILIP: the Library and Information Association, https://infolit.org.uk/ILdefinitionCILIP2018.pdf.

Coleman, S. (2013) *How Voters Feel*, Cambridge University Press.

Coleman, S. and Blumler, J. G. (2009) *The Internet and Democratic Citizenship: theory, practice and polity*, Cambridge University Press.

Cope, J. (2010) Information Literacy and Social Power. In Accardi, M. T., Drabinski, E. and Kumbier, A. (eds) *Critical Library Instruction: theories and methods*, Library Juice Press, 13–28.

Correia, A. M. R. (2002) *Information Literacy for an Active and Effective Citizenship*, White Paper prepared for UNESCO, the US National Commission on Libraries and Information Science and the National Forum on Information Literacy, for use at the Information Literacy Meetings of Experts. Prague, Czech Republic, www.researchgate.net/publication/228765129_Information_literacy_for_an_active_and_effective_citizenship.

Dahl, R. A. (1982) *Dilemmas of Pluralist Democracy: autonomy vs. control*, Yale University Press.

Dahl, R. A. (1992) The Problem of Civic Competence, *Journal of Democracy*, 3 (4), 45–59, doi:10.1353/jod.1992.0048.

Dahl, R. A. (1998) *On Democracy*, Yale University Press.

Dahl, R. A. (2006) *On Political Equality*, Yale University Press.

Dahlgren, P. (2003) Reconfiguring Civic Culture in the New Media Milieu. In Corner, J. and Pels, D. (eds) *Media and the Restyling of Politics: consumerism, celebrity and cynicism*, Sage, 151–70.

Dahlgren, P. (2004) Foreword. In van de Donk, W., Loader, B. D., Nixon, P. G. and Rucht, D. (eds) *Cyberprotest: new media, citizens and social movements*, Routledge, ix–xiii.

Davies, I. and Hogarth, S. (2004) Political Literacy: issues for teachers and learners. In Demaine, J. (ed.) *Citizenship and Political Education Today*, Palgrave Macmillan, 181–99.

Delli Carpini, M. X. and Keeter, S. (1993) Measuring Political Knowledge: putting first things first, *American Journal of Political Science*, 37 (4), 1179–1206, doi:10.2307/2111549.

Delli Carpini, M. X. and Keeter, S. (1996) *What Americans Know About Politics and Why It Matters*, Yale University Press.

Downey, J. and Fenton, N. (2003) New Media, Counter Publicity and the Public Sphere, *New Media & Society*, 5, (2), 185–202, doi:10.1177/1461444803005002003.

Downs, A. (1957) *An Economic Theory of Democracy*, Harper & Row.

Duran, R. L., Yousman, B., Walsh, K. M. and Longshore, M. A. (2008) Holistic Media Education: an assessment of the effectiveness of a college course in media literacy, *Communication Quarterly*, 56 (1), 49–68, doi:10.1080/01463370701839198.

Durndell, A. and Haag, Z. (2002) Computer Self-Efficacy, Computer Anxiety,

Attitudes towards the Internet and Reported Experience with the Internet, by Gender, in an East European Sample, *Computers in Human Behavior*, **18**, 521–35, doi:10.1016/S0747–5632(02)00006–7.

Dutton, W. H., Blank, G. and Groselj, D. (2013) *Cultures of the Internet: the internet in Britain*, Oxford Internet Survey 2013, Oxford Internet Institute, http://oxis.oii.ox.ac.uk/wp-content/uploads/2014/11/OxIS-2013.pdf.

Elmborg, J. (2006) Critical Information Literacy: implications for instructional practice, *Journal of Academic Librarianship*, **32** (2), 192–9, doi:10.1016/j.acalib.2005.12.004.

Eynon, R. and Geniets, A. (2016) The Digital Skills Paradox: how do digitally excluded youth develop skills to use the internet?, *Learning, Media and Technology*, **41** (3), 463–79, doi:10.1080/17439884.2014.1002845.

Feria-Galicia, J. (2011) Mascot Politics, Public Pedagogy, and Social Movements: alternative media as a context for critical media literacy, *Policy Futures in Education*, **9** (6), 706–14, doi:10.2304/pfie.2011.9.6.706.

Freedman, D. (2012) Web 2.0 and the Death of the Blockbuster Economy. In Curran, J., Fenton, N. and Freedman, D. (eds) *Misunderstanding the Internet*, Routledge, 69–94.

Freire, P. (2005) *Pedagogy of the Oppressed*, 30th anniversary edn, translated by Ramos, M. B., Continuum International.

Fry, K. G. (2014) What Are We Really Teaching? Outline for an activist media literacy education. In de Abreu, B. S. and Mihailidis, P. (eds) *Media Literacy Education in Action: Theoretical and Pedagogical Perspectives*, Routledge, 125–37.

Fuchs, C. (2010) StudiVZ: social networking in the surveillance society, *Ethics and Information Technology*, **12** (2), 171–85, doi:10.1007/s10676–010–9220–z.

Garrett, K. R. (2006) Protest in an Information Society: a review of literature on social movements and new ICTs, *Information, Communication & Society*, **9** (2), 202–24, doi:10.1080/13691180600630773.

Giroux, H. A. (2017) The Scourge of Illiteracy in Authoritarian Times, *Contemporary Readings in Law and Social Justice*, **9** (1), 14–27, doi:10.22381/CRLSJ9120172.

Gregory, L. and Higgins, S. (2013) Introduction. In Gregory, L. and Higgins, S. (eds) *Information Literacy and Social Justice: radical professional praxis*, Library Juice Press, 1–11.

Hakkarainen, P. (2012) No Good for Shovelling Snow and Carrying Firewood: social representations of computers and the internet by elderly Finnish non-users, *New Media & Society*, **14** (7), 1198–1215, doi:10.1177/1461444812442663.

Held, D. (2006) *Model of Democracy*, 3rd edn, Polity Press.

Hindman, M. S. (2009) *The Myth of Digital Democracy*, Princeton University Press.

Hobbs, R. (2010) *Digital and Media Literacy: a plan of action*, The Aspen Institute.

Hobbs, R., Donnelly, K., Friesem, J. and Moen, M. (2013) Learning to Engage: how positive attitudes about the news, media literacy, and video production contribute to adolescent civic engagement, *Educational Media International*, **50** (4), 231–46, doi: 10.1080/09523987.2013.862364.

Hull, G. A. and Katz, M.-L. (2006) Crafting an Agentive Self: case studies of digital storytelling, *Research in the Teaching of English*, **41**(1), 43–81, www.jstor.org/stable/40171717.

Information Literacy Meeting of Experts (2003) *The Prague Declaration: towards an information literate society*, Prague, www.unesco.org/new/fileadmin/MULTIMEDIA/HQ/CI/CI/pdf/PragueDeclaration.pdf.

Jacobs, H. L. M. and Berg, S. (2011) Reconnecting Information Literacy Policy with the Core Values of Librarianship, *Library Trends*, **60** (2), 383–94, doi:10.1353/lib.2011.0043.

Jewitt, C. (2008) Multimodality and Literacy in School Classrooms, *Review of Research in Education*, **32**, 241–67, doi:10.3102/0091732X07310586.

Kahne, J., Lee, N.-J. and Feezell, J. T. (2012) Digital Media Literacy Education and Online Civic and Political Participation, *International Journal of Communications* **6**, 1–24, doi:1932–8036/201200050001.

Kellner, D. and Share, J. (2007) Critical Media Literacy, Democracy, and the Reconstruction of Education. In Macedo, D. and Steinberg, S. R. (eds) *Media Literacy: a reader*, Peter Lang, 3–23.

Krueger, B. S. (2005) Government Surveillance and Political Participation on the Internet, *Social Science Computer Review*, **23** (4) 439–52, doi:10.1177/0894439305278871.

Livingstone, S., van Couvering, E. and Thumim, N. (2008) Converging Traditions of Research on Media and Information Literacies: disciplinary, critical, and methodological issues. In Coiro, J., Knobel, C., Lankshear, M. and Leu, D. J. (eds) *Handbook of Research on New Literacies*, Routledge, 103–32.

Livingstone, S., Wijnen, C. W., Papaioannou, T., Costa, C. and del Mar Grandío, M. (2013) Situating Media Literacy in the Changing Media Environment: critical insights from European research on audiences. In Carpentier, N., Schrøder, K. and Hallett, L. (eds) *Audience Transformations: shifting audience positions in late modernity*, Routledge, 210–27.

Luke, A. and Freedboy, P. (1997) Shaping the Social Practices of Reading. In Muspratt, S., Luke, A. and Freedboy, P. (eds) *Constructing Critical Literacies: teaching and learning textual practice*, Hampton Press, 185–225.

Lund, D. E. and Carr, P. R. (2008) Introduction: Scanning Democracy. In Lund, D. E. and Carr, P. R. (eds) *Doing Democracy: striving for political literacy and social justice*, Peter Lang, 1–32.

Mackey, T. P. and Jacobson, T. E. (2011) Reframing Information Literacy as a Metaliteracy, *College & Research Libraries*, **72** (1), 62–78, doi:10.5860/crl-76r1.

Martens, H. and Hobbs, R. (2015) How Media Literacy Supports Civic Engagement in a Digital Age, *Atlantic Journal of Communication*, **23** (2), 120–37, doi:10.1080/15456870.2014.961636.

Martin, J. A. (2015) Mobile News Use and Participation in Elections: a bridge for the democratic divide?, *Mobile Media & Communication*, **3** (2), 230–49, doi:10.1177/2050157914550664.

McChesney, R. (2013) *Digital Disconnect: how capitalism is turning the internet against democracy*, The New Press.

McCurdy, P. (2010) Breaking the Spiral of Silence: unpacking the 'media debate' within global justice movements: a case study of dissent! And the 2005 Gleneagles G8 Summit, *Interface: a journal for and about social movements*, **2** (2), 42–67, www.interfacejournal.net/wordpress/wp-content/uploads/2010/12/Interface-2-2-pp.42-67-McCurdy1.pdf.

McCurdy, P. (2011) Theorizing 'Lay Theories of Media': a case study of the dissent! Network at the Gleneagles G8 Summit, *International Journal of Communication*, **5**, 619–38, doi:1932–8036/20110619.

McGinnis, T., Goodstein-Stolzenberg, A. and Saliani, E. C. (2007) 'indnpride': online spaces of transnational youth as sites of creative and sophisticated literacy and identity work, *Linguistics and Education*, **18**, 283–304, doi:10.1016/j.linged.2007.07.006.

Mihailidis, P. and Thevenin, B. (2013) Media Literacy as a Core Competency for Engaged Citizenship in Participatory Democracy, *American Behavioral Scientist*, **57** (11), 1611–22, doi:10.1177/0002764213489015.

Mihailidis, P. and Viotty, S. (2017) Spreadable Spectacle in Digital Culture: civic expression, fake news, and the role of media literacies in 'post-fact' society, *American Behavioral Scientist*, **61** (4), 441–54, doi:10.1177/0002764217701217.

Neuman, R. W. (1986) *The Paradox of Mass Politics: knowledge and opinion in the American electorate*, Harvard University Press.

Nichols, T. (2017) *The Death of Expertise: the campaign against established knowledge and why it matters*, Oxford University Press.

Oxley, Z. M. (2012) More Sources, Better Informed Public? New media and political knowledge. In Fox, R. L. and Ramos, J. M. (eds) *iPolitics: citizens, elections, and governing in the new media era*, 25–47, Cambridge University Press.

Pangrazio, L. (2016) Reconceptualising Critical Digital Literacy, *Discourse: studies in the cultural politics of education*, **37** (2), 163–74, doi:10.1080/01596306.2014.942836.

Rapeli, L. (2014) *The Conception of Citizen Knowledge in Democratic Theory*, Palgrave Macmillan.

Reisdorf, B. C. and Groselj, D. (2017) Internet (Non-)Use Types and Motivational Access: implications for digital inequalities research, *New Media & Society*, **19** (8), 1157–76, doi:10.1177/1461444815621539.

Rosanvallon, P. (2011) *Democratic Legitimacy: impartiality, reflexivity, proximity*, translated by A. Goldhammer, Princeton University Press.

Schonfeld, W. R. (1975) Review: The Meaning of Democratic Participation, *World Politics*, **28** (1), 134–58, doi:10.2307/2010033.

Shresthova, S. (2016) Between Storytelling and Surveillance: the precarious public of American Muslim youth. In Jenkins, H., Shresthova, S., Gamber-Thompson, L., Kligler-Vilenchik, N. and Zimmerman, A. M. (eds) *By Any Media Necessary*, New York University Press, 149–85.

Sunstein, C. R. (2007) *Republic.Com 2.0*, Princeton University Press.

Theocharis, Y. (2015) The Conceptualization of Digitally Networked Participation, *Social Media + Society*, **1** (2), 1–14, doi:10.1177/2056305115610140.

Treré, E. (2015) The Struggle Within: discord, conflict and paranoia in social media protest. In Dencik, L. and Leistert, O. (eds) *Critical Perspectives on Social Media and Protest*, Rowman & Littlefield International, 163–80.

Trültzsch-Wijnen, C. W., Murru, M. F. and Papaioannou, T. (2017) Definitions and Values of Media and Information Literacy in a Historical Context. In Frau-Meigs, D., Velez, I. and Michel, J. F. (eds) *Public Policies in Media and Information Literacy in Europe: cross-country comparisons*, Routledge, 91–115.

UNESCO (2014) *Paris Declaration on Media and Information Literacy in the Digital Era*, www.unesco.org/new/fileadmin/MULTIMEDIA/HQ/CI/CI/pdf/In_Focus/ paris_mil_declaration_final.pdf.

Vaidhyanathan, S. (2018) *Antisocial Media: how Facebook disconnects us and undermines democracy*, Oxford University Press.

van Dijck, J. (2013) *The Culture of Connectivity: a critical history of social media*, Oxford University Press.

van Laer, J. and van Aelst, P. (2010) Internet and Social Movement Action Repertoires, *Information, Communication & Society*, **13** (8), 1146–71, doi:10.1080/13691181003628307.

Weissberg, R. (1974) *Political Learning, Political Choice, and Democratic Citizenship*, Prentice Hall.

2

The discourses of power, information and literacy

Andrew Whitworth

This book as a whole is concerned with the notion that information and, by extension, information literacy (IL) are political: more precisely, that information and IL are enmeshed in formal and informal decision-making systems that determine the distribution of capital, human rights, public benefits and so on. From the work of Bell (1976), through Castells (1996) and other analyses of the 'information society' (see Webster, 2014 for a review), these issues are considered most frequently at the global, macro level. Discussions of information *literacy* in respect to such macro-political and economic matters are rarer, but the gap is partly filled by the preceding chapter, and others that follow in this collection.

Befitting the common conception of IL as an attribute of individuals and communities, the focus of this chapter is on *micro*-politics: that is, the relations of power, authority and inequality that stem from everyday language and discourse. The aim is to explore how information and IL underpin political processes at this micro-level, and how dialogue, interaction and the making of judgements about information operate within information landscapes (Lloyd, 2010) that are shaped and stratified by power and authority of various kinds. This is accomplished by investigating the critical political theories of authors including Jürgen Habermas, Mikhail Bakhtin and Michel Foucault to gain insight into the ways in which IL can be applied in challenges to power and authority structures – but how it also may become part of these structures.

Politics and information

The earliest philosophers recognised the importance of applying knowledge and information to political decisions. Socrates 'preached insistently that knowledge ought to be applied to conduct in the same way as it was already applied with such success to carpentry, shoemaking or medicine' (Lindsay, 1906, xii). In Book VII of *The Republic* Plato argues to Glaucon that public affairs should never be conducted only by 'men who are poor and hungry for goods of their own' (*ibid.*, 214) as, motivated only by self-interest, they would lack the wisdom and skill to take effective decisions. Plato would 'persuade those who are to share in the highest affairs of the city to take to calculation, and embrace it in no amateur spirit . . . until they arrive by the help of sheer intelligence at a vision of the nature of numbers' (*ibid.*, 219). In other words, he affirms the importance of information, an ability to handle it, and an objective, dispassionate viewpoint, when it comes to taking effective decisions and planning (military) strategy.

The subsequent history of espionage and surveillance acknowledges the indispensability of information, whether in military campaigns or when asserting political strength at home. Propaganda and control over information dispersal have always been pillars of the power structures that underpin both totalitarian regimes and less coercive forms of authority. In the 1920s, Antonio Gramsci recognised that consent to an existing, dominant political order is not usually secured through overt force but through the application of *hegemony* (Gramsci, 1971), by which is meant political control over culture and key informational processes such as education, the legal system and the broadcast and print media. In the 1960s, Robert Dahl (1961) included 'control over information' in his analysis of key political resources. Information itself, and by implication, those trained in the effective use and application of information, have always been valuable to power-holders.

The rise of information and communications technologies has made this information-handling capability a valuable resource at the micro- as well as macro-political level. Zurkowski's (1974) seminal definition of information literacy stresses the importance of IL in sustaining economic competitiveness, democratic legitimacy and liberal political institutions, such as a free press. All depend on the resource that is information. However, this is not a free good: work in processing and understanding information is necessary before it can be usable (Zurkowski, 1974, 1). Zurkowski argues that the (US) state should allocate the required resources to develop IL in individuals and communities, stating that this is an essential investment to support the 'Information Services Environment' that underpins liberal capitalism (Zurkowski, 1974, 25: Whitworth, 2014, 33). This plea, made also by contemporaries like Burchinal (1976), anticipates the coming diffusion of information technology outside business and science and into the home and community. For these authors, IL is defined as akin to Plato's lauding of 'calculation', something that can elevate the quality of decision making and understanding of relevant issues (Owens, 1976, 27): '(V)oters with information literacy are in a position to make more intelligent decisions than citizens who are information illiterates. The application of information resources to the process of decision making to fulfil civic responsibilities is a vital necessity.'

Such views remain cogent in debates about the role of disinformation (a.k.a. 'fake news'), surveillance and data mining in the 2016 electoral shocks in the UK and USA (see Chapters 1 and 4 in this book). This is a debate with concerns beyond just the conventional expressions of political participation, in which political legitimacy stems from conformity to the formal-legal democratic process, including activities such as voting, contacting elected officials, membership of political parties, unions, etc. Any definition of politics must also include less normative activities such as membership of community and/or activist groups, protests or boycotts. Informal engagement with political information, such as sharing a link on Facebook, or reading a political blog, must also be considered. New technologies may have given rise to new conduits for propaganda and surveillance, but they also add to the 'repertoires' of how people can express themselves politically (Norris, 2002, 190), repertoires that do not take the legitimacy of extant political institutions and discourses for granted:

> When understood radically, democracy is about the processes of public
> decision making to which economic, social and cultural institutions must be
> subjected in order to be legitimate and binding upon citizens. Such a radical
> concept of democracy is concerned to *judge* social, economic and political
> institutions, not to presuppose their legitimacy.
>
> (Angus, 2001, 10)

The role of education is paramount in developing an informed citizenry who are in a position to make these judgements effectively. Giroux (2011, 71; cited in Smith, 2015, 2) is clear that civic education and critical pedagogy are crucial in sustaining pluralism, inclusiveness and active debate around key political issues. Smith (2015) explores how the information and digital literacy of the teenagers in her study were bound up with both their ability, and opportunity, to make political judgements. *Informed* political judgements are not just a factor of the amount or availability of information; nor of the delegation of decision making to 'professional' politicians. They depend also an ability to *discern* (see Chapter 8 in this book), understand where information is relevant, make connections and evaluate impacts. Political judgements depend on people learning to navigate 'information landscapes' (Lloyd, 2010) which, like all such landscapes, are complex and context-specific.

This is an ideal, though. While the basic processes of conventional and non-conventional politics can be explored within programmes of 'civics' education, making a good, informed judgement in a particular place and time requires engagement with a complex information landscape, as well as weighing the competing interests of many different stakeholders. Complex decisions with potentially significant impacts for certain groups become political precisely because they are complex and potentially significant, and this can retard the making of good judgements. Many voters and other political actors lack *confidence* when it comes to making political decisions, particularly, but not only, the young (Henn and Foard, 2012; Smith, 2015, 23). Andersen, Heath and Sinnott (2002, cited in Smith, 2015, 37) 'discuss how people are able to "get by" when participating through heuristics, or information shortcuts, and follow cues from influential figures in their lives so that they can act *as if* they were politically knowledgeable without actually possessing political knowledge.'

In addition to this complexity, lack of confidence and, generally, despair regarding the effectiveness of political action (Gilroy-Ware, 2017), there is uneven provision of information, particularly online. Contrary to Zurkowski's vision of an essentially open and unbiased 'Information Services Environment', the information landscape within which informed political decisions must be made is often not balanced or neutral. It is not just that information is deliberately concealed or distorted, though this can happen (see the case of the 1989 Hillsborough disaster, discussed below). The technological operations of social media software like Facebook also contribute to political polarisation. Likes, retweets, bots and auto-fill trap users in 'filter bubbles' (Pariser, 2011) that retard the ability to synthesise and make connections between issues (Shenk, 1997), something essential to making informed political judgements. In 2014 the Pew Research Center showed how political polarisation between Republican and Democrat voters had not just increased, but become extreme in the era of social media – and this analysis does not even account for US citizens and residents who would not identify with either of these parties.

Being aware of political issues, engaging with active political participation, these are factors not just of whether individuals have been 'educated' in civics, but also of being embedded in an information landscape that is more conducive to activism. Smith (2015, 17–18) cites Dinas (2014) who found that children of politically engaged parents were more likely to be engaged themselves.

Conversely, individuals might be part of information landscapes – at home, school, work – that promote apathy and non-participation. Smith points out that while many sources of political socialisation can be seen as explicitly informational (texts, dialogues), 'some of the more abstract and structural sources [of political feeling] may not be consciously acknowledged' (Smith, 2015, 18). The opinions of family members, and the reading matter (particularly newspapers) which were typically available in a home, were influential in how young people developed political opinion – whether through agreement with these viewpoints, or rejection of them. Either way, Smith notes that: '[t]he relationship between political knowledge and attitudes is complex and not based on purely rational systems of thought; therefore any development of critical information literacy must take this into account' (Smith, 2015, 44).

Forms of power

The concept of the autonomous individual, rationally assessing a variety of information sources from the landscape around them before making informed judgements, is a key trope of liberal views of democracy, but also an ideal. As well as the unevenness of actual information landscapes, instead of being individualistic observers:

> humans make meaning in social contexts . . . we are strongly influenced in our thinking by the groups, organisations and institutions in which we live and work. Individuals join and interact in organisations and, to varying degrees, absorb their norms, rules and categories of thought.
>
> (Blaug, 2010, 4)

We are like 'centaurs, part human, part organisation' (*ibid.*). From this viewpoint, a 'pure', individualist democracy can be seen as 'a disorganised and inefficient clamour of different voices' (*ibid.*, 23); hence the appeal of *power,* brought to bear to reduce and simplify this complexity, and streamline decision making.

Dennis H. Wrong (1995) outlines a classification scheme for the forms of power and influence that can be asserted in interpersonal exchanges. At the top level of the schema lie *force*; *manipulation*; *persuasion*; and *authority*. Each form of power can, and does, shape information to fulfil its ends. Particular opinions, individuals, communities and texts can either be given elevated status and prominence in a landscape, or be obscured, excluded. Using force to achieve political ends, in an extreme sense, annuls information and judgement altogether:

more likely, propaganda will be brought to bear to justify its use. Manipulation seeks to conceal the fact that judgements are being made, but shapes an information landscape in ways that direct people toward the 'proper' decision. Persuasion is more benign (Wrong, 1995, 32–34); see below, and the discussion of Habermas, for more detail on how this type of deliberate influence works with information.

Wrong divides the concept of 'authority' into further sub-types: coercive (e.g. fascism); induced (authority secured through offering rewards for compliance); legitimate (the authority of the police and judiciary); personal (authority stemming from respect or love) and competent authority. This last is (Wrong, 1995, 53) 'a power relation in which the subject obeys the directives of the authority out of belief in the authority's superior competence or expertise to decide which actions will best serve the subject's interests and goals'. The classic example of competent authority is the doctor giving advice to a patient. If the doctor, based on a diagnosis, provides the patient with the information that suggests they should quit drinking alcohol, while authoritative, this is not backed by legal force and the patient is free to ignore it. Nor is the statement depending on persuasion. Its authority is instantiated not in the force of the argument, but in the doctor's role, and recognised competence in that role. This recognition, in the case of the doctor and in many other (but not all) competent authorities, is supported by the institution of a *profession*.

Competent authority is usually depicted as benign, and asserted only in specific fields. One would be a lot less likely to accept the doctor's authority if he or she was offering advice on how to vote. But Friedson (1968) notes how the institution of professionalisation often leads to an elision of competent and legitimate authority. Professions secure and maintain the ability to regulate their relevant environment, and constrain who can act in the field: e.g. to prescribe drugs, speak in court, or award degrees. In the final section of this chapter, which considers IL more specifically, the argument is made (and cf. O'Connor, 2009) that the library profession has achieved a similar (if not complete) regulation over IL, perhaps to the detriment of its political credentials.

Such regulation, and the authority and institutional structures which support it, do have value in making decisions in a timely and effective manner. But disparate 'cognitive cultures' (Blaug, 2010, 86) can develop between those who hold such authority and those on whom it is asserted. Within organisations and institutions, multiple information landscapes emerge, between which dialogue and open communication is replaced by organisational diktat and limited information flows. Wrong (1995, 71) writes that it is in the interests of power-holders to diversify the forms of power that are brought to bear on the subjects of power. The different forms of power and authority in his classification rarely function in isolation.

Hillsborough 1989: a case study

A case study is useful at this point (see also Whitworth, 2017), as an illustration of how information landscapes and public opinion can be shaped and distorted by multiple forms of political power acting in concert. On 15 April 1989, 96 supporters of Liverpool Football Club were killed in a crush at the Hillsborough stadium, Sheffield, UK. The events were broadcast live on BBC television. Within a few minutes of the disaster becoming apparent, the TV commentary announced that the cause of the crush had been fans without tickets forcing a gate to gain entry to the stadium. This discursive move – the blaming of unruly football fans for the deaths – was repeated and embellished in newspapers over the following days, culminating in *The Sun*'s front page on 19 April. Headlined 'The Truth', it stated that while emergency services were trying to help victims, hooligans assaulted policemen and picked the pockets of corpses.

Families of the victims, backed by football supporters' groups and the community of the city of Liverpool (which launched a boycott of *The Sun* that persists to this day), campaigned to have the inquest verdict of accidental death, overturned and further investigations launched into the cause of the disaster. Despite acknowledgements as early as 1990, in a report compiled by Lord Justice Taylor (Taylor, 1990), that the actual cause of the disaster had been the failure of police control, it took until April 2016, 27 years later, before an inquest formally accepted that Liverpool fans had no culpability whatsoever. Legal responsibility was instead assigned to a variety of authorities including the police officer in charge on the day (who had no previous experience of managing such events and had not conducted an inspection of the stadium) and institutions including South Yorkshire Police, Sheffield Wednesday FC (the owners of the stadium, which had an invalid safety certificate), and the Football Association.

The extraordinary length of time that it took for this version of events to emerge from beneath the initial, official discourse of 'hooliganism' can be attributed to two things. First, the assertion of various forms of competent and legitimate authority (that of the police, the coroner, the judiciary, health and safety authorities, and journalists); second, that those with most to lose from the disaster (the police) were precisely those with the most privileged and immediate access to the public sphere, and could thereby shape relevant information landscapes from the start. BBC commentators made the first announcement of the cause of the disaster – fans forcing the gate – but as they bore no witness to events outside the ground, this information must have been fed to them. Yet whether done deliberately or not, this was later revealed to be misinformation of the most profound significance, as were the later accusations made in *The Sun*. On 10 October 2014, officer Gordon Sykes testified to the Hillsborough inquest (Conn, 2014) that the stories of looting and attacks on police during the disaster were false, largely made in police bars afterwards, fed to the press by White's, a Sheffield press agency, and run as *The Sun*'s lead story almost verbatim. Victims had no such privileged access to the public sphere.

Information about the disaster was therefore configured and presented in ways that deflected scrutiny of core issues, including the cause of the disaster itself, the handling of the initial public enquiry, and the subsequent role of the mainstream media in spreading mis- (and dis-) information. 'Hidden transcripts' (Scott, 1990) always existed, however, embodied within the memories of survivors and the contradictions and tensions between these and the official discourse. To have these transcripts revealed, and the official position finally altered, required a process of community *learning* that needed to be undertaken by these political (and politicised) actors, and their moving into different information landscapes, particularly that of the law and judicial system.

Like other examples of state-corporate cover-ups, such as the scandals involving contaminated pharmaceuticals such as Thalidomide and Factor 8, for culpability to be properly assigned in these cases, dominant versions of events needed to be *critiqued,* regardless of their presentation as 'truth' via the use of manipulation, legitimate authority and competent authority. The challenge to the dominant information landscape around Hillsborough was a *rational* one, but it was not – and could not – wholly be conducted through the normative, formal political system. It emerged instead from the micro-level, using a range of media to promulgate an alternative discourse that eventually displaced the official position, backed as it was by propaganda and various other forms of political power and influence over information flows. Throughout this process there were a number of politicians prominent in the media, such as Bernard Ingham and Boris Johnson, who continued to push the 'official line' that Liverpool fans were to blame (Mulholland, 2012).

On the other hand, very similar, but less 'rational', processes can challenge authority in ways that turn out to have damaging consequences, such as the campaign that questioned the safety of the MMR (Measles, Mumps and Rubella) vaccine (Thompson, 2008). To guard against the emergence of what Thompson calls 'counterknowledge', and steer clear of a relativist position where if enough people critique an authority (despite the lack of grounds to do so) then their critique should be accepted, a normative core must remain in any political theory of information and IL.

Theories of discourse

A rich tradition of political philosophy focuses on the micro-levels of discourse and how the influence asserted over ideas and action at this micro-level can accumulate into broader cultural and political change: and to do so rationally and normatively, not simply through the popularity of 'alternative' viewpoints. The remainder of this chapter considers the work of three influential authors in this tradition, Jürgen Habermas, Mikhail Bakhtin and Michel Foucault.

Jürgen Habermas

Habermas is a successor to the work of 'Frankfurt School' thinkers such as Horkheimer and Adorno (1972) and Marcuse (1964), as well as, less directly, other second-generation Marxists such as Antonio Gramsci (1971). All were concerned to explain the 'failure' of Marxism and recognised the dangers of the forms of 'rationality' promulgated by the Enlightenment, which had brought an end to widespread want and suffering, but at the cost of developments such as high-technology warfare, control of discourse through the mass media, and consumerism. But with rationality seen as totalitarian and all-pervasive, the Frankfurt School struggled to outline alternatives beyond irrational forces such as love, art and anger – the sort of reactions that help sustain counterknowledge (Thompson, 2008). Habermas sought to move beyond this dead end, not to reject rationality but reconstruct it, arguing that only in a society in which a general notion of reason can be evoked can political decisions be justified.

However, the discursive background against which such judgements are made has been distorted. Habermas describes how the active public political sphere has been transformed into 'a manipulated public sphere in which states and corporations use "publicity" in the modern sense of the word to secure for themselves a kind of plebiscitary acclamation' (Outhwaite, 1996, 7). These entities manipulate the public sphere in a hegemonic and technocratic fashion, their activities removed from rational control. Yet Habermas maintains that through public communication and communicative structures, such controls can be re-established. Hence his development of the idea of 'communicative rationality' in the *Theory of Communicative Action* (Habermas, 1984, 1987).

Communicatively rational action is oriented not to fulfilling goals, but reaching consensus. While real-world deliberative fora are frequently distorted, nevertheless, the *ideal* is of free information and participation in decision-making processes by all who are affected by them. Thereby, for Habermas, rationality

> ... can be measured by the degree of openness or closure in commun-
> ication; ... the goals of truth, freedom and justice are not mere utopian
> dreams, but are anticipated in ordinary communication; and ... the goal of
> emancipation is presupposed in the constitution of the species as linguistic
> beings.
>
> (Ray, 1993, 26–7)

The possibility of consensus in any given communicative exchange exists because of the shared background that Habermas calls the 'lifeworld' – in essence, an amalgam of all extant information landscapes. But Habermas notes how sub-regions of this lifeworld have been differentiated from others, through *colonisation* by the 'steering media' of money and power (Habermas, 1987, 180–5), which come to substitute for communicative rationality – persuasion (to use Wrong's term), the force of the better argument – when it comes to making decisions. There is a reification of institutions and the forms of authority embedded within them, and a consequent devaluing of dialogue and critique, the idea that *authoritative* decisions can be made, or at least informed, by public debate based on available and relevant information.

Two important elements of Habermas's work are particularly significant for IL. First, the importance of *scrutiny and ongoing validation* of judgements. In *Justification and Application* (1993) Habermas acknowledges that real discourses are imperfect. Judgements resulting from them, even if consensual at the time of their making, are provisional. Circumstances will change, new information emerge, consequences be manifested. Therefore, there is a need for ongoing *validation* of judgements, periodically lifting them up to (public) scrutiny. This is not just a plea to attend to injustices such as Hillsborough, but to be constantly *vigilant* (Blaug, 1999) over authority, and the information landscapes that sustain it.

Habermas's other significant contribution is to recognise that the discourses that thereby test validity claims (1984, 8–10), always take place in a particular *context*:

> It would be utterly pointless to engage a practical discourse without a
> horizon provided by the lifeworld of a specific social group and without real

conflicts in a concrete situation in which the actors consider it incumbent upon them to reach a consensual means of negotiating some controversial social matter. Practical discourses are always related to the concrete point of departure of a disturbed normative agreement. These antecedent disruptions determine the topics that are up for discussion.

(Habermas, 1990, 103)

Mikhail Bakhtin

The essentiality of context when it comes to making informed judgements about information and practice is also recognised by key writers on IL such as Lloyd (2010). Here, it provides a connection with another writer whose ideas are significant for understanding IL, at the level of discourse: Mikhail Bakhtin (see also Whitworth, 2014, 119 ff).

Bakhtin and Habermas:

> . . . both assert the special importance of dialogic realms wherein relationships of power are partly neutralised by being brought into the foreground . . . [and thereby] help to define a more ethical world by demystifying some of the ways in which domination is embedded in acts of speech and communication.

(Garvey, 2000, 371)

Habermas has been criticised as being mired in theory and difficult to apply to practice. For example, Benhabib (1994) observes that despite the apparent importance of context, Habermasian discourse ethics is too general and lacking in practical guidance to be useful in real-world political fora. But Bakhtin's formulation of this idea of a 'dialogic realm' does not have the universalist (and thus idealistic) character of consensus as a unifying force (Gardiner, 2004, 30). Bakhtin's worldview is one where dialogue itself is pre-eminent. All meaning, all agency and transformation, is generated by dialogic interaction. The world is a 'polyphony', one where many voices speak, each making 'utterances' that respond to what has been said before, and can be responded to in turn. Through these multiple and constantly occurring interactions, new ideas and circumstances arise, and judgements are made.

Bakhtin's ideas affirm the notion that IL is 'prosaic' (Morson and Emerson, 1990, 15), often taking place where it is 'hardly noticeable' (*ibid.*, 23):

For Bakhtin, literacy is applicable to every utterance, written or spoken, and not limited only to specialised texts. . . He recognises the reality of authority. . . but also that, because of the nature of language, no 'final state' is possible in a communicative situation. Thus, there can be no absolute authority. Everything contains the possibility of change and transformation within itself at multiple levels, from the single utterance up to the structures of language and communication . . .

(Whitworth, 2014, 120)

For Bakhtin, political legitimacy comes via dialogue, which plays a constitutive role in human decision making and creativity. Multiple practices and ways of making judgements about information that have developed in different contexts can come together in dialogue: a space where each participant's utterances, and the bases for them, are open to scrutiny. The ontological basis for these judgements is not, as it is for Habermas, a universalist 'lifeworld' that lies behind every speech act. Instead, Bakhtin acknowledges that judgements are always formed within a specific physical and temporal location. Bakhtin calls this the 'chronotope' (Bakhtin, 1986, 42): a term derived from the Greek words for time and place. The chronotope is the horizon of the speaker, the landscape in which they are present (Holquist, 2009). It defines 'parameters of value' (Morson and Emerson, 1990, 369) for judgements. A judgement made in a specific chronotope can never be replicated, just as no utterance ever has exactly the same meaning when made again – even the fact of its repetition is a form of response, one that causes micro-adjustments to information landscapes.

The contextual nature of these judgements means that dialogue is innately creative, giving rise to new possibilities and practices (Whitworth, 2014, 122). It is in the differences between chronotopes that there is *agency* and transformation for Bakhtin. Information landscapes are all 'imperfectly suited to their present use – and for that very reason relatively adaptable to future uses, to which they will also be acceptably but not optimally suited' (Morson and Emerson, 1990, 292). The richness of human discourse means we each individually act at the nexus of many landscapes, and it is through dialogue that the boundaries between landscapes are crossed. Transference across boundaries is essential, as all dialogues are ultimately imperfect as decision making fora, as already noted: they require further review and ongoing scrutiny and (normative) legitimation (Habermas, 1993). This can only take place if, at times, participants 'engage in role-playing, to assume the perspectives and interests of others and give them equal weight to their own in the course of argumentation about the general acceptability of the consequences of proposed norms' (Eckersley, 1999, 26–7). This advocacy, representing the interests of other (absent) parties in a decision, is fundamental to the idea of active or 'deep' citizenship (Clarke, 1996). Bakhtin, too, recognises the importance of boundary-crossing: the ability to speak credibly (in other words, with 'authority') in different genres and contexts, and thereby to bring to these contexts new and different perspectives, to translate issues from one discourse to another.

The value of diversity has been particularly promoted in IL through the work of Christine Bruce and colleagues (Bruce, Edwards and Lupton, 2006; Bruce, 2008). The different 'frames' of IL that these authors outline include the *relational* frame of IL, where IL is developed in learners through encouraging their 'experience of variation'. Simply exposing learners to different perspectives is not sufficient however. As Freire notes (1985, 49): '. . . to be an act of knowing, the adult literacy process demands among teachers and students a relationship of authentic dialogue. True dialogue unites subjects together in the cognition of a knowable object, which mediates between them.' Thus, the relational frame requires learners to have the chance to explore these different landscapes, and experience variation with reference to a 'knowable object' that can encourage dialogue across the boundaries of a context and its information landscape. It is the role of IL educators to help learners explore and navigate different information landscapes, and thus help them make judgements about contexts with which they are unfamiliar (Webster and Whitworth, 2017).

In summary, a Bakhtinian perspective sees political legitimacy and rationality as dependent on discourse, dialogue and diversity. But this is not literacy as the unquestioning (and thus relativist) embrace of diversity. Dialogue is the tool by which one exercises judgements and selectivity, developing an understanding of how to translate between settings, cross boundaries and build networks, all of which allow the validity of particular courses of action to be not just asserted, but investigated and scrutinised after application (cf. Habermas, 1993). It was through this kind of cognitive work that the Hillsborough justice campaign achieved enough social pressure for the political authorities to eventually accede to their demands for a fresh inquest and verdict.

Michel Foucault

A third perspective on the relationship between discourse, information and power comes from the work of Michel Foucault. The title of his book *Power/Knowledge* (1980) makes it clear that he sees these two concepts as closely related, though as Kendall and Wickham (1999, 55) point out, to claim that he thinks they are the *same* is a 'vulgar reading' of his work. Instead, Foucault sees power in the social realm as, at one level, not dissimilar to electrical power: flowing through systems and potentially accessible by all. It is when power is drawn upon that knowledge can form – but at the same time, stratification occur and control over discourses be asserted.

Foucault's ideas have developed from his studies of the 'archaeology' of knowledge(s) (Foucault, 1972), particularly in the contexts of penology and criminality (1977), sexuality (1978) and medicine and mental health (1973). In each case his archaeological investigations suggest how coercive, legitimate and competent authorities assert power to define discourses, and create information landscapes, backed up by institutions, that coerce people to conform to these definitions. Categorisations become endemic: for example, definitions of 'sane' or 'insane' that accord with the discourses of 'madness', its forms, limits and manifestations, that are promulgated by the mental health establishment.

A political question that must be asked about IL is: who shapes the discourses that define the limits of the IL concept, its definitions and manifestations, in education and elsewhere? Critten (2016) notes how the Association of College and Research Libraries (ACRL) has asserted particular influence thanks, first, to its *Standards* published in 2000. O'Connor (2009) also 'uncovered the American political mythologies and assumptions inherent in the conception of information literacy, as reflected in the ACRL standards' (Julien and Williamson, 2011, n. p.). The ACRL's move to the 2015 *Information Literacy Framework* (ACRL, 2015) was an attempt to be less prescriptive, but, as a body 'ascribed with [competent] authority by academic librarians, ACRL's presence in the Framework document still gives the Framework a sensibility of prescriptiveness, of being a set of standards, even as it was purposefully defined *not* to be a set of standards' (Critten, 2016, 27). And the move to the Framework did not change, as if overnight, how librarians were teaching IL. The practices that they had developed around the Standards still constitute a dominant discourse (Downey, 2016, 22).

Foucault is a critical theorist whose ideas can uncover oppressive dimensions often concealed within 'emancipatory' educational practice (*pace* Brookfield, 2005, 121). For example, a recent study by Webster and Gunter (2018) draws on Foucault to investigate how, and in what ways, authority over information practices can be distributed across a learning community when that community's information landscape has been shaped by authoritative discourses, in this case those of the tutor and institution. Webster and Gunter's analysis is based on recorded dialogues within 20 small groups of learners on a postgraduate course.

Each group worked collaboratively on complex tasks that required them to make a range of judgements about information and technology in order to solve problems – thus, to exhibit information literacy. A particular conduit of power and authority in this setting was the fact that these dialogues were subjected to grading, with grades being assigned based on both group and individual performance. Linking good IL practice to the award of grades and qualifications is a way of encouraging and rewarding it, but also an imposition of one person's (or institution's) authority over practice, and the information landscape that has been built around it. In response, will students subsequently engage with information practices in ways that empower them, or will they present a 'persona', a practice/identity nexus, that they sense will be rewarded (what Wrong calls, authority by inducement)?

Webster and Gunter recognise various 'Foucauldian' processes as present in how students exhibit IL in this setting, including surveillance and normalisation. Students disciplined each other when it came to their work. Note this quote from a student, for example (Webster and Gunter, 2018, 78):

> I felt I had to impress people and so I didn't want to be too controversial and I wanted just to be really encouraging to everyone. I certainly didn't feel free to write anything . . . I definitely felt that I modified my behaviour but only as far as what I would do in a professional environment.

What *authority* is being asserted here? As with all real situations there is a mixture: Webster and Gunter (2018) present evidence of personal authority (students wanting to please the tutor because they like him); authority by inducement (get a good mark). There is also competent authority – 'the tutor knows best' – about how to develop students' information practice. But at the same time Webster and Gunter (2018, 81) are clear that some students, at least, have developed their own authority within these settings. They learn to engage in dialogue in ways that help define the IL practices of the group, in ways that not only accord with the perceived expectations of the marking rubric, but emerge in ways that allow these IL capabilities to expand beyond the parameters of the original, tutor-created environment, and thus bring new resources into the information landscapes being constantly created by the practices within these groups. Thus, this is a view of power to which IL is not subservient. Instead, IL is intimately entwined with how individuals acquire authority.

Conclusion

The intention of this chapter has been to provide some bases for thinking about the relationship between information literacy, democracy, citizenship and political engagement. It is the job of the remaining chapters in this book to explore, in more depth, how this relationship plays out in specific contexts. Nevertheless, some concluding remarks are worth making here regarding what the critical theories of Habermas, Bakhtin and Foucault have to say about IL and how this field has been conceptualised.

Since IL began to coalesce as a concept and field of study in the 1970s, a number of authors have argued for a critical, politically aware approach. For instance, Hamelink (1976), inspired by Freire, lauds community-controlled media that can provide an 'alternative to news' for those groups ill-served by the corporate-dominated mainstream. But the absorption of IL into the library, a process which started in the 1980s (see Whitworth, 2014, 48 ff), has meant that the discourses of the field are dominated by the library perspective. While many excellent investigations of 'critical information literacy' exist, even if they do not call it that (see for example Pawley, 2003; Elmborg, 2006; Downey, 2016), these investigations are of IL as enacted within a library setting. This places limits on how much the critical practices can attend to the application of IL in prosaic, everyday dialogues, and the way power is promulgated through these dialogues. Critical theory calls into doubt any idea that librarians (and they alone?) can bring a politically 'neutral' perspective to an educational space. Downey provides several case studies of where librarians, working with critical pedagogy in IL, attempt to position themselves as 'peers' to the students, a position of 'non-authority' and 'non-expertise' (see the case of 'Jack' in Downey, 2016, 87). It is only towards the end of the book that Downey acknowledges (*ibid.*, 161) that '[a]s educators in their own right, librarians should not pretend to be neutral and they should also not hold to the false notion that libraries are neutral.'

This position offers little basis to reflect on how the library profession asserts its competent authority (to use Wrong's term) to have defined IL in the discourse. Attempts to annul authority and expertise also risk reinforcing the dominant discourse of librarians as passive and powerless, and the typical one-shot IL instruction offered by libraries is highly limiting when it comes to establishing dialogues, experiencing variation and allowing for the transformation of information practices among learners. In any case, higher education is a context of its own, defining its boundaries in particular ways and by no means always an inclusive space. Where people do engage with HE, this is usually for a limited time. Bakhtin's prosaic view of literacy demonstrates, emphatically, that to see IL instruction as something only the library is 'qualified' to undertake (or has 'competent authority' in, using Wrong's term) is itself a way of bounding it and limiting access to the domain.

Engagement with the politics of discourse, as explored by Habermas, Bakhtin and Foucault amongst others, thus emphasises the need for IL to extend out of the library and out of HE (Smith, 2015, 55). Critten (in Downey, 2016, 5–6) declares that if IL must be situated in a context to have meaningful application, then it needs to be situated *in politics*, not a 'neutral' academic setting. These are the areas of concern of several other chapters in this book.

In summary, then, general themes which have emerged from this discussion of critical theory and are relevant to this book's interest in democracy, inclusion and citizenship are, first, that IL is what is brought to bear when, in interpersonal discourses, we explore the legitimacy of judgements about information and scrutinise validity claims (see also Whitworth, 2016, 71–4). Teaching IL involves creating and sustaining environments in which diverse perspectives are empowered to not only exist, but to come together in dialogue about 'knowable objects' that have relevance across boundaries, and allow translation to occur between these different landscapes and the chronotopes within them. Critical, political IL education involves the development of techniques and tools, but also empathy, the ability to engage in dialogue, collaboration and production, all of which enhance the ability to navigate information landscapes, including, most critically, those that are not one's own; and through doing so, develop the capacity to make judgements about the normative applicability of proposed courses of action in one's own and in other contexts. IL is, and will never, be, a fixed point; it must always be adaptable to new challenges, forms of power and hegemony that seek to control and conceal information and limit the ability of most people to make informed and meaningful political judgements. These abilities, and thus IL itself, are bound up with political power and authority and can never be separated from them.

References

ACRL (Association of College and Research Libraries) (2015) *Framework for Information Literacy for Higher Education*, www.ala.org/acrl/standards/ilframework.

Andersen, R., Heath, A. and Sinnott, R. (2002) Political Knowledge and Electoral Choice, *British Elections & Parties Review*, **12** (1), 11–27.

Angus, I. (2001) *Emergent Politics: an essay on social movements and democracy*, Arbeiter Ring.

Bakhtin, M. (1986) *Speech Genres and Other Late Essays*, ed. by C. Emerson and M. Holquist, University of Texas Press.

Bell, D. (1976) The Coming of the Post-industrial Society, *The Educational Forum,* **40** (4), 574–9.

Benhabib, S. (1994) Deliberative Rationality and Models of Democratic Legitimacy, *Constellations*, **1** (1), 6–52.

Blaug, R. (1999) The Tyranny of the Visible: problems in the evaluation of anti-institutional radicalism, *Organization*, **6** (1), 33–56.

Blaug, R. (2010) *How Power Corrupts*, Palgrave Macmillan.

Brookfield, S. (2005) *The Power of Critical Theory for Adult Learning and Teaching*, Open University Press.

Bruce, C. (2008) *Informed Learning*, Association of College & Research Libraries.

Bruce, C., Edwards, S. and Lupton, M. (2006) Six Frames for Information Literacy Education: a conceptual framework for interpreting the relationships between theory and practice, *Innovation in Teaching and Learning in Information and Computer Sciences*, **5** (1), 1–18.

Burchinal, L. G. (1976) The Communications Revolution: America's third century challenge. In *The Future of Organizing Knowledge: papers presented at the Texas A & M University Library's Centennial Academic Assembly*, 24 September, Texas A & M University Library.

Castells, M. (1996) *The Rise of the Network Society. The Information Age: economy, society, and culture*, vol. I, (Information Age Series), Blackwell.

Clarke, P. B. (1996) *Deep Citizenship*, Pluto Press.

Conn, D. (2014) Hillsborough Inquest: police admit Sun report of fans looting corpses was false, *The Guardian*, 10 October, www.theguardian.com/uk-news/2014/oct/10/hillsborough-inquest-police-admit-sun-report-fans-looted-corpses-false.

Critten, J. (2016) Death of the Author(ity): repositioning students as constructors of meaning in information literacy instruction. In McNicol, S. (ed.) *Critical Literacy for Information Professionals*, Facet Publishing, 19–29.

Dahl, R. A. (1961) *Who Governs?: Democracy and power in an American city,* Yale University.

Dinas, E. (2014) Why Does the Apple Fall Far from the Tree? How early political socialisation prompts parent-child dissimilarity, *British Journal of Political Science*, **44** (4), 827–52.

Downey, A. (2016) *Critical Information Literacy: foundations, inspiration and ideas,*

Library Juice Press.

Eckersley, R. (1999) The Discourse Ethic and the Problem of Representing Nature, *Environmental Politics*, **8**, 24–49.

Elmborg, J. (2006) Critical Information Literacy: implications for instructional practice, *Journal of Academic Librarianship*, **32** (2), 192–9.

Foucault, M. (1972) *The Archaeology of Knowledge*, translated Sheridan Smith A.M., Pantheon.

Foucault, M. (1973) *The Birth of the Clinic*, translated Sheridan Smith A.M., Tavistock.

Foucault, M. (1977) *Discipline and Punish*, Sheridan Smith A.M., Vintage.

Foucault, M. (1978) *The History of Sexuality: an introduction*, Vol. 1, Vintage.

Foucault, M. (1980) *Power/Knowledge*, Random House.

Freire, P. (1985) *The Politics of Education: culture, power, and liberation*, Greenwood Publishing Group.

Friedson, E. (1968) The Impurity of Professional Authority. In Becker, H., Geer, B., Riesman, D. and Weiss, R. (eds) *Institutions and the Person*, Aldine, 25–34.

Gardiner, M. E. (2004) Wild Publics and Grotesque Symposiums: Habermas and Bakhtin on dialogue, everyday life and the public sphere, *The Sociological Review*, **52** (1), 28–48.

Garvey, T. G. (2000) The Value of Opacity: a Bakhtinian analysis of Habermas's discourse ethics, *Philosophy and Rhetoric*, **33** (4), 370–90.

Gilroy-Ware, M. (2017) *Filling the Void: emotion, capitalism and social media*, Duncan Baird Publishers.

Giroux, H. A. (2011) *On Critical Pedagogy*, Continuum.

Gramsci, A. (1971) *Prison Notebooks*, Lawrence & Wishart.

Habermas, J. (1984) *The Theory of Communicative Action. Vol 1: Reason and the Rationalization of Society*, Heinemann.

Habermas, J. (1987) *The Theory of Communicative Action. Vol 2: Lifeworld and System – A Critique of Functionalist Reason*, Polity Press.

Habermas, J. (1990) *Moral Consciousness and Communicative Action*, Polity Press.

Habermas, J. (1993) *Justification and Application: remarks on discourse ethics*, Polity Press.

Hamelink, C. (1976) An Alternative to News, *Journal of Communication*, **20**, 120–3.

Henn, M. and Foard, N. (2012) Young People, Political Participation and Trust in Britain, *Parliamentary Affairs*, **65** (1), 47–67.

Holquist, M. (2009) The Role of Chronotope in Dialogue. In Junefelt, K. and Nordin, P. (eds) *Proceedings from the Second International Interdisciplinary Conference on Perspectives and Limits of Dialogism in Mikhail Bakhtin*, Stockholm, 3–5 June, 9–17.

Horkheimer, M. and Adorno, T. (1972) *The Dialectic of Enlightenment*, Scabury.

Julien, H. and Williamson, K. (2011) Discourse and Practice in Information Literacy and Information Seeking: gaps and opportunities, *Information Research*, **16** (1).

Kendall, G. and Wickham, G. (1999) *Using Foucault's Methods*, Sage.

Lindsay, A. D. (ed.) (1906) Plato: *The Republic,* Everyman.

Lloyd, A. (2010) *Information Literacy Landscapes: information literacy in education, workplace and everyday contexts*, Chandos Publishing.

Marcuse, H. (1964) *One-Dimensional Man: studies in the ideology of advanced industrial society,* Routledge and Kegan Paul.

Morson, G. S. and Emerson, C. (1990) *Mikhail Bakhtin: creation of a prosaics*, Stanford University Press.

Mulholland, H. (2012) Boris Johnson Apologises for Hillsborough Article, *The Guardian*, 12 September, www.theguardian.com/football/2012/sep/13/boris-johnson-apologises-hillsborough-article.

Norris, P. (2002) *Democratic Phoenix: reinventing political activism*, Cambridge University Press.

O'Connor, L. (2009) Information Literacy as Professional Legitimation: a critical analysis, *Journal of Education for Library and Information Science*, **50** (2), 79–89.

Outhwaite, W. (ed.) (1996) *The Habermas Reader*, Polity Press.

Owens, M. (1976) State, Government and Libraries, *Library Journal,* **101** (1), 19–28.

Pariser, E. (2011) *The Filter Bubble: what the internet is hiding from you*, Penguin.

Pawley, C. (2003) Information Literacy: a contradictory coupling, *Library Quarterly*, **73** (4), 422–42.

Pew Research Center (2014) www.people-press.org/2014/06/12/political-polarization-in-the-american-public.

Ray, L. J. (1993) *Rethinking Critical Theory: emancipation in the age of global social movements*, Sage.

Scott, J. C. (1990) *Domination and the Arts of Resistance*, Yale University Press.

Shenk, D. (1997) *Data Smog: surviving the information glut*, Harper Collins.

Smith, L. (2015) *Critical Information Literacy and Political Agency*, PhD thesis submitted to the University of Strathclyde, UK.

Taylor, S. P. (1990) *The Hillsborough Stadium Disaster: 15 April 1989: inquiry by the Rt Hon Lord Justice Taylor: final report: presented to Parliament by the Secretary of State for the Home Department by command of Her Majesty*, HM Stationery Office.

Thompson, D. (2008) *Counterknowledge*, Atlantic.

Webster, F. (2014) *Theories of the Information Society*, 4th edn, Routledge.

Webster, L. and Gunter, H. (2018) How Power Relations Affect the Distribution of

Authority: implications for information literacy pedagogy, *Journal of Information Literacy*, **12** (1), 68–85.

Webster, L. and Whitworth, A. (2017) Distance Learning as Alterity: facilitating the experience of variation and professional information practice, *Journal of Information Literacy*, **11** (2), 69–85.

Whitworth, A. (2014) *Radical Information Literacy: reclaiming the political heart of the IL movement*, Chandos Publishing.

Whitworth, A. (2016) 'Anyone Can Cook': critical literacy in the workplace. In McNicol, S. (ed.) *Critical Literacy for Information Professionals*, 65–78, Facet Publishing.

Whitworth, A. (2017) Lessons from the Borg Cube: information literacy and the knowledge of difference, Keynote speech at European Conference on Information Literacy (ECIL) 20 September, St Malo, France.

Wrong, D. H. (1995) *Power: its forms, bases and uses*, 2nd edn, Transaction.

Zurkowski, P. G. (1974) *The Information Service Environment: relationships and priorities,* Report presented to the National Commission on Libraries and Information Science, Washington DC.

3

What intellectual empathy can offer information literacy education

Andrea Baer

Introduction

This chapter explores the roles that affect, social identity and beliefs play in how people engage with information about politically and emotionally charged issues and the implications for information literacy education, particularly in politically polarised times. Considering research from cognitive psychology and education, I also suggest ways to move beyond traditional approaches to information literacy that tend to focus on logic and 'objectivity' while neglecting the significance of personal beliefs and social identity to information behaviours. I give particular focus to philosopher Maureen Linker's concept of 'intellectual empathy' – 'the cognitive-affective elements of thinking about identity and social difference' (Linker, 2014, 12). Intellectual empathy, I argue, is crucial for the kind of critically reflective information literacy that is especially needed in order to foster democratic dialogue and civic engagement in an increasingly diverse and global world.

Background

On the morning of 9 November 2016, I walked into my information literacy classroom at the University of West Georgia disoriented and disillusioned, unsure how to begin talking about a final research project and unsure how much that assignment really mattered now. Along with many other US citizens and residents, I had woken up to news that Donald Trump would be the 45th President of the United States, after he had run a highly divisive campaign that repeatedly played on fears that a more ethnically, racially, and religiously diverse society was a threat to the country's prosperity and 'values'.

That morning I asked myself how I would start class. My lesson plan seemed ridiculous now, dismissive of the elephant in the room. The previous evening students at an election viewing event had sat on two opposite sides of the room: they had self-segregated themselves by race and political alliances. I had also heard of white students heckling black students about the final outcome of the election. These were signs of the racial and political tension on my campus about which I had heard, but had not witnessed directly. While this wasn't too surprising given my geographic location (a small town in a conservative state) and the student population (racially diverse and primarily first-generation students from the state of Georgia), I hadn't had to confront this reality in the same way before. This was new territory, and I wasn't sure where or how to step.

Reconsidering my approach to the day's class, I discovered the resource *Returning to the Classroom after the Election* from the University of Michigan's Center for Research on Learning and Teaching (Center for Research on Learning and Teaching, University of Michigan, 2016). I decided to follow some of its recommendations, which were intended to acknowledge students' current mental and emotional states and to better enable a more connected and engaged classroom. Later that morning I began the class with an acknowledgement of the mix of emotions and thoughts that students might be having at this moment, and I allowed time for students to share their reactions in a respectful manner. Many of my students, like me, were dazed and unsure if they were in a dream. Most stared into the distance as if in disbelief; some smiled with quiet reserve. Most remained silent, but a few chose to speak about the vitriol expressed on both sides of the political divide and the undeniable divisions in the country. People listened; people felt uncomfortable. There were no resolutions, except that I would strive to foster an inclusive classroom environment founded on mutual respect and a shared goal for learning together.

Looking back almost two years later, I see that this was a pivotal point in my teaching. Not because of a sudden radical change in my teaching approaches, but because of a gradual process of rethinking my conceptions of information literacy and my pedagogical priorities and approaches. Though throughout my librarian career I have believed that the affective, social and political are crucial (and too often neglected) dimensions of information literacy, my teaching often did not adequately reflect their importance. The current socio-political moment in the USA, and more specifically my experience of teaching on a racially and politically diverse campus in the conservative state of Georgia, has pushed me – along with many other educators – to reconsider what I most want students to carry with them when they leave my classroom. Gradually my classes are coming to better reflect that, even if there will always be some tension between my hopes and the realities.

A broader approach to information literacy

The charged rhetoric that has come into sharp relief in the USA since 2016 asks educators and citizens to pose deeper questions about our social structures, discursive practices and interpersonal relationships. We need new ways of engaging in civic life, and new ways of engaging with our students, regardless of their political views or their backgrounds. In the light of research on political polarisation and motivated reasoning, simply teaching students to be well-informed, how to spot 'fake news' or how to search a database for empirical research may be helpful, but these alone are not enough. And they are probably not the most important things to teach. We need new approaches to and new conceptions of information literacy and information literacy education. As danah boyd wrote (boyd, 2017), '[w]e need to get creative and build the social infrastructure necessary for people to meaningfully and substantively engage across existing structural lines. . . . [W]e need to focus on the underlying issues at play. No simple band-aid will work.'

Recently other information literacy educators and scholars have similarly called for new conceptions of information literacy and new pedagogical approaches that foreground the powerful role that beliefs and cognitive biases play in information behaviours. Nicole Cooke has explored the unsettling ways that emotion can influence people's information behaviours, and in particular their engagement with disinformation. As she observed in a keynote conference presentation in 2019, 'Despite knowing better intellectually, people fall prey to their emotional responses to information because our not so latent fears, prejudices, boredom, anxiety and any number of other emotion-based impulses are powerful and convincing, even if our "heads" tell us otherwise' (Cooke, 2019, n.p.). Geoff Walton (Walton, 2017) and Mark Lenker (Lenker, 2016), expressing similar concerns, have argued for expanding conceptions of information literacy and information literacy education in order to better address the roles of affect, beliefs and cognitive biases in information literacy. As Walton argues, we need to develop understandings of information literacy that acknowledge the significance of 'psychological notions of worldview, misinformation, confirmation bias, motivated reasoning and epistemic beliefs' in how people engage with and evaluate information (Walton, 2017, 137). Similarly, Lenker asserts that we can broaden the scope of information literacy education 'to include more than just knowledge of information and its sources' but also 'knowledge of how people interact with information, particularly the ways that motivated reasoning can influence citizens' interactions with political information' (Lenker, 2016, 511). As Cooke, Walton and Lenker illustrate, educators need to address the deeper roots of what influences human thinking and information behaviours, often in unconscious ways.

These deeper roots include the role of beliefs and social identity in how people seek, evaluate, share and use information. The self-reflective approaches to information literacy education that I consider in this chapter invite students to become more self-aware learners who are better positioned to engage critically and responsibly with their local and global communities. More specifically, 'intellectual empathy', an ability to consider the viewpoints, experiences and reasoning of others and to appreciate how social identity and social difference may influence our beliefs, can enable the self-reflective and socially engaged qualities needed when engaging with information.

In this chapter I focus in particular on Maureen Linker's conception of intellectual empathy. It offers a lens through which to engage with issues of social identity and social difference that can be sources of human connection, as well as sources of divisiveness. Linker's work on teaching critical thinking and fostering intellectual empathy offers a great deal to information literacy educators who explore with students the affective, cognitive, social and political dimensions of information literacy that are often unrecognised but nonetheless powerfully influence individual and collective thought and discourse. The concept of intellectual empathy can be a powerful means through which to encourage in students the curiosity, openness and criticality that are essential to reflective inquiry and civic engagement.

Linker's pedagogical approaches are alternatives to the often combative nature of political and academic discourse, which she relates to a tradition of adversarial argument in Western culture. Linker instead models ways to encourage self-reflection, open inquiry and appreciation of social difference. Such abilities better enable individuals to recognise how our social identities and beliefs can influence how we seek out, evaluate and use information. Without an awareness of this relationship, it is far more difficult to examine information and ideas critically. Because most people want to view themselves as reasonable and critical thinkers, our own biases and motivated reasoning can be difficult to examine. Linker's work helps to make this work more approachable and meaningful.

To provide further context for the relevance of Linker's work to information literacy education at (and beyond) this socio-political moment, I first discuss research on the relationship between socio-political beliefs, motivated reasoning and information behaviours. Then, considering their influence on how we reason and how we engage with information, I explore how the concept of intellectual empathy can inform approaches to information literacy education and how it has influenced the design of my information literacy credit course.

The ideas in this chapter are largely born out of my experiences teaching at the time of this writing (2018) in the southern USA. However, political polarisation and social conflict are hardly unique to my class setting or my geographic location. I hope that the pedagogical concepts and strategies that I consider can encourage critical and reflective inquiry far beyond my immediate environment.

Socio-political beliefs, motivated reasoning and information behaviours

Critically examining evidence and arguments and engaging in critical thought and inquiry is much easier when our views align with those of others or when examining issues about which we don't have strong beliefs. It is far more difficult when considering viewpoints, evidence and arguments that challenge long-held beliefs or our sense of self or of social belonging. This is well supported by research on motivated reasoning, which indicates that our evaluation of evidence and arguments is driven largely by pre-existing beliefs, convictions or motivations, more so than critical evaluation of evidence. As much as we as humans may wish to believe that our choices and logic are rational and well-informed, numerous psychological studies suggest that we have far less conscious understanding of and control over our decisions and judgements than we realise (Lodge and Taber, 2005; Taber and Lodge, 2016; Druckman, 2012). We regularly engage in 'motivated reasoning' – thinking that is heavily influenced, often unconsciously, by our own beliefs and agendas.

Motivated reasoning tends to be especially strong when we feel passionately about an issue, as is often the case with political and social issues. Thus, evaluating evidence accurately and examining arguments critically is especially challenging when encountering information about political or contentious issues, which often evokes strong pre-existing beliefs and emotions. As Milton Lodge and Charles S. Taber have found, when individuals engage with information about social and political issues, they are especially prone to automatic cognitive responses that are shaped by pre-existing beliefs and biases (Lodge and Taber, 2005; Taber and Lodge, 2016). Moreover, a number of research studies indicate that individuals who are more informed about an issue are likely to perform more poorly in evaluating the accuracy of information than those who are less informed. This is probably because those who are more knowledgeable about an issue are also likely to have already formulated strong opinions about that issue and thus to be more resistant than others with less strong views to reconsidering their beliefs (Lodge and Taber, 2005; Taber and Lodge 2016; Kahne and Bowyer, 2017). While educators in particular might like to believe that those who are better informed will make sounder and more reasoned decisions, research on motivated reasoning indicates that this is often not true.

Motivated reasoning does serve some functions. Political and social issues frequently remind people of their core values, beliefs and social connections, all of which are vital to a sense of self and social belonging. Thus, humans have good reason to think in ways that keep those aspects of themselves and their experiences intact. But people may tell themselves that they have reached certain conclusions through a careful consideration of all of the evidence when that is not necessarily the case. In a similar way, most individuals tend to believe that if they are well-informed on an issue, they are better equipped to examine fairly evidence and arguments about that issue.

Politically polarised climates present further obstacles to critical thinking and dialogue. In the USA this became particularly evident amidst the heated rhetoric of the 2016 Presidential campaign, as family members and previous friends 'unfriended' one another on Facebook when it became too difficult to see views or statements that felt threatening or even hostile to their identities, lifestyles or deeply held beliefs and values. In such environments, how does one engage with the 'other side', or is it even a good idea to do so?

In such climates a common and understandable impulse is to retreat to insulated communities and echo chambers, to places that provide some sense of solace from the messiness of our social and political environments. While this inclination can be helpful in many contexts, if we remain within those chambers, if they become our only spaces of residence rather than places of respite in which we recharge before engaging with a wider – but also respectful – circle of people, polarisation will most likely grow even further (this is not to say that one should expose oneself to hateful or destructive rhetoric, as I discuss shortly). Studies by the Pew Research Center suggest that these echo chambers and information silos that we help to construct worsen polarisation (Pew Research Center, 2016, 2017; Barthel and Mitchell, 2017). Not only do we become less aware of the perspectives of others with differing views and the information to which they are exposed; we also become more hostile toward those with differing views (Pew Research Center, 2016). Such circumstances tend to strengthen the human tendency towards motivated reasoning and a dismissal of varying perspectives.

The answer, however, is not as simple as merely listening to other respectfully expressed viewpoints. Research on confirmation bias shows that having one's own views challenged can result in a 'backfire effect' that further reinforces those views, especially is they are strong. Interestingly, among the ways to reduce the likelihood of this backfire effect is by making information less threatening. Reframing information can have a powerful effect, as can self-affirmation exercises like writing about an experience in which you felt good about yourself after acting according to a value that is important to you (Hardisty, Johnson and Weber, 2010). Such research suggests that a disarming approach, like the intellectual empathic mindset that Linker encourages (described in more detail later in this chapter), may reduce the likelihood of the backfire effect.

As such studies show, highly contentious issues often evoke strong beliefs because these issues tend to feel personal. For example, how can an immigrant or a Muslim not have strong feelings about the US ban on immigrants from certain Muslim countries? Or how can a working-class student who has been told from an early age onward that illegal immigration explains why their family can't get a living wage be empathetic to individuals working in the USA illegally and with whom they have had little interaction? Beliefs about such issues are often inextricable from individuals' social identities and senses of self. And those issues have become especially heated as political polarisation has grown. Having one's beliefs questioned or considering alternatives to them can feel like a threat to one's sense of self and to one's community (and in some cases it may well be).

It is easy to feel paralysed when looking at the current political climate and the daily news. This all points to the importance – and the challenges – of ensuring that information literacy education addresses issues of social identity and difference, and their influence on beliefs and information behaviours.

For most educators this is less familiar and less comfortable terrain. We may understandably fear mis-stepping despite good intentions. Part of my own uncertainty comes from recognising that I, like many educators, possess a certain social privilege, in my case as a middle-class and educated individual. I am also white, cisgender, able-bodied and a US citizen, which results in certain social privileges that distance me from social inequities that affect many of my students on a deeply personal level. But the alternative, to do nothing out of fear of mis-stepping, is an even greater risk. Linker's conception of intellectual empathy has helped me explore ways to rethink my teaching in light of these complex realities.

Intellectual empathy and critical thinking

The term 'intellectual empathy' is often referenced without being clearly defined. This reflects the concept's complexity and the challenge of adequately describing it. But outlining what intellectual empathy involves is a useful starting point for conversations about how education can foster more reflective and empathic thought. Among the first places that the term 'intellectual empathy' appears is in Richard Paul's work on 'intellectual virtues'. Intellectual virtues are capacities that are vital to both cognitive and moral development and without which 'intellectual development is circumscribed and distorted' (Paul, 2000, 163). These virtues include 'intellectual humility, courage, integrity, perseverance, empathy and fairmindedness' (Paul, 2000, 166).

Intellectual empathy, as defined by Paul (2000, 169), involves the ability 'to imaginatively put oneself in the place of others in order to genuinely understand them'. This is critical to considering varying perspectives and to critically reading and evaluating sources that may not align with one's pre-existing views, capacities that are vital to true inquiry and democratic dialogue. As Paul continues, intellectual empathy

> . . . requires the consciousness of our egocentric tendency to identify truth with our immediate perceptions or long-standing thought or belief. This trait correlates with the ability to reconstruct accurately the viewpoints and reasoning of others and to reason from premises, assumptions, and ideas other than our own. This trait also correlates with the willingness to remember occasions when we were wrong in the past despite an intense conviction that we were right, and with the ability to imagine our being similarly deceived in a case at hand.
>
> (Paul, 2000, 169)

Paul's discussion of intellectual empathy and other 'intellectual virtues' articulates the value of more holistic pedagogical approaches that encourage reflection on one's own experiences and perceptions and their relationship to those of others.

More recently, Linker has explored the importance of intellectual empathy. She examines how issues of social identity and social difference can be barriers or bridges to more critical thought (elements to which Paul gives less attention). For her, 'intellectual empathy' is 'the *cognitive-affective* elements of thinking about identity and social difference' (Linker, 2014, 12). This requires deliberate reflection on the roles that social identity and social difference play in human beliefs and reasoning. Linker's approach, informed by the work of Miranda Fricker, is rooted in an understanding that 'many insights into judgements about credibility, reliable testimony, and rationality are lost if we fail to face the complexities of social difference, privilege, power, and disadvantage' (Linker, 2011, 113; Fricker, 2007).

Intellectual empathy offers ways to examine evidence and arguments more critically than is possible if individuals are unaware of their own positionality (various social identities and the privileges and disadvantages that come with them) and how they influence their worldviews and relationships to others. Empathy here is a matter of thinking, feeling and reflection. As Linker explains in 'Do Squirrels Eat Hamburgers?: intellectual empathy as a remedy for residual prejudice':

> The intellectually empathic person seeks to develop empathic responses so as to gain a better ground epistemologically – not only with regard to her own beliefs but with regard to the assessment of evidence more generally. Thus, the objective of intellectual empathy is not to imagine that one can simply feel what another person is feeling but rather that one treat the reports of others, particularly those whose social experiences are vastly different from one's own, as credible sources of information for reflectively assessing one's own system of belief.
>
> (Linker, 2011, 125)

This approach is distinct from traditional (and more pervasive) representations of critical thinking that describe evidence and reason as 'objective' and uninfluenced by a speaker's social context or identity. Despite the prevalence of 'objective' models of reasoning and argumentation, research on motivated reasoning repeatedly shows that one's beliefs and sense of social belonging are highly influential in their reasoning and evaluation of evidence, arguments, and information sources. Moreover, when a person identifies with a dominant group, it is much easier to dismiss or to silence the views of those in non-dominant groups. To ignore the powerful roles that social identity and social difference play in reasoning and argumentation is likely to make one more susceptible to cognitive biases that prevent deeper and more critical thought.

At the same time that intellectual empathy emphasises the importance of valuing and listening to the experiences and perspectives of others, this does not mean that any individual viewpoint is just as valid as that of another. Suggesting otherwise runs the risk of absolute relativism, according to which facts, evidence, and certain material realities (e.g., climate change, social inequalities) are inconsequential. For Linker, an intellectually empathic listener does not dismiss the importance of evidence and reasoning. Instead they are able to think more critically because they are 'attuned to rhetorical contexts involving social difference'. Such an individual considers social difference when 'assess[ing] the consistency and coherence of their own beliefs and feelings before making an interpretive judgement' (Linker, 2011, 124).

For Linker (2011, 125, 133) developing our reasoning in this way involves four key skills:

1 Beginning with the perspective of mutual compassion.
2 Acknowledging 'that advantage and disadvantage occur within a matrix of intersecting social properties' (as is described in Kimberly Crenshaw's concept of intersectionality).
3 Recognising that social privilege tends to be invisible to those with that privilege.
4 Recognising 'maybe it's you' judgements, in which an interpreter dismisses a speaker's claim because the interpreter views the related issue as social rather than personal, and learning 'to treat these judgements as opportunities for information and evidence'.

These capacities, Linker believes, work together to better enable individuals to recognise, assess, and reduce residual prejudice. Diminishing such prejudice is vital both for creating a more just society and for enabling the kind of reflective, critical thought for which scholars like Fricker hope (Linker, 2011, 125; Fricker, 2007; Lipman, 2003; Lakoff, 2009).

I would also add to Linker's conception of intellectual empathy that some viewpoints may not be perspectives with which to empathise. As danah boyd argues,

Empathy is a powerful emotion, one that most educators want to encourage. But when you start to empathize with worldviews that are toxic, it's very hard to stay grounded. It requires deep cognitive strength. Scholars who spend a lot of time trying to understand dangerous worldviews work hard to keep their emotional distance.

(boyd, 2018, n.p.)

Linker's four skills of intellectual empathy are crucial for exercising discernment about the limitations of empathy, though Linker does not discuss those skills in these terms.

Linker's book *Intellectual Empathy and Social Justice* (Linker, 2014), a text for college students on critical thinking, illustrates practical applications of her conception of intellectual empathy. Here she invites students to consider how their own backgrounds, experiences and social identities influence their beliefs, thinking and social interactions. She simultaneously introduces students to the science of how the human brain forms and maintain beliefs and how this affects human reasoning, interpersonal relationships, public and political discourse and larger issues of social justice.

Linker also emphasises the influential and often unrecognised role that cognitive biases related to social identity and difference can play in reasoning and argumentation. As she explains, because issues of social identity and difference often are deeply personal, it can be particularly difficult 'to find arguments that rely on reasons and justification rather than insults and hostility' (Linker, 2014, 81). Because of their personal nature, we often have automatic and visceral 'gut-level' responses when engaging with such issues. Moreover, issues of social identity and difference are 'imbued with a history of inequality and opposition, which constrains not only our choices but also our concepts and our language'. In the context of information literacy, these constrained choices include whether we seek out information that challenges or complicates our own beliefs; how we evaluate the evidence and arguments in that information; and whether, how and why we use that information for particular purposes.

Linker's work suggests that critical thinking requires more than analytical skills alone: one also needs to become more cognisant of the roles that identity, affect and cognition play in one's engagement with information. These are aspects of information literacy that generally receive limited attention, despite their powerful influence on how people think and engage with information. They are also probably the hardest aspects of information literacy to teach, and they require time and a venture into less certain territory. But these barriers begin to lessen when educators engage with the work of others like Linker.

Intellectual Empathy and Social Justice offers strategies and key concepts that help individuals to recognise when they or others may be reacting unreflectively to issues of social identity and difference and to develop constructive responses to such moments. Two of the book's foundational concepts have been particularly useful to me in structuring my information literacy course around the theme of cognitive bias:

1 the web of belief, a metaphor for how we form, preserve or change our beliefs and

2 the 'adversary method' of argumentation, which describes the traditional Western approach of 'winning an argument', which often limits critical thought and a consideration of social differences.

These interconnected concepts provide points of departure for exploring how beliefs, reasoning and people's relationships to information are largely shaped by social identities, experiences and environments in ways that often are not always visible.

The 'web of belief'

The web of belief – a metaphor for how people form, maintain or change beliefs – provides a foundation for *Intellectual Empathy and Social Justice* (Quine, 1951; Linker, 2014). As Linker explains, our beliefs are like a spider's web: each belief is connected to the others, and a change to one part of the web inevitably affects the other parts. Because people prefer to have a strong web, they generally resist changes to it. Individuals are particularly reluctant to make changes that lead to instability, as is the case if a core belief that lies at the web centre is challenged.

Core beliefs are the strongest and often the oldest beliefs. They are therefore the most difficult to change. Often these beliefs are closely tied to one's sense of self, to social identity and to core values. At the edges of the web are peripheral beliefs, which are the least resistant to change, since they do not cause radical shifts in the entire web. Intermediary beliefs reside somewhere between the centre and the outer edges of the web.

For the most part the web of belief helps people think and act efficiently throughout the day, but it can also limit the ability to think critically. For example, the web of belief illustrates how all individuals are susceptible to confirmation bias (the tendency to believe information that aligns with pre-existing beliefs and to reject information that misaligns with those beliefs), since confirmation bias helps people preserve stable webs.

The web of belief provides a foundation for Linker's later focus on the relationship between issues of social identity and difference, beliefs and argument. As she discusses, social identity plays a significant role in cognitive judgement and in views of social and political issues, particularly when those issues call to mind 'core beliefs' that have shaped much of one's sense of self and one's thinking over time. Thus, thinking critically about information that may not fit into one's core beliefs often requires examining one's social identity in relation to one's web of belief. This web metaphor is particularly valuable when entering conversations about issues that often are more contentious, as it enables students and teachers to recognise a shared humanity that can ground and re-ground challenging discussions.

The adversary method of argument and co-operative reasoning

Another foundational concept in *Intellectual Empathy and Social Justice* is the 'adversary method' of argumentation. The adversary method, a term introduced by feminist philosopher Janice Moulton, describes the aggressive rhetoric and approaches to argument that are characteristic of much of Western culture and scholarship (Moulton, 1983). As Moulton describes it, an adversarial approach encourages individuals either to uphold or to refute arguments in their entirety and to make the judgement that an argument is either completely right or wrong, rather than considering if some elements of an argument are useful while other elements should be questioned or could be modified and thus strengthened. The adversary method discourages individuals from examining an issue in relation to evidence and perspectives that complicate their own argument and that could actually be used to strengthen that argument. Thus an adversarial approach tends to encourage more simplistic thinking, rather than an appreciation of nuance and complexity.

According to philosopher Catherine E. Hundleby's analysis of critical thinking textbooks, the adversary method dominates much of higher education (Hundleby, 2010). Reporting on this research, Linker explains that this approach undermines critical thinking: 'Because we view those with whom we argue as opponents and not collaborators, we are not positioned to hear their claims with any openness or willingness that would enable us to see how their conclusions are related to our own' (Linker, 2014, 87). Such an approach to argument reinforces one's own biases and assumptions and allows one to keep their 'web of belief' intact in its current form.

I would add that this does not mean that claims that are based on a complete disregard for well-founded evidence (e.g., denial of climate change) or that dismiss universal human dignity and rights (e.g., white supremacy) should be considered legitimate topics for debate. Such ideas often shut down dialogue more than they open it. Hateful rhetoric can also have a silencing effect, particularly for students from marginalised groups who may feel less free to speak. Such argument also does not align with the skills of intellectual empathy that Linker describes in 'Do Squirrels Eat Hamburgers' (e.g., beginning with mutual compassion, recognising that social privilege is often invisible to those who have that privilege).

The combative qualities of adversary argument, which are typically associated with masculinity, have overall made argumentation more accessible to individuals who generally experience a greater degree of social privilege. As Hundleby writes, '[t]he pervasiveness and authority of adversarial argumentation suppresses forms of discourse more available to people who are socially marginalised, regardless of their personal preferences, their comfort levels with different styles of communication, or their cognitive abilities' (Hundleby, 2013, 3). Not only does the adversary method reinforce traditional power structures. It also limits true critical thought because it is driven by attempts to 'win an argument' and to poke holes in another person's reasoning, rather than by a genuine interest in deepening understanding (Hundleby, 2013; Moulton, 1983; Linker, 2014). Though oppositional argument may be at times useful, Hundleby and Linker express concern about when it is presented as the only available approach (Linker, 2014, 87).

While the adversary method that Linker describes is characteristic of much of teaching about argumentation, more co-operative approaches to argument can encourage deeper and more critical thought. Co-operative reasoning, an alternative that Linker proposes in *Intellectual Empathy and Social Justice*, draws from Linker's principles of intellectual empathy (outlined in 'Do Squirrels Eat Hamburgers?'). As she writes:

> Co-operative reasoning involves thinking and reasoning co-operatively about social identity and difference, because when we reason in an adversarial manner, we fail to access the relevant feelings, experiences, and data that are all necessary for understanding the oppressive aspects of social identity. We need to think through these issues together, and this means hearing about how each of us experiences social systems and social categories.
>
> (Linker, 2014, 96)

Such co-operative reasoning involves mutual respect, as well as an acknowledgement that social privilege tends to be invisible to those who have it. Linker recommends that when others express experiences of injustice, individuals consider their own privileges and keep an open mind before jumping to conclusions about that other person's experiences. Using this frame of mind is likely to reduce the negative effects of one's own conscious and unconscious biases and to enable us to be more reflective and civically engaged community members, both within and outside of our classrooms.

Intellectual empathy and information literacy pedagogies

As the title of this chapter implies, the concept of 'intellectual empathy' has been an important catalyst for thinking about my instructional work in new ways. The 2016 US Presidential election and its aftermath prompted me to re-envision my credit-bearing information literacy course, as well as my view of information literacy education more broadly. Over the past two years I have continued to reshape my information literacy course, and Linker's work and the questions it raises have come to play an increasingly significant role in my curriculum.

The most obvious change to my course design has been the course theme, cognitive bias and information behaviours. This focus provides a lens through which students can reflect on the social, political and personal nature of information, while also developing concrete information skills. The class explores topics such as how individuals form, maintain and change beliefs; the powerful and important role that personal beliefs and identity play in information behaviours and the challenges of evaluating information related to issues about which a person feels strongly (as is often the case with political and social issues).

Given the course theme, the web of belief provides a helpful metaphor from the very beginning of the semester. It serves as a touchstone as the class explores the relationship between cognitive bias and information behaviours, common forms of cognitive bias (including confirmation bias and implicit bias) and possibilities for and challenges to counteracting cognitive biases. The adversary method of argumentation and alternatives to it are introduced one to two weeks after the web of belief. This encourages the class to consider how Western and academic cultures and political and public discourses can reinforce cognitive biases and limit thinking.

Taken together, the web of belief and the adversary method are intended to help the class to make better sense of the intense political polarisation that is now particularly evident in the USA and elsewhere. These concepts are relevant to the various ways that students develop their understandings of information as social, political and personal and of themselves as active agents in complex information environments.

Political polarisation and the web of belief

An essential aspect of the course is considering the current socio-political moment in the USA and its influence on political and public discourse, including in the online environments that have become prevalent in everyday life. The concepts of the web of belief and the adversary method prove useful as participants reflect on their own information habits and personal experiences in relation to research on political polarisation and media habits.

Toward the beginning of the course the class reads the first chapter of *Intellectual Empathy and Social Justice*, entitled 'The Web of Belief'. Students reflect on the relevance of this concept to the course theme. Various course materials build on the concept of the web, as students consider issues like the spread of misinformation in politically polarised climates and the human impulse to maintain our webs of belief. Research from the Pew Research Center, such as the 2014 report *Political Polarization and Media Habits* (Mitchell et al., 2014) and the more recent 2017 report *The Partisan Divide on Political Values Grows Even Wider* (Pew Research Center, 2017), provide evidence for the increased ideological divisions in the USA and suggest the significance that information behaviours and online news sources play in this polarisation. Brief videos like 'Why Our Brains Love Fake News' and 'How You Can Burst Your Filter Bubble' draw connections between our beliefs, confirmation bias and online information environments (Above The Noise, Public Broadcasting, 2017; BBC Trending, 2017).

Evaluating source credibility and source bias

The web of belief is also a powerful concept for teaching about source bias and source credibility. This metaphor illustrates how one's worldview and beliefs are often closely tied to one's experiences, background and sense of self and social belonging. This creates an opening for reflecting on the influence that identity and experience often have on the representation and the interpretation of facts and evidence.

A related resource, the video *How Journalists Minimize Bias* (from Facing History's lesson unit 'Facing Ferguson: new literacy in a digital age'), illustrates that identity and perspective can shape the creation and the consumption of the news. The 6½-minute video consists of interviews with journalists on their experiences reporting on the events surrounding the death of Michael Brown, an African-American youth killed by a police officer in Ferguson, Missouri, in 2014. These reporters discuss the difficulties of gathering and evaluating information on this event as the story unfolded. They articulate that facts and evidence remain vital to understanding events and the issues surrounding them, at the same time that critically examining their own biases and perspectives enables them to provide more accurate and balanced reporting. Awareness of one's own identity, worldviews and biases (not a denial of these) can strengthen one's ability to critically evaluate information (Facing History and Ourselves & the News Literacy Project, n.d.).

Among the challenges the journalists discuss is being cognisant of their own biases in order to resist any inclination to dismiss evidence that might not support their own immediate assumptions or preconceptions. Reporter Yamiche Alcindor, a black woman, articulates how an awareness of one's background and experiences can strengthen one's ability to critically evaluate and report on news events. She also reflects that some audience members may prematurely and unfairly draw conclusions about the nature of her reporting when they see that she is African-American. Her thoughts about reporting on Ferguson strike a chord with many students, in particular those who have themselves been affected by police brutality or by negative perceptions of well-intentioned law enforcement officers. Alcindor, like other reporters featured in this video, conveys the importance of seeking out differing perspectives and interpretations of facts and evidence and evaluating that information critically. The ability to critically analyse information, she suggests, is strengthened by one's awareness of their identity, beliefs and various alliances and groups of social belonging.

Facing implicit bias

Recognising and reducing biases is, however, hardly simple, especially when those biases are implicit and deeply rooted in a culture and in personal and collective histories. Most people, myself included, would rather view ourselves as fair and unbiased, but research on implicit bias presents the unsettling reality that implicit biases are part of being human. Our brains begin to create associations from the day that we are born, and most of these association are automatic and unconscious. The longer those associations are reinforced, the stronger they become and the more challenging they are to reshape. The enslavement of blacks in the USA, violence and sexual abuse against women, the stigmatisation of anyone veering outside the heterosexual or gender norms and the dehumanisation of anyone who looks different – these are just a few examples of how past and present powerfully shape human perceptions of and relationships and responses to other individuals and social groups. Asking students to examine this reality and how it affects our judgements, behaviours and relationships is a tall order.

Acknowledging implicit bias may be easier when a class is first introduced to concepts like the web of belief and the adversary method, as my teaching experiences thus far suggest. The web of belief and alternatives to the adversary method draw attention to a shared humanity and encourage mutual respect, openness and non-defensiveness. As research on de-biasing indicates, feeling less threatened better enables individuals to examine information that may be unsettling (Sherman and Cohen, 2002; Cohen et al., 2007).

To encourage students to consider how implicit biases may influence human thinking and behaviours, I also invite them to take a version of the Implicit Association Test (IAT), created by researchers interested in implicit social cognition that is beyond conscious awareness. The IAT measures implicit biases through an online activity in which participants make very quick and automatic associations between certain images and words. For example, an IAT related to racial bias involves relating positive or negative terms like good or bad to images of black or white people. IAT participants are not given time to think, so their implicit biases are likely to surface. Though a person may intend to treat and to view all individuals with the same degree of respect, because implicit bias is learned unconsciously and begins to form at a very early age, it develops without one making a choice about it.

I present the IAT as an optional bonus activity, since taking the test involves giving consent to researchers to collect the data from completed tests. Students are asked to explain how the test measures implicit bias, and to reflect on their experience completing the test. They are not asked to share the results of their test, though some choose to do so. The IAT can be eye-opening; it may help students gain a better understanding of how profoundly implicit biases affect our thinking, and it makes apparent the relevance of the web of belief to our everyday thinking and behaviours. The fact that most of us share similar implicit biases, regardless of our social identities, may help students to recognise that cognitive biases are part of being human and that working to counteract them can be a shared goal.

Researching on cognitive bias

All of the above materials and activities help to build toward a final research project, in which students develop and explore a research question related to cognitive bias. (The project consists of (1) a research statement in which each student articulates their question, its significance and key issues and themes evident from their information-gathering and analysis and (2) a corresponding annotated bibliography.) This project provides an opportunity for students to apply and to build on what they have learned about cognitive biases, as they seek out varying perspectives and critically evaluate a range of information sources.

Since beginning to teach this course through the lens of cognitive bias, I find that students are more invested in and engaged with their research. They generally develop more nuanced research questions and are more strategic in searching for and evaluating sources. The time that is given to developing a fuller awareness of the influence of beliefs, identity, cognition and affect on reasoning and information behaviours provides a meaningful context for students' research and better enables them to develop research skills that have more traditionally been associated with information literacy instruction. My experiences thus far suggest that students are developing stronger research and information skills in my course than previously and, moreover, that they are taking away a deeper awareness of the intersections between identity, belief and information behaviours, aspects of information literacy that have far-reaching implications for fostering democratic dialogue and civic engagement.

Conclusion

As I continue to explore approaches to teaching that encourage intellectual empathy in both myself and my students, I, along with students, face new questions and moments of discomfort and uncertainty. But I believe it is worth those moments of unease when the principles of intellectual empathy that Linker offers guide our interactions. As danah boyd again reflects:

> The path forward is hazy. We need to enable people to hear different perspectives and make sense of a very complicated – and in many ways, overwhelming – information landscape. We cannot fall back on standard educational approaches because the societal context has shifted. . . . We need to get creative and build the social infrastructure necessary for people to meaningfully and substantively engage across existing structural lines. . . . [W]e need to focus on the underlying issues at play. No simple band-aid will work.
>
> (boyd, 2017)

The societal context that boyd describes will continue to shift, potentially in more hopeful and empathic directions. Information literacy educators have a powerful role to play, as we work with students to foster intellectually empathic spaces and communities.

References

Above The Noise, Public Broadcasting (2017) *Why Do Our Brains Love Fake News?*, www.youtube.com/watch?v=dNmwvntMF5A.

Barthel, M. and Mitchell, A. (2017) Americans' Attitudes about the News Media Deeply Divided along Partisan Lines, *Pew Research Center's Journalism Project blog*, 10 May, www.journalism.org/2017/05/10/americans-attitudes-about-the-news-media-deeply-divided-along-partisan-lines.

BBC Trending (2017) *How Can You Burst Your Filter Bubble?*, www.youtube.com/watch?v=mh1dLvGe06Y.

boyd, d. (2017) Did Media Literacy Backfire?, *Data & Society: Points,* 5 January, https://points.datasociety.net/did-media-literacy-backfire-7418c084d88d#.b0e5tqxzs.

boyd, d. (2018) You Think You Want Media Literacy . . . Do You?, *Data & Society: Points*, 9 March, https://points.datasociety.net/you-think-you-want-media-literacy-do-you-7cad6af18ec2.

Center for Research on Learning and Teaching, University of Michigan (2016) Returning to the Classroom after the Election, *CRLT Blog* blog, 9 November, www.crlt.umich.edu/node/93815.

Cohen, G. L., Sherman, D. K., Bastardi, A., Hsu, L., McGoey, M. and Ross, L. (2007) Bridging the Partisan Divide: self-affirmation reduces ideological closed-mindedness and inflexibility in negotiation, *Journal of Personality and Social Psychology*, **93** (3), 415–30, https://doi.org/10.1037/0022-3514.93.3.415.

Cooke, N. A. (2019) The Dark Side of Information Behavior (Keynote Conference Presentation). *18th Annual Information Literacy Summer: News Media and Disinformation: Making Sense in Today's Information Landscape*. Moraine Valley Community College Library. https://informationliteracysummit.org/keynote-speaker/.

Druckman, J. N. (2012) The Politics of Motivation, *Critical Review*, **24** (2), 199–216.

Facing History and Ourselves & the News Literacy Project (n.d.) *How Journalists Minimize Bias*, www.facinghistory.org/resource-library/video/how-journalists-minimize-bias, accessed 3 July 2018.

Fricker, M. (2007) *Epistemic Injustice: power and the ethics of knowing*, Oxford University Press. www.oxfordscholarship.com/view/10.1093/acprof:oso/9780198237907.001.0001/acprof-9780198237907.

Hardisty, D. J., Johnson, E. J. and Weber, E. U. (2010) A Dirty Word or a Dirty World? Attribute framing, political affiliation, and query theory, *Psychological Science*, **21** (1), 86–92.

Hundleby, C. E. (2010) The Authority of the Fallacies Approach to Argument Evaluation, *Informal Logic*, **30** (3), 279–308.

Hundleby, C. E. (2013) Critical Thinking and the Adversary Paradigm, *APA Newsletters*, **13** (1), 2–8.

Kahne, J. and Bowyer, B. (2017) Educating for Democracy in a Partisan Age: confronting the challenges of motivated reasoning and misinformation, *American Educational Research Journal*, **54** (1), 3–34, https://doi.org/10.3102/0002831216679817.

Lakoff, G. (2009) Empathy, Sotomayor, and Democracy: the conservative stealth strategy, *Huffington Post*, 30 May, www.huffingtonpost.com/george-lakoff/empathy-sotomayor-and-dem_b_209406.html.

Lenker, M. (2016) Motivated Reasoning, Political Information, and Information Literacy Education, *Portal: Libraries and the Academy*, **16** (3), 511–28.

Linker, M. (2011) Do Squirrels Eat Hamburgers? intellectual empathy as a remedy for residual prejudice, *Informal Logic*, **31** (2), 110–38.

Linker, M. (2014) *Intellectual Empathy: critical thinking for social justice*, University of Michigan Press.

Lipman, M. (2003) *Thinking in Education*, 2nd edn, Cambridge University Press.

Lodge, M. and Taber, C. S. (2005) The Automaticity of Affect for Political Leaders, Groups, and Issues: an experimental test of the hot cognition hypothesis, *Political Psychology*, **26** (3), 455–82.

Mitchell, A., Gottfried, J., Kiley, J. and Matsa, K. E. (2014) Political Polarization & Media Habits, *Pew Research Center's Journalism Project blog,* 21 October, www.journalism.org/2014/10/21/political-polarization-media-habits.

Moulton, J. (1983) A Paradigm of Philosophy: the adversary method. In Harding, S. and Hintikka, M. B. (eds) *Discovering Reality: feminist perspectives on epistemology, metaphysics, methodology, and philosophy of science*, Springer, https://doi.org/10.1007/0-306-48017-4_9.

Paul, R. (2000) Critical Thinking, Moral Integrity and Citizenship: teaching for the intellectual virtues. In Axtell, G. (ed.) *Knowledge, Belief and Character: readings in virtue epistemology*, Roman & Littlefield Publishers, 163–75.

Pew Research Center (2016) *Partisanship and Political Animosity in 2016*, http://assets.pewresearch.org/wp-content/uploads/sites/5/2016/06/06-22-16-Partisanship-and-animosity-release.pdf.

Pew Research Center (2017) *The Partisan Divide on Political Values Grows Even Wider*, www.people-press.org/2017/10/05/the-partisan-divide-on-political-values-grows-even-wider.

Quine, W. V. (1951) Two Dogmas of Empiricism, *The Philosophical Review*, **60** (1),

20–43, https://doi.org/10.2307/2181906.

Sherman, D. K. and Cohen, G. L. (2002) Accepting Threatening Information: self-affirmation and the reduction of defensive biases, *Current Directions in Psychological Science*, **11** (4), 119–23, https://doi.org/10.1111/1467-8721.00182.

Taber, C. S. and Lodge, M. (2016) The Illusion of Choice in Democratic Politics: the unconscious impact of motivated political reasoning, *Political Psychology*, **37** (February), 61–85, https://doi.org/10.1111/pops.12321.

Walton, G. (2017) Information Literacy is a Subversive Activity: developing a research-based theory of information discernment, *Journal of Information Literacy*, **11** (1), 137–55.

4

The 'post-truth' world, misinformation, and information literacy: a perspective from cognitive science

Stephan Lewandowsky

The Party told you to reject the evidence of your eyes and ears. It was their final, most essential command.

(George Orwell, *1984*)

Just remember, what you're seeing and what you're reading is not what's happening.

(Donald Trump, 24 July 2018)

Introduction

There has been increasing concern with the growing infusion of disinformation, or 'fake news', into public discourse. Fact-checkers have reported that Donald Trump has been making more than six false or misleading statements every day during his term in office thus far. This chapter explores three questions that arise from this situation:

1 Is disregard for the truth really an acceptable hallmark of contemporary politics? If so, how is this possible and what factors contributed to this state of affairs? I review research that shows how among partisans, endorsement of a politician has become decoupled from his or her perceived veracity. This may reflect disenchantment with the current political system and its 'elite'.
2 What are the political and psychological consequences of the 'post-truth' world? I survey the many findings that suggest that, once acquired, misinformation 'sticks' in memory and is difficult to dislodge. In addition

to those direct consequences of misinformation, it has indirect fallouts that may undermine the democratic process.

3   What is the appropriate response to this situation? I review the difficulties associated with debunking misinformation and suggest instead that 'inoculating' people against misinformation before it is presented is a more successful strategy. I contrast psychological approaches with the idea of 'technocognition', which blends findings from cognitive science with the design of information architectures that are more resilient to the spreading of misinformation.

'Post-truth' was nominated word of the year by Oxford dictionaries in 2016, to describe 'circumstances in which objective facts are less influential in shaping public opinion than appeals to emotion and personal belief'.[1] A year later, Collins dictionaries declared 'fake news' to be the next word of the year, to refer to 'false, often sensational, information disseminated under the guise of news reporting'.[2] The concern with truth – or indeed its absence – was largely triggered by two political events in 2016 that had global ramifications and that arguably involved an unprecedented extent of deception and misinformation: the Brexit referendum in the UK and the election of Donald Trump in the USA. During the Brexit referendum, the public's 'epistemic rights' – that is, their right to be adequately informed – were serially violated by the British tabloids (Watson, 2018), and during the US Presidential campaign, independent fact-checker *PolitiFact* judged 70% of all statements by Donald Trump to be false or mostly false.

At the time of this writing, in mid-2018, the events of 2016 have turned out to be harbingers of a continued concern with the truthfulness of public discourse. By May 2018, the *Washington Post* had collated more than 3,000 false or misleading claims that President Trump had made, barely 18 months into his term, for an average of nearly 6½ false claims a day (Kessler, Rizzo and Kelly, 2018). Breaking with longstanding practice, premier American newspapers such as the *New York Times* now routinely refer to Donald Trump's 'lies' rather than using more circumspect language such as referring to statements as 'misleading' or 'false'.

The President's amply-demonstrated disregard for the truth has, however, incurred remarkably little political cost. According to the Rasmussen daily tracker poll (Rasmussen Reports, 2019), President Trump's approval ratings in 2018 to date have been largely indistinguishable from former President Obama's ratings during the equivalent period of his presidency. Among Republicans, Trump's average weekly approval has been at 86% in 2018, compared to 35% on average among Democrats (Gallup, 2019).

This situation invites at least three questions. First, is disregard for the truth really an acceptable hallmark of contemporary politics? If so, how is this possible and what factors contributed to this state of affairs? Second, what are the political and psychological consequences of the 'post-truth' world? Third, what is the appropriate response to this situation? I take up these questions in turn.

The political viability of disregard for the truth

Do voters really disregard the truthfulness of a candidate? Are they truly unconcerned with facts? Or do voters who support Donald Trump share his view that the media are 'enemies of the people' that publish 'fake news' (Pengelly, 2018), and that the President actually speaks the truth? If so, how can that belief be sustained in light of so much contrary evidence by independent fact-checkers?[3]

Corrections of falsehoods but not feelings

Several lines of evidence suggest that, at least in the USA, partisan supporters of politicians do not link their voting intentions and favourability ratings to the perceived veracity of a candidate. In a recent experiment, conducted during the US primary campaign in 2016, Briony Swire and colleagues (Swire et al., 2017) presented more than 2000 online participants with statements made by Donald Trump on the campaign trail. Half the statements shown to participants were true (e.g., 'the US spent $2 trillion on the war in Iraq') and the other half consisted of false claims (e.g., 'vaccines cause autism'). Participants indicated their belief in those statements on an 11-point scale (from 'definitely false' to 'definitely true'). Participants were then presented with corrections of the false statements and affirmations of the correct statements. On a subsequent test, belief ratings changed according to the information presented: all participants, including Trump supporters, believed statements less after they were identified as false, and they believed them more after they were affirmed as being correct. However, for Trump supporters there was no association between the extent to which they shifted their belief when a statement was corrected and their feelings for President Trump or their intention to vote for him. Thus, it seems that President Trump's false claims did not matter to his supporters – at least, they did not matter sufficiently to alter their feelings or voting intentions.

The same result was obtained in a study by Nyhan et al. (2017) using a slightly different methodology. They presented participants with a single incorrect claim made by Donald Trump (about crime rates), which was followed by various different types of correction and a single belief rating. Trump supporters again showed that they were sensitive to the corrections, in comparison to a control condition that did not receive any correction. However, just as in the study by Swire et al. (2017), the correction had no effect on participants' favourability ratings of Donald Trump.

The basic pattern of results was replicated yet again in an as-yet unpublished study by my team, led by Briony Swire, in which we also included supporters of Bernie Sanders and used some of Sanders' statements in addition to Donald Trump's. Although the data contain some nuances, as a first approximation it is clear that Sanders supporters differed little from Trump supporters in their dissociation between perceptions of factual accuracy on the one hand, and support for their favoured candidate on the other.

These data leave us with a conundrum: on the one hand, recent research has shown that even partisans are sensitive to corrections of false statements by their favoured candidate. On the other hand, acceptance of those corrections and the ensuing appropriate belief adjustment appear to have no effect on partisans' support for their favoured candidate. Several resolutions to this conundrum have been proposed.

Authenticity versus truthfulness

There is no doubt that partisanship affects information processing in a large number of ways (for an overview, see, e.g. Bavel and Pereira, 2018). Arguably, those effects reflect the trade-off between the rewards that are offered by a strong partisan identity and those offered by being concerned with accuracy or truth. Specifically, by identifying strongly with a political party, people can satisfy a variety of needs and social goals – such as a sense of belonging (Jost, 2017), generating a sense of certainty or 'closure' (Kruglanski and Webster, 1996), or having a platform to exercise their moral values (Tetlock, 2003). If fulfilment of those goals is valued more strongly than achieving accuracy or truthfulness, then people may act in ways that are seemingly at odds with indisputable facts.

A particularly striking example of such behaviour was observed in a recent study by Schaffner and Luks (2018), who presented participants with two side-by-side photographs of the inaugurations of Barack Obama in 2009 and Donald Trump in 2017. In the condition of greatest interest here, the photographs were unlabelled and participants were asked to choose the photo that had more people in it. There is no doubt that far more people attended Obama's inauguration than Trump's (in addition to the photos taken from the Washington monument by the US National Parks Service, ridership of the DC Metro by 11 a.m. on

Trump's inauguration day was the lowest for any inauguration since 2005).

Schaffner and Luks found that among non-voters and Clinton voters, 3% and 2% of respondents, respectively, chose the incorrect picture (i.e., the picture from Trump's inauguration with far fewer people). Among Trump voters, this proportion was 15%. When the data were broken down further by level of education of respondents, the error rate rose to 26% among highly educated Trump voters, compared to 1% for highly educated Clinton voters. For participants with low education, the gap between Trump (11%) and Clinton (2%) voters was considerably smaller. Given that inauguration attendance had become a matter of controversy at the time the study was conducted, with Trump's press secretary claiming that it was 'the largest audience ever to witness an inauguration period – both in person and around the globe,' the results of Schaffner and Luks identify an instance in which people's partisan identity trumped clear and unambiguous perceptual evidence.

Lest one think that this is an isolated instance, an NBC poll conducted in April 2018 revealed that 76% of Republicans thought that President Trump tells the truth 'all or most of the time' (Arrenge, Lapinski and Tallevi, 2018). By contrast, only 5% of Democrats held that view. Clearly, partisanship is a major determinant of people's views of truthfulness, what counts as facts, and even their own perceptions of photographs.

However, I argue that partisanship by itself is insufficient to explain people's tolerance for dishonesty or their willingness to distrust their own eyes. In a recent, as yet unpublished, study conducted in Australia by my team led by Ullrich Ecker at the University of Western Australia, we found that Australian partisans *did* adjust their feelings about their favoured politicians when confronted with evidence for their lack of truthfulness. What, then, explains American partisans' willingness to dissociate their preferences for politicians from their truthfulness?

A recent set of studies helps shed light on this question. Hahl, Kim and Sivan (2018) proposed that flagrant lies may actually *enhance* the appeal of a 'lying demagogue' when those lies are perceived as violations of norms – such as truth-telling – that are associated with a political system whose legitimacy is in question. That is, people who feel that the political system is in a crisis of legitimacy will consider *any* norm violation by a politician as a mark of his or her authenticity. Thus, the more blatantly Donald Trump is lying, the more his supporters may consider him to be their authentic champion, simply because blatant lies are considered unacceptable by the 'establishment'.[4]

Hahl, Kim and Sivan supported their argument with two studies in which participants were presented with brief vignettes pertaining to a (fictitious) election to a student government. In one condition, participants were led to believe that the student government was subject to a crisis of legitimacy by being told that 'the student government president often meets with college administrators and board members' and that a scheduled debate 'would be unfair, since the moderator was an administrator and knew one of the candidates'. In another condition this information was replaced by positive comments about the student government. Participants were then provided with more information about the campaign, which either identified one of the candidates as telling a flagrant lie or telling the truth. Participants judged the 'lying demagogue' candidate to be more authentic than the honest candidate in the condition in which the student government was painted as being in a crisis of legitimacy. Conversely, when no crisis was perceived, the 'lying demagogue' was judged to be *less* authentic than the honest candidate.

Crucially, these results were confined to those participants who were led to sympathise with the candidate in question by considering him to be a member of the same outgroup as the participant. Participants who were not led to sympathise with the candidate never considered him to be authentic. Hahl, Kim and Sivan thus identified two components that must be present before liars can be considered authentic: first, partisanship, and second, a shared sense of grievance caused by a crisis of legitimacy. Each factor on its own is insufficient to create the perception of authenticity when a political candidate is flagrantly violating the truth.

The consequences of 'post-truth' politics

It is a truism that a functioning democracy relies on a well-informed populace. Widespread misinformation can engender collective preferences very different from those that would be observed if people were not misinformed (Kuklinski et al., 2000). The issues and processes just reviewed therefore cannot be without adverse consequences for individuals and society as a whole.

Misinformation and the individual

Misinformation sticks. Erasing 'fake news' from one's memory is a challenging task, even under the best of circumstances; that is, in the psychological laboratory when participants are motivated to be accurate and are free from distraction (for a review, see Lewandowsky et al., 2012). When circumstances are less than ideal, the persistence of misinformation can take on epic proportions. To illustrate, consider the mythical weapons of mass destruction (WMDs) that were alleged to be in Iraq and that were cited as the reason for the invasion of 2003. The constant drumbeat of 'WMD, WMD, WMD' in the media and among politicians in the lead-up to the invasion, followed by innumerable media reports of 'preliminary tests' that tested positive for chemical weapons during the early stages of the conflict – but ultimately were never confirmed by more thorough follow-up tests – created a powerful impression that those weapons had been discovered. The impression was so powerful that notable segments of the American public continued to believe, for up to a decade after the absence of WMDs had become the bipartisan official US position, either that the USA had found WMDs in Iraq or that Iraq had hidden the weapons so well that they escaped detection. Jacobson (2010) reviewed polling data from 2006 through 2009 and found that around 60% of Republicans (and around 20% of Democrats) believed in the existence of Iraqi WMDs, with little evidence of a decline of those false beliefs over time. A poll from December 2014[5] pegged erroneous beliefs in WMDs at 51% for Republicans and 32% for Democrats, confirming the longevity of those false beliefs.

A particularly concerning aspect of the psychology of misinformation is that it can stick in people's memory even when they acknowledge a correction, and even when people *know* that a piece of information is false. This 'continued influence effect' of misinformation has been demonstrated innumerable times (Chan et al., 2017; Lewandowsky et al., 2012; Swire and Ecker, 2017), including in the context of the Iraq war. In a study conducted during the initial stages of the invasion of Iraq, colleagues and I presented participants with specific war-related items from the news media, some of which had been subsequently corrected, and asked for ratings of belief as well as memory for the original information and its correction (Lewandowsky et al., 2005). We found that among US participants, even those individuals who were certain that the information had been retracted continued to believe it to be true. This dissociation between overt statements of disbelief or acknowledgement of a correction on the one hand, and the continued reliance on the incorrect information on the other, is what makes misinformation so pernicious. I discussed the study by Swire et al. (2017) at the outset, where we showed that Trump partisans are able to adjust their explicit belief in a claim by Donald Trump in response to a correction, but that those corrections had no effect on their feelings for the candidate. It turns out that even with material that is less politically charged (e.g., a story about a fictitious warehouse fire: Ecker et al., 2011; Johnson and Seifert, 1994; Wilkes and Leatherbarrow, 1988), this dissociation can be observed. An overt acknowledgement by participants that they have received a correction does not preclude their reliance on information they now know to be false when subsequently drawing inferences.

Misinformation and society

It requires little imagination to realise that misinformed individuals are unlikely to make optimal decisions, and that even putting aside one's political preferences, this can have adverse consequences for society as a whole. For example, following the unsubstantiated – and now thoroughly debunked (DeStefano and Thompson, 2004; Godlee, Smith and Marcovitch, 2011) – claim of a link between childhood vaccinations and autism, numerous parents (largely in the UK) decided not to immunise their children. These misinformation-driven choices led to a marked increase in vaccine-preventable diseases, and substantial effort and expenditure were required to resolve this public-health crisis (Larson et al., 2011; Poland and Spier, 2010).

The toxic fallout from misinformation is not limited to those direct consequences. Other more insidious fallouts may involve people's reluctance to believe in facts altogether. There have been numerous demonstrations that the presence of misinformation undermines the effects of accurate information. Van der Linden et al. (2017) showed that when participants were presented with both a persuasive fact and a related piece of misinformation, belief overall was unaffected – the misinformation cancelled out the fact. McCright et al. (2016) found that the presence of a contrarian counter-frame cancelled out valid climate information, and the same effect was also observed by Cook, Lewandowsky and Ecker (2017).

The insidious fallout from misinformation is particularly pronounced when the misinformation is packaged as a conspiracy theory. There have been repeated demonstrations that exposure to conspiratorial discourse, even if the claims are dismissed, makes people less likely to accept official information (Einstein and Glick, 2015: Jolley and Douglas, 2013; Raab et al., 2013). To illustrate, in one study exposure to a conspiracy claim – namely, that the US Bureau of Labor Statistics manipulated unemployment data for political reasons – adversely affected trust in government services and institutions, including those *unconnected* to the conspiratorial allegations (Einstein and Glick, 2015).

Misinformation does not just misinform. It also undermines democracy by calling into question the knowability of information altogether. And without knowable information deliberative democratic discourse is called into question (for an elaboration of those concerns, see Lewandowsky, Ecker and Cook, 2017). Fortunately, we are not entirely powerless in confronting the 'post-truth' malaise.

Recovering from the 'post-truth' world

The political context

Science sometimes cannot help but be political, at least in the eyes of some stakeholders: for example, when medical researchers determine that smoking causes lung cancer, public reporting of their results is likely to create political fallout. When climate scientists alerted the world to the risks from greenhouse gas emissions, the political fallout echoed around the world and continues to do so decades later. Likewise, any researcher on misinformation will sooner or later encounter political fallout from their work. I argue that the political context and implications of misinformation must be understood and considered by researchers (for details, see Lewandowsky, Ecker and Cook, 2017).

In particular, it must be borne in mind that disinformation is not a coincidental by-product of some other activity but is, usually, disseminated by political actors for a specific purpose. That is, much like climate denial (Lewandowsky, Cook and Lloyd, 2016), 'post-truth' politics is best considered a rational strategy that is deployed in pursuit of political objectives. By implication, post-truth politics may cease when its effectiveness is curtailed by a change in the political environment.

Although effecting that political change is beyond the purview of cognitive science, researchers can contribute to the process in various ways. One particularly intriguing example is a field experiment conducted on US state legislators by Nyhan and Reifler (2015). They randomly assigned incumbents to one of two groups before the 2012 election. One group was sent letters outlining the risks to their reputation and re-election chances if they were caught making statements of questionable accuracy. The other group was sent letters indicating merely that research on politicians' accuracy was being conducted without specifying any details. The group that was alerted to the reputational costs on inaccuracy was substantially less likely to receive negative ratings from fact-checkers. It appears that state-level politicians are quite sensitive to the reputational impact of inaccuracies (or at least they were in 2012).

Similarly, there is at least preliminary evidence that issuing a public commitment to honest conduct, known as the 'Pro-Truth Pledge' (Tsipursky, Votta and Mulick, 2018), is effective in enhancing the integrity of conduct of the signatories. Anecdotal evidence suggests that some of the signatories who are politicians, publicly corrected their own social-media postings when alerted to inaccuracies after taking the Pledge. In a further small-scale analysis of the Facebook posts of 20 signatories, a significant increase in the accuracy of posted content was observed after the Pledge had been taken (Tsipursky, Votta and Roose, 2018).

Cognitive scientists (myself included) have also contributed to a 2018 report by the UK House of Commons Digital, Culture, Media and Sport Committee (2018) that investigated 'fake news'. The report drew the headline conclusion that tech companies should be held liable for use of 'harmful and misleading material' on their sites.

In summary, the large-scale dissemination of misinformation is political, and hence the solution must also be largely political. There are indications that at least some political actors are sensitive to the reputational costs incurred by inaccurate statements, and are willing to express a commitment to greater accuracy. Nonetheless, even within this larger context, it is important to understand how individuals' cognitive systems respond to debunking of misinformation.

Debunking of misinformation

There is broad agreement in the literature that corrections of misinformation are successful only if the correction is accompanied by an alternative explanation, or if suspicion is aroused over the initial source of the misinformation. That is, telling people that negligence was *not* a factor in a story about a fictitious warehouse fire (after negligence was first implied) is insufficient for them to dismiss that information. Telling people instead that arson, rather than negligence, was to blame for the fire, successfully eliminates reliance on the initial misinformation (e.g., Ecker, Lewandowsky and Tang, 2010; Ecker et al., 2015; Johnson and Seifert, 1994).

If a causal alternative is not available – as, for example, when attempting to rebut conspiracy theories about the disappearance of Malaysian Airlines flight MH370 over the Indian Ocean – arousing suspicion about the source of misinformation may be another technique to achieve debunking. For example, when mock jurors are admonished to disregard tainted evidence presented as part of a mock trial when reaching a verdict, they demonstrably continue to rely on that tainted evidence. The reliance occurs even though jurors indicate that they disregarded the evidence. Reliance disappears only when jurors are made suspicious of the motives underlying the dissemination of the tainted evidence in the first place, for example because it may have been planted by the prosecutor's office (Fein, McCloskey and Tomlinson, 1997). These difficulties associated with debunking can be circumvented if people are made aware of misinformation *before* it is presented or if they can acquire generic skills that enable them to filter out disinformation.

Inoculation and information literacy

There is growing evidence that people can avoid being misled if they are warned that they might be misinformed or if their attention is drawn to particular techniques by which they might be misled (Cook, Lewandowksy and Ecker, 2017; Ecker, Lewandowksy and Tang, 2010; van der Linden et al., 2017). This process is known as 'inoculation' or 'prebunking' and it was summarised as follows:

> There are two elements to an inoculation: (1) an explicit warning of an impending threat and (2) a refutation of an anticipated argument that exposes the imminent fallacy. For example, an inoculation might include (1) a warning that there exist attempts to cast doubt on the scientific consensus regarding climate change, and (2) an explanation that one technique employed is the rhetorical use of a large group of 'fake experts' to feign a lack of consensus. By exposing the fallacy, the misinformation (in this case, the feigned lack of consensus) is delivered in a 'weakened' form. Thus, when people subsequently encounter a deceptive argument, the inoculation provides them with a counter-argument to immediately dismiss the misinformation.
>
> (Cook et al., 2017, 4)

The success of inoculation has been established in several experiments (Cook, Lewandowksy and Ecker, 2017; van der Linden et al., 2017). To illustrate with an example from climate change, our team showed that people can be inoculated against disinformation efforts by climate deniers by presenting participants with (1) a warning that attempts are made to cast doubt on the scientific consensus for political reasons, and (2) an explanation that one disinformation technique involves appeals to dissenting 'fake experts' to feign a lack of scientific consensus. We illustrated the 'fake-expert' approach by drawing attention to the historical attempts of the tobacco industry to undermine the medical consensus about the health risks from smoking with advertising claims such as '20,679 Physicians say "Luckies are less irritating"'. By exposing the fake-expert disinformation strategy at the outset, the subsequent misinformation (in this case, the feigned lack of scientific consensus on climate change) was defanged and people's responses to various climate-related test items did not differ from a control condition that received no misinformation about the consensus. By contrast, in the absence of inoculation, the misinformation involving 'fake experts' had a discernible detrimental effect.

Misinformation sticks and is hard to dislodge. But we can prevent it from sticking in the first place by alerting people to how they might be misled.

In a slightly different context, Merpert et al. (2018) showed that members of the public can be readily trained to identify statements in a politician's speech that could, in principle, be subject to fact-checking. This is an important skill because opinions, by definition, are not subject to fact-checking, and differentiation of opinions from factual assertions is therefore a necessary first step before fact-checking of suitable items can commence.

Available research indicates that there *is* a path towards educating the public about post-truth discourse. However, that path is filled with pitfalls and, by itself, cannot overcome the 'post-truth' malaise. An alternative approach therefore goes beyond cognitive science and seeks to incorporate technological solutions.

Technocognition

This approach has been labelled 'technocognition' (Lewandowsky, Ecker and Cook, 2017) and invites an interdisciplinary approach to the design of information architectures. Core to the approach is the incorporation of principles borrowed from behavioural economics to 'nudge' (Thaler and Sunstein, 2008) people against spreading of misinformation by designing better information architectures. To illustrate with an example from behavioural economics, organ donation rates have been shown to quintuple by merely changing the default; that is, moving from 'opt-in' to an 'opt-out' system (Johnson and Goldstein, 2003). I argue that similar principles could apply to information technology, and there are some recent pointers in that direction.

To illustrate, reader comments on online articles and posts are known to affect other readers' impressions and behavioural intentions (Lee, 2012; Stavrositu and Kim, 2015; Winter and Krämer, 2016). The mere tone of blog comments can affect people's attitudes towards scientific issues they do not understand well: uncivil comments have been shown to polarise readers' views on nanotechnology (Anderson et al., 2013). The recognition that blog comments can have toxic consequences is of growing concern to internet information providers. One particularly innovative response to this problem was launched by the Norwegian broadcaster NRK. The NRK experimented with the requirement that readers must pass a brief comprehension quiz before being permitted to post comments (Lichterman, 2017). This simple measure cannot help but eliminate uninformed comments and it may also serve to deter 'trolls' who are unlikely to expend the effort necessary to overcome this threshold for involvement. Crucially, no one is censored in the process, because once the quiz has been passed people are free to comment as per usual.

Other possible avenues for exploration involve redesign – or at least re-evaluation – of recommender systems. Recommender systems have become an unavoidable and constant companion in our lives. For example, whenever we watch a YouTube video, the experience will be accompanied by a panel of thumbnails that is providing us with further movies to choose from. Those suggestions are far from random but are customised on the basis of our viewing history and, possibly, other variables that we are unaware of. There is no evidence that consumers know how recommender systems operate, and to date these highly sophisticated tools have flourished without much legislative supervision or constraint (though see Ricci, Rokach and Shapira, 2015, for some pointers to discussion of regulations).

There is evidence that the YouTube recommender system, for example, can lead users to become immersed in an ideological bubble in a few clicks once they have watched a single extremist video and then follow YouTube's recommendations (O'Callaghan et al., 2015). A particularly troubling implication of the YouTube recommender system is that *counter-extremist* messages, deployed (e.g., by educational institutions) with the intent to inoculate users *against* extremist messages, may inadvertently draw viewers further into extremist content (Schmitt et al., 2018). Because YouTube's recommendations favour highly-active channels, extremist content – known to be produced at a rapid pace – is likely to be ranked ahead of counter-extremist messages that take more time to produce (Bartlett and Krasodomski-Jones, 2015).

Fortunately, these problems constitute only one side of the coin: there is also evidence that algorithmic correction of misinformation shows promise (Bode and Vraga, 2015). Likewise, in at least one instance common recommender-system algorithms have been shown to yield at least as much diversity of recommended news content as the human editors of a quality newspaper (Möller et al., 2018). A debate about how diversity can be achieved as a design principle of recommender systems has commenced in the literature (Helberger, Karppinen and D'Acunto, 2018), and in my view those discussions will bear fruit in the near future. I mentioned at the outset how the misinformation disseminated by the Leave campaign during the Brexit referendum violated people's epistemic rights (Watson, 2018). It is notable that similar arguments have been made outside any specific context or event about personalisation more generally. Based on analysis of case law of the European Court of Human Rights, Eskens, Helberger, and Moeller (2017) argued that news personalisation, *per se*, may impinge on people's right to receive information.

Conclusion

We live in an environment that is drenched in misinformation, 'fake news' and propaganda, not because of an unavoidable accident but because it has been created by political actors in pursuit of political and economic objectives. We therefore do not face a natural disaster but a political problem. On the positive side, this implies that, unlike for earthquakes or tsunamis, a solution is likely to exist and ought to be achievable. On the negative side, it means that the solution is unlikely to involve more (or better) communication alone. As Brulle, Carmichael and Jenkins (2012, 185) noted in the context of climate change, 'introducing new messages or information into an otherwise unchanged socioeconomic system will accomplish little'.

Post-truth politics is a tool in a struggle for power in societies and over the very nature of liberal democracies, and communication alone cannot resolve such deep-seated political conflicts. Instead, their resolution requires political mobilisation and public activism (Brulle, Carmichael and Jenkins, 2012). The contribution from cognitive science is therefore limited to highlighting how people's thinking and acting might facilitate or hinder such mobilisation.

Notes

1 https://en.oxforddictionaries.com/word-of-the-year/word-of-the-year-2016.
2 www.collinsdictionary.com/woty.
3 There is some debate about whether non-partisan fact-checking is reliable or even possible (Amazeen, 2015; Uscinski and Butler, 2013). Critics point to issues such as ambiguities in what constitutes a 'fact' and an inevitable selection bias because fact-checkers cannot cover all statements (Uscinski and Butler). I consider those issues to be valid concerns but they do not negate the fact that sometimes politicians make claims that are unequivocally incompatible with the available evidence and that can – and should – be identified as false.
4 By a similar process, education may also be devalued when it is seen as an attribute of the 'establishment'. In a recent Pew poll, the majority of Republicans, by a 58% to 36% margin, considered colleges and universities to have a *negative* effect on the way things are going in the country (www.pewresearch.org/fact-tank/2017/07/20/republicans-skeptical-of-colleges-impact-on-u-s-but-most-see-benefits-for-workforce-preparation). Among Democrats, the opinion was split the other way by a 72% (positive) to 19% (negative) margin.

5 https://view2.fdu.edu/publicmind/2017.

References

Amazeen, M. A. (2015) Revisiting the Epistemology of Fact-checking, *Critical Review*, 27, 1–22, doi:10.1080/08913811.2014.993890.

Anderson, A. A., Brossard, D., Scheufele, D. A., Xenos, M. A. and Ladwig, P. (2013) The 'Nasty Effect:' online incivility and risk perceptions of emerging technologies, *Journal of Computer-Mediated Communication*, 19, 373–87, doi:10.1111/jcc4.12009.

Arrenge, A., Lapinski, J. and Tallevi, A. (2018) Poll: Republicans who think Trump is untruthful still approve of him, *NBC News*, 2 May, www.nbcnews.com/politics/politics-news/poll-republicans-who-think-trump-untruthful-still-approve-him-n870521.

Bartlett, J. and Krasodomski-Jones, A. (2015) *Counter Speech: examining content that challenges extremism online*, Demos, www.demos.co.uk/wp-content/uploads/2015/10/Counter-speech.pdf.

Bavel, J. J. V. and Pereira, A. (2018) The Partisan Brain: an identity-based model of political belief, *Trends in Cognitive Sciences, 22,* 213–24.

Bode, L. and Vraga, E. K. (2015) In Related News, That Was Wrong: the correction of misinformation through related stories functionality in social media, *Journal of Communication*, 65, 619–38.

Brulle, R. J., Carmichael, J. and Jenkins, J. C. (2012) Shifting Public Opinion on Climate Change: an empirical assessment of factors influencing concern over climate change in the U.S., 2002–2010, *Climatic Change*, 114, 169–88, doi:0.1007/s10584-012-0403-y.

Chan, M.-p. S., Jones, C. R., Jamieson, K. H. and Albarracín, D. (2017) Debunking: a meta-analysis of the psychological efficacy of messages countering misinformation, *Psychological Science*, doi:10.1177/0956797617714579.

Cook, J., Lewandowsky, S. and Ecker, U. K. H. (2017) Neutralizing Misinformation Through Inoculation: exposing misleading argumentation techniques reduces their influence', *PLOS ONE*, 12, e0175799, doi:10.1371/journal.pone.0175799.

DeStefano, F. and Thompson, W. W. (2004) MMR Vaccine and Autism: an update of the scientific evidence, *Expert Review of Vaccines*, 3, 19–22, doi:10.1586/14760584.3.1.19.

Ecker, U. K. H., Lewandowsky, S. and Tang, D. T. W. (2010) Explicit Warnings Reduce But Do Not Eliminate the Continued Influence of Misinformation, *Memory & Cognition*, 38, 1087–1100, doi:10.3758/MC.38.8.1087.

Ecker, U. K. H., Lewandowsky, S., Swire, B. and Chang, D. (2011) Correcting False Information in Memory: manipulating the strength of misinformation encoding and its retraction, *Psychonomic Bulletin & Review*, **18**, 570–8.

Ecker, U. K. H., Lewandowsky, S., Cheung, C. S. C. and Maybery, M. T. (2015) He Did It! She Did It! No, She Did Not! Multiple causal explanations and the continued influence of misinformation, *Journal of Memory and Language*, **85**, 101–15.

Einstein, K. L. and Glick, D. M. (2015) Do I Think BLS Data Are BS? The consequences of conspiracy theories, *Political Behavior*, **37**, 679–701, doi:10.1007/s11109-014-9287-z.

Eskens, S., Helberger, N. and Moeller, J. (2017) Challenged by News Personalisation: five perspectives on the right to receive information, *Journal of Media Law*, **9**, 259–84, doi:10.1080/17577632.2017.1387353.

Fein, S., McCloskey, A. L. and Tomlinson, T. M. (1997) Can the Jury Disregard That Information? The use of suspicion to reduce the prejudicial effects of pretrial publicity and inadmissible testimony, *Personality and Social Psychology Bulletin*, **23**, 1215–26, doi:10.1177/01461672972311008.

Gallup (2019) *Presidential Approval Ratings — Donald Trump*, https://news.gallup.com/poll/203198/presidential-approval-ratings-donald-trump.aspx [retrieved 23 July].

Godlee, F., Smith, J. and Marcovitch, H. (2011) Wakefield's Article Linking MMR Vaccine and Autism was Fraudulent: clear evidence of falsification of data should now close the door on this damaging vaccine scare, *BMJ: British Medical Journal*, **342**, 64–6.

Hahl, O., Kim, M. and Sivan, E. W. Z. (2018) The Authentic Appeal of the Lying Demagogue: proclaiming the deeper truth about political illegitimacy, *American Sociological Review*, **83**, doi:10.1177/0003122417749632.

Helberger, N., Karppinen, K. and D'Acunto, L. (2018) Exposure Diversity as a Design Principle for Recommender Systems, *Information, Communication & Society*, **21**, 191–207, doi:10.1080/1369118X.2016.1271900.

House of Commons, Digital, Culture, Media and Sport Committee (2018) *Disinformation and 'fake news': interim report*, Fifth Report of Session 2017–19, https://publications.parliament.uk/pa/cm201719/cmselect/cmcumeds/363/363.pdf.

Jacobson, G. C. (2010) Perception, Memory, and Partisan Polarization on the Iraq war, *Political Science Quarterly*, **125**, 31–56.

Johnson, E. J. and Goldstein, D. (2003) Do Defaults Save Lives?, *Science*, **302**, 1338–9.

Johnson, H. M. and Seifert, C. M. (1994) Sources of the Continued Influence Effect: when misinformation in memory affects later inferences, *Journal of Experimental*

Psychology: Learning, Memory and Cognition, **20**, 1420–36.

Jolley, D. and Douglas, K. M. (2013) The Social Consequences of Conspiracism: exposure to conspiracy theories decreases intentions to engage in politics and to reduce one's carbon footprint, *British Journal of Psychology*, **105**, 35–56, doi:10.1111/bjop.12018.

Jost, J. T. (2017) Ideological Asymmetries and the Essence of Political Psychology, *Political Psychology*, **38**, 167–208, doi:10.1111/pops.12407.

Kessler, G., Rizzo, S. and Kelly M. (2018) President Trump has Made 3,001 False or Misleading Claims So Far, *Washington Post*, 1 May, www.washingtonpost.com/news/fact-checker/wp/2018/05/01/president-trump-has-made-3001–false-or-misleading-claims-so-far.

Kruglanski, A. W. and Webster, D. M. (1996) Motivated Closing of the Mind: 'seizing' and 'freezing', *Psychological Review*, **103**, 263–83.

Kuklinski, J. H., Quirk, P. J., Jerit, J., Schwieder, D. and Rich, R. F. (2000) Misinformation and the Currency of Democratic Citizenship, *Journal of Politics*, **62**, 790–816.

Larson, H. J., Cooper, L. Z., Eskola, J., Katz, S. L. and Ratzan, S. C. (2011) Addressing the Vaccine Confidence Gap, *The Lancet*, **378**, 526–35.

Lee, E.-J. (2012) That's Not The Way It Is: how user-generated comments on the news affect perceived media bias, *Journal of Computer-Mediated Communication*, **18**, 32–45, http://dx.doi.org/10.1111/j.1083–6101.2012.01597.x.

Lewandowsky, S., Cook, J. and Lloyd, E. (2016) The 'Alice in Wonderland' Mechanics of the Rejection of (Climate) Science: simulating coherence by conspiracism, *Synthese*, **195**, 175–96, doi:10.1007/s11229–016–1198–6.

Lewandowsky, S., Ecker, U. K. H. and Cook, J. (2017) Beyond Misinformation: understanding and coping with the post-truth era, *Journal of Applied Research in Memory and Cognition*, **6**, 353–69, doi:10.1016/j.jarmac.2017.07.008.

Lewandowsky, S., Stritzke, W. G. K., Oberauer, K. and Morales, M. (2005) Memory for Fact, Fiction, and Misinformation: the Iraq War 2003, *Psychological Science*, **16**, 190–5, doi:10.1111/j.0956–7976.2005.00802.x.

Lewandowsky, S., Ecker, U. K. H., Seifert, C., Schwarz, N. and Cook, J. (2012) Misinformation and its Correction: continued influence and successful debiasing, *Psychological Science in the Public Interest*, **13**, 106–31, doi:10.1177/1529100612451018.

Lichterman, J. (2017) This Site is 'Taking the Edge Off Rant Mode' by Making Readers Pass a Quiz Before Commenting, *Nieman Lab*, www.niemanlab.org/2017/03/this-site-is-taking-the-edge-off-rant-mode-by-making-readers-pass-a-quiz-before-commenting.

McCright, A. M., Charters, M., Dentzman, K. and Dietz, T. (2016) Examining the Effectiveness of Climate Change Frames in the Face of a Climate Change Denial Counter-Frame, *Topics in Cognitive Science*, **8**, 76–97, doi:10.1111/tops.12171.

Merpert, A., Furman, M., Anauati, M. V., Zommer, L. and Taylor, I. (2018) Is That Even Checkable? An experimental study in identifying checkable statements in political discourse, *Communication Research Reports*, **35**, 48–57, doi:10.1080/08824096.2017.1366303.

Möller, J., Trilling, D., Helberger, N. and van Es, B. (2018) Do Not Blame it on the Algorithm: an empirical assessment of multiple recommender systems and their impact on content diversity, *Information, Communication & Society*, **21**, 959–77, doi:10.1080/1369118X.2018.1444076.

Nyhan, B. and Reifler, J. (2015) The Effect of Fact-checking on Elites: a field experiment on U.S. state legislators, *American Journal of Political Science*, **59**, 628–40, doi:10.1111/ajps.12162.

Nyhan, B., Porter, E., Reifler, J. and Wood, T. (2017) *Taking Corrections Literally But Not Seriously? The effects of information on factual beliefs and candidate favorability*, https://www.ssrn.com/abstract=2995128.

O'Callaghan, D., Greene, D., Conway, M., Carthy, J. and Cunningham, P. (2015) Down the (White) Rabbit Hole: the extreme right and online recommender systems, *Social Science Computer Review*, **33**, 459–78, doi:10.1177/0894439314555329.

Pengelly, M. (2018) Trump Blasts Back After New York Times Publisher Decries 'Enemy of the People' Attacks, *The Guardian*, 30 July, www.theguardian.com/media/2018/jul/29/new-york-times-washington-post-trump-attacks-press-warning.

Poland, G. A. and Spier, R. (2010) Fear, Misinformation, and Innumerates: How the Wakefield paper, the press, and advocacy groups damaged the public health, *Vaccine*, **28**, 2361–2.

Raab, M. H., Auer, N., Ortlieb, S. A. and Carbon, C.-C. (2013) The Sarrazin Effect: the presence of absurd statements in conspiracy theories makes canonical information less plausible, *Frontiers in Psychology*, **4**, 453, doi:10.3389/fpsyg.2013.00453.

Rassmussen Reports (2019) www.rasmussenreports.com/public_content/politics/trump_administration/prez_track_jul27 [retrieved 23 July].

Ricci, F., Rokach, L. and Shapira, B. (2015) *Recommender Systems: introduction and challenges*, Springer.

Schaffner, B. F. and Luks, S. (2018) Misinformation or Expressive Responding? What an inauguration crowd can tell us about the source of political misinformation in surveys, *Public Opinion Quarterly*, **82**, 135–47.

Schmitt, J. B., Rieger, D., Rutkowski, O. and Ernst, J. (2018) Counter-messages as Prevention or Promotion of Extremism?! The potential role of YouTube recommendation algorithms, *Journal of Communication*, doi:10.1093/joc/jqy029.

Stavrositu, C. D. and Kim, J. (2015) All Blogs Are Not Created Equal: the role of narrative formats and user-generated comments in health prevention, *Health Communication*, **30**, 485–95, doi:10.1080/10410236.2013.867296.

Swire, B. and Ecker, U. K. H. (2017) Misinformation and its Correction: cognitive mechanisms and recommendations for mass communication. In Southwell, B., Thorson, E. A. and Sheble, L. (eds) *Misinformation and Mass Audiences*, University of Texas Press.

Swire, B., Berinsky, A. J., Lewandowsky, S. and Ecker, U. K. H. (2017) Processing Political Misinformation: comprehending the Trump phenomenon, *Royal Society Open Science*, **4**, 160802, doi:10.1098/rsos.160802.

Tetlock, P. E. (2003) Thinking the Unthinkable: sacred values and taboo cognitions, *Trends in Cognitive Sciences*, **7**, 320–4.

Thaler, R. H. and Sunstein, C. R. (2008) *Nudge: improving decisions about health, wealth, and happiness*, Yale University Press.

Tsipursky, G., Votta, F. and Mulick, J. A. (2018) A Psychological Approach to Promoting Truth in Politics: the Pro-Truth Pledge, *Journal of Social and Political Psychology*, **6**, 271–90, doi:10.5964/jspp.v6i2.856.

Tsipursky, G., Votta, F. and Roose, K. M. (2018) Fighting Fake News and Post-truth Politics with Behavioral Science: the Pro-Truth Pledge, *Behavior and Social Issues*, **27**, 47–70, doi:10.5210/bsi.v.27i0.9127.

Uscinski, J. E. and Butler, R. W. (2013) The Epistemology of Fact Checking, *Critical Review*, **25**, 162–180.

van der Linden, S., Leiserowitz, A., Rosenthal, S. and Maibach, E. (2017) Inoculating the Public Against Misinformation about Climate Change, *Global Challenges*, **1**, 1600008, doi:10.1002/gch2.201600008.

Watson, L. (2018) Systematic Epistemic Rights Violations in the Media: a Brexit case study, *Social Epistemology*, **32**, 88–102, doi:10.1080/02691728.2018.1440022.

Wilkes, A. L. and Leatherbarrow, M. (1988) Editing Episodic Memory Following the Identification of Error, *Quarterly Journal of Experimental Psychology: Human Experimental Psychology*, **40**, 361–87.

Winter, S. and Krämer, N. C. (2016) Who's Right: the author or the audience? Effects of user comments and ratings on the perception of online science articles, *Communications: The European Journal of Communication Research*, **41**, 339–60.

5

Media and information literacy: intersection and evolution, a brief history

Jesús Lau and Alton Grizzle

Introduction

This chapter discusses the evolution of the media and information literacy (MIL) concept, and the framework for understanding the 'intersection' between media literacy (ML) and information literacy (IL). The aim is to offer a brief history and a general introduction to MIL and the work and actions deployed by UNESCO. The chapter is useful to those who are interested in becoming familiar with this subject. This is a bibliographic and exploratory text, not an in-depth study.

Concept evolution: media and information literacy – the historical place of IL and ML

UNESCO created the MIL concept in 2007 by merging two separate terms, stating that MIL '. . . empowers citizens to understand the functions of media and other information providers, to critically evaluate their content, and to make informed decisions as users and producers of information and media content.' (UNESCO, 2017c; see also Grizzle, 2013). The organisation prefers not to give a classic definition of MIL, focusing instead on delineating the key learning objectives, outcomes or competencies of MIL. The argument here is that it is hard to capture all the essentials of MIL in one short paragraph. Furthermore, when one considers the hundreds of definitions of media literacy and information literacy, with their myriad of entry points and emphases, non-expert stakeholders may be confused (Grizzle, 2013 and Grizzle, 2014a). MIL skills are elements vital to the exercising of human rights, as established by Article 1 of the Universal Declaration of Human Rights, 'all human beings are born free and equal in dignity and rights . . .' (United Nations, 2006). It is a right that is also recognised in the UN Sustainable Development Goals that have a human rights approach, where public information access and other fundamental freedoms are included specifically in target 16.10 (United Nations, 2015). UNESCO has made several great efforts to promote MIL skills as vital elements in the exercise of human rights are several but best summarised in the book *Media and Information Literacy: enhancing human rights and countering radicalization and extremism* (Grizzle, 2016). MIL skills and their role in democracy, participation and social, economic and political engagement, as well as in personal well-being, have also been a concern for UNESCO.

The history behind the composite concept began, on the other hand, at UNESCO headquarters in Paris, where the Communication and Information Division (currently called Freedom of Expression and Media Development), and the Knowledge Societies Division, both under the umbrella of the Communication and Information Sector, were working on IL and ML on separate fronts. This organisation recognised that this approach did not benefit from synergies and compromised greater impact (Grizzle and Wilson, 2011). The isolated work that both Divisions undertook in IL and ML had been ongoing for some years. In the case of IL, UNESCO began paying attention to the subject around 2003, when it co-sponsored the Information Literacy Meeting of Experts, organised by the United States National Commission on Library and Information Science, and the National Forum on Information Literacy (NFIL) in Prague, Czech Republic, where 23 countries from all continents were represented, releasing the seminal manifesto *Towards an Information Literate Society* (UNESCO, 2003). This was UNESCO's first meeting on IL and probably the first international meeting to discuss the importance and the role of IL in society, even though national and local conferences had taken place several years earlier, such as the ones in the USA in the 1980s. One early example is LOEX (Library Orientation Exchange), founded in 1971 (see Behrens, 1994, for additional background). After Prague, UNESCO organised a follow-up meeting two years later, the High Level Colloquium on Information Literacy and Lifelong Learning at the Alexandria Library, Alexandria, Egypt, that in turn released the manifesto *Beacons of the Information Society – Alexandria Statement on Information Literacy and Lifelong Learning*. This time, the meeting was led by UNESCO with the co-sponsorship of NFIL (Devotion, 2012). Following these two meetings, UNESCO also provided financial support to the then recently upgraded IFLA (International Federation of Library Associations and Institutions) Section on Information Literacy in 2005.

UNESCO's funding for IFLA came from one of the Sector's two programmes: the Information for All Programme (IFAP) that was created in 2000. IFAP is supported by 'governments of the world that . . . pledged to harness the new opportunities of the information age to create equitable societies through better access to information'. IFAP had a Thematic Debate on Information Literacy at UNESCO, Paris, France in 2005 that put IL as a key intergovernmental concern at UNESCO (UNESCO, 2017a). At the same time, IFLA's Information Literacy Section published its *Guidelines on Information Literacy for Lifelong Learning* (Lau, 2006), an international standard that became a guide to IL international opportunities. The economic resources that UNESCO gave to IFLA-funded key projects, such as the compilation of an international directory of IL resources, *Information Literacy: an international state-of-the-art report* (Lau, 2007) and the organisation of an international contest to create an IL logo and a marketing IL manual (Lau and Cortés, 2009). This joint UNESCO-IFLA work created a greater momentum and was followed by other UNESCO initiatives such as the writing of the guidelines *Towards Information Literacy Indicators* (Catts and Lau, 2008). Another early action of UNESCO, under IFAP sponsorship, was the delivery of the Training-the-Trainers in Information Literacy (TTT) Workshop Project that offered 11 workshops '. . . to enable people to reap the full benefits of the emerging knowledge societies' (Boekhorst and Horton, 2009). This itinerant workshop was offered in places such as Alexandria, Ankara, Cape Town, Granada, Lima, Montego Bay, Port Dickson, Pattala, Quebec, Tallinn and Wuhan; other courses were added later, such as the one offered in Botswana in 2007. This IFAP training was an effective IL awareness programme around the world, where 761 participants from 99 countries took part. Another project was to organise five continental IL conferences, but owing to a lack of funding, only one was held – the European Conference on Information Literacy (ECIL) – but as a self-funded and independent congress. It reached its 6th edition in 2018 and has taken place in Ankara, Dubrovnik, Tallinn, Prague, St Malo and Oulu. This is a successful independent congress that, despite its continental focus, has been the most international conference to date, as audiences normally come from all five continents. IFAP, in a few words, has been a crucial programme in supporting MIL, and the most active country member has been the Russian Federation, which has organised national IFAP MIL conferences and meetings (see Tables 5.1 and 5.2 in the final sections of this chapter) with important proceedings and manifestos. IL has traditionally been more academic, with developments of standards since the 1990s at school level, and landmark standards at university level in the early start of the century. The term dates from 1974 but began developing in the 1980s and reached sizeable impact in the 1990s. Therefore, IL has been a key activity for libraries for at least three decades (Behrens, 1994).

Information skills have been a concern that has been reflected in the organisation of conferences and meetings in the Western world, such as the British LILAC – Librarians' Information Literacy Annual Conference, since 2005 (LILAC, 2018); ECIL – European Conference on Information Literacy, since 2013 (ECIL, 2017); CCLI – California Conference on Library Instruction, since 2004 (CCLI, 2018); LOEX – Library and Orientation Exchange, since 1971 (LOEX, 2018); DHI – Encuentro sobre Desarrollo de Habilidades Informativas – in Mexico, since 1997 (UACJ, 2017); and similar conferences in Argentina and Brazil and Europe. IL has also made an important contribution to developing academic competency standards, the best-known of which is the US standard issued by ACRL (2000), followed by other national equivalents in the UK (SCONUL, 1999), Australia and New Zealand (Bundy, 2004) and Mexico (Cortés et al., 2012), in addition to the international version generated by IFLA (Lau, 2006). The most recent normative academic IL developments have been the IL conceptual frameworks that offer more holistic, institutional or community approaches to creating an information culture, as exemplified notably by the ACRL (2016) and the CILIP frameworks (CILIP, 2018).

At the same time, developments were taking place in MIL. UNESCO unified this IL tradition with similar practices to develop ML competency standards. This merging or blending of approaches enriched the UNESCO MIL strategy and related resources (Grizzle, 2013). UNESCO's Freedom of Expression and Media Development Division oversaw the development of the 'Media and Information Literacy (Wilson, Grizzle, Tuazon, Akyempong and Cheung, 2011) for Teachers' a pioneering work that was ' . . . forward looking, drawing on present trends toward the convergence of radio, television, Internet, newspapers, books, digital archives and libraries into one platform – thereby, for the first time, presenting MIL in a holistic manner' (Grizzle and Wilson, 2011). The drafting of such guidelines involved experts from various subject areas, including media and communication, information and library sciences, technology, education and curriculum development. UNESCO convened a series of expert group meetings in Paris as well as validation meetings with other experts in Africa, Asia and the Caribbean. The expert groups that contributed to the consultations on the MIL curriculum for teachers supported the UNESCO thrust for MIL to be considered as a composite concept. Despite some resistance from expert communities, UNESCO remained committed to an integrated and interdisciplinary approach to MIL development. Both divisions promoted the same competencies as goals for citizens. Such goals had more similarities than differences, which become clear in the discussion of this chapter's following sections.

It was not easy for experts to accept the merging of the terms 'IL' and 'ML'. IL experts argued that information is a much broader term that includes media as a sub-component, an argument still made by IL experts such as Whitworth (2009), who for example states that IL is itself a concept that integrates multi-literacies, including ML. The argument is best summarised by the statement that all media can convey information but not all information is media. Media experts, on the other hand, emphasised that information is a part of ML, and that the field of ML is broader than that of IL. They argued that ML includes an analysis of the production, ownership, distribution, regulation and control of media and information, in addition to the focus on media and information messages and their audiences (Grizzle and Torras Calvo, 2013). In coining the term 'Media and Information Literacy', UNESCO was careful to ensure a holistic approach, giving equal prominence to the strengths of the two concepts. The acronym MIL was adopted without a semantic order but with the aim of creating an abbreviation that sounded good phonetically. As Grizzle (2015, 107) writes in his reflection on how measuring MIL relates to the push to measure sustainable development goals, 'there is an urgent need for media and information literacy (MIL) or information and media literacy revolution (whichever juxtaposition is preferred by the reader)'. The MIL term is currently 11 years old! Due to the continued efforts of UNESCO and its partners to expand the MIL agenda globally, the MIL concept is slowly taking hold in academic spheres and in local communities globally.

Convergence of terms

IL and ML share the learning goals of having an information-literate citizen. However, some experts would argue that both fields differ to some extent in the information medium and the way media and information are accessed. CILIP's active Information Literacy Group in the UK states, in its newly released 2018 definition of IL, that 'Information literacy is the ability to think critically and make balanced judgements about any information we find and use. It empowers us as citizens to develop informed views and to engage fully with society' (CILIP, 2018). Proponents of IL have traditionally focused on what can be called formal or perhaps academic information sources, such as journal articles, books, and other printed serial and monographic materials. Yet, even IL experts have been calling for IL initiatives to exit the realms of higher education levels or research in formal workplace settings and, as with MIL, to take on a more societal and community-based context (Grizzle, 2014a, 102).

Consider also the following definition of ML proposed by the National Association of Media Literacy in the USA:

> [ML] is seen to consist of a series of communication competencies, including the ability to access, analyze, evaluate, and communicate information in a variety of forms, including print and non-print messages. Media literacy empowers people to be both critical thinkers and creative producers of an increasingly wide range of messages using image, language, and sound.
>
> (NAMLE, 2019)

When one compares both definitions, and with close textual analysis, they approximate to very similar meanings (*ibid.*).

MediaSmarts (2018), Canada's national media literacy organisation, considers that 'Media is constructed; that audiences negotiate meaning; that media have commercial, social and political implications; and that each medium has a unique aesthetic form that affects how content is presented. . .'. Principles are 'equally applicable to watching TV news as to searching for health information online.' In a more specific skill-oriented definition, it also states that '. . . media literacy includes the competencies required to access media on a basic level, to analyze it in a critical way based on certain key concepts, to evaluate it based on that analysis and, finally, to produce media oneself. This process of learning media literacy skills is media education.' However, as general and comprehensive as such definitions are, mass media lie at the heart of ML: social networks, video, news, television, among other multimedia content. Both fields do address all communication means, but their differences are that the core media for one field are sometimes peripheral to the other, and vice versa. The ML field tends to include media that are produced by both major industries, alternative media outlets, and individual producers, that can include pop culture as well as high culture 'texts' and can be evaluated by those working within the industry, and by audiences. Other experts argue that both literacies also differ in the evaluation of the content, and the focus on such content, as well as in the way media and information are accessed or delivered to the end user (see Figure 5.1 opposite).

Another distinction, argued by some proponents, is in the origin of both literacies. IL sprang up from the library and information science field, mainly in

Information – IL	◄ Convergence ►	Mass media – ML
• Books • Monographs • Journals • Serials • Patents • Business	**Perceived content formats**	• News • Newspapers • Television • Radio • Visual • Social networks
• Investigative research • Peer-reviewed • Long process to edit • Editorial industry validation • Citations are crucial	**Content validation**	• Investigative research • Industry validation • Long process of editing • Sometimes impromptu preparation given the nature of media
• Groups – more selective • Reading skills are needed • Less digested – more cognitive demand	**Perceived audience**	• More general mass audience, and often targeted groups • Audio-visual message, reading and viewing skills needed • 'Sound bite 'or dramatic visuals
• User has to search • Retrieval-evaluation skills required • ICT maker blurred boundaries	**Perceived access**	• Media follows/targets user • Skills to filter/reject and analyse media message • Creation/production skills are also required
• Educational use/business • Long-term decision making	**Perceived main purpose for use**	• Entertainment and education focus • Daily and long-term decision-making
• More printed-text • Usually academically produced	**Perceived aesthetics**	• More audiovisual • Industry-/government-produced, large and small companies – mainstream and alternative
• Librarians • Info-collection use concerns • Educators • Quality information concern	**Perceived skill promoters**	• Mass media specialists • Media production understand truth versus bias concern • Focus on aesthetics, design

Figure 5.1 *Foundational characteristics of IL and ML*

school and academic libraries. Therefore, IL is more resource-oriented, as libraries have an interest in higher demand and more effective use of their collections and information services by their learning community – students, teachers, professors and researchers. This is a population that tends to give more weight to primary information when teaching or doing research. In the world of libraries, mass media tend to get less attention in education, especially in higher education, as they are considered a less reliable source of information. ML, on the other hand, has been part of the world of primary and secondary education, where educators have been concerned with providing students with the skills needed to assess and analyse the media that surrounds them, as well as develop media production and digital literacy skills. However, Grizzle (2015) and other experts have shown that when taken from definitional and competencies perspectives, IL, ML and even digital literacy converge. Grizzle reviewed broad competencies of information literacy, media literacy and digital literacy as articulated by various experts. He writes:

> . . . closer analysis. . . reveals that there is more agreement than departures on what are the key competencies. Symmetry exists across almost all the competencies though primarily from different viewpoints and standpoints with diverging yet converging emphases. These ever converging emphases are often crowded out by 'noise channels' of communication on MIL.
>
> (Grizzle, 2015, 111)

Current technological developments are reducing the boundaries between media and information, as formally defined by both fields. Media is increasingly becoming part of formal academic studies. So, as new digital production evolves, the differences between both fields continue to lessen. As seen in Figure 5.1, in more precise terms, both fields cover all sorts of communication means, methods and texts. Figure 5.1 also breaks down into the perceived foundational characteristics of IL and ML from the point of view of content format, content validation, audience, access, main purpose of use, aesthetics and skills promoters. A key point for readers to note is that there is varying convergence across these characteristics of IL and ML.

The Five Laws of MIL: towards unification to impact human rights

In a classic case of UNESCO's practice of historicity and foresight, Grizzle and Singh (2016) brought back S. R. Ranganathan to life. He was a powerful and renowned 'forefather'and is known as the father of information and library science in India. He is respected around the world for the Five Laws of Library Science. Grizzle and Singh proposed the Five Laws of MIL as a way to offer further bases and principles to unify information, media and technological competencies (see Figure 5.2 opposite). The authors noted that this is what

Ranganathan, 'the man, the visionary, the leader, the scholar, the unifier, the teacher, and the librarian of librarians' (Grizzle and Singh, 2016, 26), would have wanted to see.

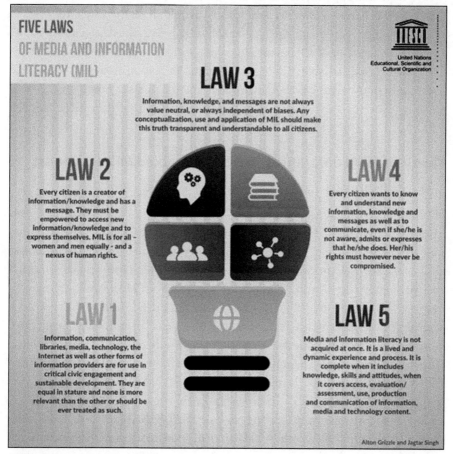

Figure 5.2 *The Five Laws of MIL*

The Five Laws of MIL are not discussed here, given the brevity of this chapter. However, it must be emphasised that collaboration between these fields can strengthen their actions, because each of them makes its own outstanding contributions to the rapidly converging disciplines of information studies and media and communication studies. There are many benefits to this harmonised approach, chief among which are the potential impact of MIL on sustainable development and human rights. It is partly through improving their critical information, media and technological competencies that people can enjoy the full benefits of their rights. As Grizzle noted:

> A rights-based approach to media and information literacy and to sustainable development . . . can play a crucial role in perceptions of the 'other' by encouraging reporting, research and analysis as well as the design and implementation of development interventions that are objective, evidence-based, inclusive, reliable, ethical and accurate, and by encouraging individuals to take sound actions based on their rights and the rights of other.
>
> (Grizzle, 2016, 12)

Meetings and conferences that have enabled MIL awareness

Global GAPMIL Week predecessors

Meetings and conferences, as well as publications, have helped achieve the emergence and consolidation of MIL, to enable UNESCO to gain consensus. The five early meetings that shaped the concept, most of which were led by UNESCO, are listed in Appendix 3 of this chapter. After these seminal meetings and conferences, the Global Alliance for Partnerships on Media and Information Literacy was created in 2013. A UNESCO-led umbrella MIL organisation '. . . dedicated to developing active and informed citizens by promoting media and information literacy around the world' (Onumah, 2014; Grizzle, 2014b). GAPMIL has representatives and organisations from more than 80 countries (Wilson and Habermehl, 2016). UNESCO supported GAPMIL in setting up chapters in Europe, North America and Latin America to address issues in United Nations regions. These are still in their embryonic stages and need consolidation. With the present explosion of disinformation and the concomitant global debates and call for action, there is now a momentum to strengthen GAPMIL, as noted by Grizzle in a statement to the GAPMIL network members. UNESCO's collaboration with the Swedish International Development Agency will be assisting with finances. UNESCO calls on other development partners to join in. A leading MIL UNESCO partner has been the United Nations Alliance of Civilizations (UNAOC) that was ' . . . established in 2005, as the political initiative of the then UN Secretary-General and co-sponsored by the governments of Spain and Turkey' to explore the roots of polarisation between societies and cultures today. . .' (UNAOC, 2018). UNESCO and UNAOC jointly created the MILID initiative, the University Cooperation Programme on Media and Information Literacy and Intercultural Dialogue within the framework of UNESCO's University Twinning and Networking programme (UNITWIN) (Grizzle, Torrent and Tornero Perez, 2013). 'The MILID University Network currently consists of 19 universities from all regions of the world' (UNESCO, 2017b). Other partners of the UNESCO's MIL strategy have been the European Commission, SIDA, Japanese Funds in Trust, and the Nordic Information Centre for Media and Communication Research (NORDICOM). In corporation with the GAPMIL Regional Chapters, these partners advanced many projects and platforms for debates around MIL development (see Table 5.1).

Table 5.1 *Global MIL Week predecessors*

2011	Media and Information Literacy Intercultural Dialogue Network (MILID), UNESCO and United Nations Alliance of Civilizations (UNAOC)	Fez, Morocco
2012	MILID Week Meeting, UNESCO and the Autonomous University of Barcelona	Barcelona, Spain
2013	Global Forum for Partnership on MIL (GFPMIL), UNESCO, SIDA, and	Abuja, Nigeria
	MILID Week (2nd) UNESCO, UNAOC and University of Cairo	Cairo, Egypt
2014	Media and Information Literacy and Intercultural Dialogue (MILID) Week UNESCO, Tsinghua International Center of Communication (TICC)	Beijing, China
	First European Media and Information Literacy Forum, 'Media and Information Literacy in the Digital Age' UNESCO, Autonomous University of Barcelona, and the European Commission	Paris, France
	Latin American and Caribbean Media and Information Literacy UNESCO, UNAM, Public Broadcasting System of Mexico, and the Autonomous University of Barcelona, and the Autonomous University of Mexico	Mexico City, Mexico
2015	Regional Forum on Media and Information Literacy in MENA Region, UNESCO, SIDA, Arab League, the University of Cairo, Autonomous University of Barcelona	Cairo, Egypt
2016	Second European Media and Information Literacy Forum, 'Media and Information Literacy in Europe: Citizens' Critical Competencies for a Rights-Based, Transparent, Open, Secure, Inclusive Information Environment' UNESCO, European Commission, and the Government of Latvia (National Library of Latvia)	Khanty-Mansiysk, Russian Federation Riga, Latvia

Continued

Table 5.1 *Continued*

	International Conference on Media and Information Literacy for Building Culture of Open Government, UNESCO and the Government of the Khanty-Mansi Autonomous Area – Ugra, Russian Federation	Khanty Mansiysk, Russian Federation

Global MIL Week

After the various MIL meetings and conferences organised or promoted by 'NESCO (see Table 5.1, and Appendices 1 and 2 of this chapter), a major celebration was institutionalised in 2015 under the name Global MIL Week, an event that includes several features and activities (see Table 5.2). The last Global MIL Week in 2018 had as its theme 'Media and Information Literate Cities: voices, powers and change makers', and was organised by UNESCO, UNAOC, the Media and Information Literacy and Intercultural Dialogue (MILID) University Network and the UNESCO-initiated Global Alliance for Partnership on MIL (GAPMIL), in Lithuania and Latvia. Nearly 300 participants from over 80 countries gathered, including government representatives, MIL experts, academics, technological intermediaries, representatives from libraries and museums, and youth leaders, who attended the Feature Conference (a congress event), the 8th MILID Conference. A third component was the Youth Agenda Forum, attended by about 200 youth participants. Global MIL Week is the peak event among events from many corners of the world. In 2018, it also included 130 events and activities, some local and some with nationwide impact, held in 52 countries and organised before, during or after Global MIL Week by different MIL stakeholders (Grizzle, 2018). A new framework was adopted during this peak week: the Global Framework for MIL Cities that 'entails the vision of building bridges between local government authorities' and NGOs' activities, non-formal and informal educators, and MIL related networks. The Conference called on UNESCO and other international, regional and national partners to take the necessary steps to operationalise MIL Cities (UNESCO, 2018).

Since 2013, in addition and as part of Global MIL week, UNESCO, UNAOC and NORDICOM, in collaboration with MILID, have produced a MILID Yearbook that is generally based on the papers presented during the feature conference, or contributions by representatives of the MIL community and stakeholders. A list of the Yearbooks and links to their full texts is included in Appendix 4. Global MIL Week also includes, within the Feature Conference, an award ceremony to '... recognize significant work and contributions in the field of Media and Information Literacy (MIL), and [to] honour individuals or organisations who have demonstrated excellence and leadership in integrating MIL into their activities and practice on a local or global level' (UNESCO, 2019). The full week and global events have mostly, so far, been ML-related participations/content, therefore, there is a great opportunity to the library and information sector to take part in this major MIL celebration.

Table 5.2 *Global MIL Week celebrations*

2015	Media and Information Literacy Week 2015, and Feature MILID Conference: 'Celebrating Connectivity Across Cultures'. UNESCO, National Association of Media Literacy Education (NAMLE) and Temple University	Philadelphia, USA
2016	Global MIL Week Feature Conference, 'Media and Information Literacy: new paradigms for intercultural dialogue' UNESCO, University of Sao Paulo, MILID, GAPMIL, and other partners	São Paulo, Brazil
2017	Global MIL Week Feature Conference, 'Media and Information Literacy in Critical Times: re-imagining ways of learning and information environments' UNESCO, University of the West Indies, MILID, GAPMIL, and other partners	Kingston, Jamaica
2018	Global MIL Week Feature Conference GAPMIL, MILID, 'Media and Information Literate Cities: voices, powers, and change makers' UNESCO, Vytautas Magnus University and University of Latvia, MILID, GAPMIL, SIDA, Twitter and other partners	Kaunas, Lithuania and Riga, Latvia

Other international conferences

The well-established conferences, not to mention institutions, still keep their individual focus on either IL or ML, even though within their programmes there are some contributions that cover the convergence of both fields. Such is the case of the European Conference on Information Literacy (ECIL), the Librarians' Information Literacy Annual Conference (LILAC), and the US conferences such as the California Conference on Library Instruction and the leading work of the Association of College and Research Libraries, that cover only IL in their programming. On the media literacy side, a similar pattern exists. The leading National Association for Media Literacy Education Conference in the USA (NAMLE, 2019), and the China (West Lake) Media Literacy Summit Forum organised by Communications University of Zhejiang (CUZ, formerly Zhejiang University of Media Communications) (ZUMC, 2014) that has run over seven biannual conferences, retain their focus on ML; as does the International Conference on Media Literacy in China, held in

Beijing. Originally, ZUMC included the MIL concept in the Forum's name and call for papers – but this was dropped in the subsequent two events. However, some speakers at these conferences have discussed MIL, as stated, in their presentations. There is thus still a long way to go before full acceptance of the MIL concept, but progress has been made, resulting in some collaboration, cooperation and recognition from both fields at least at UNESCO events and within its publications (see Appendix 2 for a full list of main publications). In future, more interdisciplinary links are needed to achieve greater progress in fostering MIL skills within schools, the family, the workplace and in people's daily lives.

Conclusions

It's been a steep road towards the acceptance of MIL as a concept, and towards reaching the current state since UNESCO coined the term 11 years ago. The pragmatic merging of the term was a call for the disciplines of media and information literacy, as well as technological literacy, to join their professional efforts, so as to more effectively reach their shared goals: developing citizens' skills of access, evaluation and wise use of information, so that they benefit from and contribute to knowledge and to the increasingly digital society, regardless of the stage of national or local development. IL has made a great contribution to MIL before and during the time span of this compound concept. Both ML and IL have sometimes displayed differences in their focus on the communication medium, whose production and distribution characteristics shape the way users access and use information. At the core of this conceptual merging are the individual users and the mass audiences – the same ones who need MIL. Building synergies through co-operation and collaboration benefit such populations. UNESCO, as the prime global organisation in the education, communication and information fields, has taken a leading role to reach consensus around MIL and expand the concept through meetings, conferences and publications (see Appendix 2). The evolution of MIL to the consolidation stage has taken place thanks to myriad UNESCO actions and to the response of professional organisations and institutions from different fields, recognising that they work towards the same learning goal. In the next stage for MIL, greater collaboration is open to members of both fields. The intersection of their goals is clear, and the concept is ready for further evolution.

References

ACRL (Association of College and Research Libraries) (2000) *Information Literacy Competency Standards for Higher Education*, www.ala.org/acrl/standards/informationliteracycompetency.

ACRL (Association of College and Research Libraries) (2016) *Framework for Information Literacy for Higher Education*, www.ala.org/acrl/standards/ilframework.

Behrens, S. J. (1994) A Conceptual Analysis and Historical Overview of Information Literacy, *College & Research Libraries*, **55** (4), 309–22, https://crl.acrl.org/index.php/crl/article/view/14902/16348.

Boekhorst, A. K. and Horton, W. (2009) Training-the-Trainers in Information Literacy (TTT) Workshops Project, Final Report to UNESCO, *International Information & Library Review*, **41** (4), 224–30, https://doi.org/10.1080/10572317.2009.10762818.

Bundy, A. (2004) *Australian and New Zealand Information Literacy Framework Principles, Standards and Practice*, 2nd edn, https://www.utas.edu.au/__data/assets/pdf_file/0003/79068/anz-info-lit-policy.pdf.

Catts, R. and Lau, J. (2008) *Towards Information Literacy Indicators*, UNESCO, http://unesdoc.unesco.org/images/0015/001587/158723e.pdf.

CCLI (2018) 2004 Workshop Collaborating for a Cure: moving students beyond the online quick fix, California Conference on Library Instruction, www.cclibinstruction.org/workshops-conferences/2004-workshop.

CILIP (2018) *CILIP Definition of Information Literacy 2018*, CILIP: the Library and Information Association, https://infolit.org.uk/ILdefinitionCILIP2018.pdf.

Cortés, J., González, D., Lau, J., Moya, A. L., Quijano, A., Rovalo, L. and Souto, S. (2012) *Normas Sobre Alfabetización Informativa En Educación Superior*, https://www.uv.mx/veracruz/usbi/files/2012/09/DeclaratoriaTercerDHI.pdf.

Devotion, G. S. (2012) High-Level Colloquium on Information Literacy and Lifelong Learning, Alexandria, Egypt, www.ifla.org/files/assets/information-literacy/publications/high-level-colloquium-2005.pdf.

ECIL (2017) 'ECIL 2013', European Conference on Information Literacy, 2017, http://ecil2013.ilconf.org.

Grizzle, A. (2013) Media and Information Literacy as a Composite Concept: the UNESCO perspective. In Carlsson, U. and Culver, S. H. (eds) *Media and Information Literacy and Intercultural Dialogue,* International Clearinghouse on Children, Youth and Media, NORDICOM, University of Gothenburg, Sweden.

Grizzle, A. (2014a) Enlisting Media and Informational Literacy for Gender Equality and Women's Empowerment. In Vega Montiel, A. (ed) *Media and Gender: a scholarly agenda for the Global Alliance on Media and Gender*, UNESCO.

Grizzle, A. (2014b) MIL, Intercultural Dialogue and Global Citizenship (Academic Introduction). In Culver, S. H. and Kerr, P. (eds) *Global Citizenship in a Digital World*, International Clearinghouse on Children, Youth and Media, NORDICOM, University of Gothenburg, Sweden.

Grizzle, A. (2015) Measuring Media and Information Literacy: implications for the sustainable development goals. In Singh, J., Grizzle, A., Yee, S. J. and Culver, S. H. (eds) *Media and Information Literacy for the Sustainable Development Goals*, MILID Yearbook 2015, NORDICOM, University of Gothenburg.

Grizzle, A. (2016) A Context: MIL as a Tool to Counter Hate, Radicalization, and Violent Extremism. In Singh, J. and Kerr, P. (eds) *Media and Information Literacy: enhancing human rights and countering radicalization and extremism*, International Clearinghouse on Children, Youth and Media, NORDICOM, University of Gothenburg, Sweden.

Grizzle, A. (2018) *When Media and Information Literacy Penetrates City Life*, MIL Week 2018 Conference report, 21 November, https://en.unesco.org/news/when-media-and-information-literacy-penetrates-city-life.

Grizzle, A. and Singh, J. (2016) Five Laws of Media and Information Literacy as Harbinger of Human Rights. In Singh, J., Kerr, P. and Hamburger E. (eds) *Media and Information Literacy: enhancing human rights and countering radicalization and extremism*, International Clearinghouse on Children, Youth and Media, NORDICOM, University of Gothenburg, Sweden.

Grizzle, A. and Torras Calvo, M. C. (2013) *Media and Information Literacy Policy and Strategy Guidelines*, UNESCO.

Grizzle, A. and Wilson, C. (eds) (2011) *Media and Information Literacy Curriculum for Teachers*, UNESCO.

Grizzle, A., Torrent, J. and Tornero Perez, J. M. (2013) MIL as a Tool to Reinforce Intercultural Dialogue: an introduction. In Carlsson, U. and Culver, S. H. (eds) *Media and Information Literacy and Intercultural Dialogue*, International Clearinghouse on Children, Youth and Media, NORDICOM, University of Gothenburg, Sweden.

Lau, J. (2006) *Guidelines on Information Literacy for Lifelong Learning*, IFLA, www.ifla.org/files/assets/information-literacy/publications/ifla-guidelines-en.pdf.

Lau, J. (2007) *Information Literacy: an international state-of-the-art report*, Veracruz, Mexico.

Lau, J. and Cortés, J. (2009) *Integrating the Information Literacy Logo: a marketing manual*, InfoLitGlobal, http://infolitglobal.org/logo/en/manual.

LILAC (2018) LILAC 2005, Librarians' Information Literacy Annual Conference, www.lilacconference.com/lilac-archive/lilac-2005.

LOEX (2018) Past and Future Conferences, LOEX Annual Conference, www.loexconference.org/2018/past-future.html.

MediaSmarts (2018) *Media Literacy Fundamentals*, MediaSmarts, Canada's Centre for Digital and Media Literacy, http://mediasmarts.ca/digital-media-literacy/general-information/digital-media-literacy-fundamentals/media-literacy-fundamentals#key.

Onumah, C. (2014) Developing Media and Information Literacy: a case study of Nigeria. In Culver, S. H. and Kerr, P. (eds) *Global Citizenship in a Digital World*, International Clearinghouse on Children, Youth and Media, NORDICOM, University of Gothenburg, Sweden.

NAMLE (2019) *Media Literacy Defined*, NAMLE: National Association for Media Literacy Education, https://namle.net/publications/media-literacy-definitions.

SCONUL (1999) *Information Skills in Higher Education*, briefing paper prepared by the SCONUL Advisory Committee on Information Literacy, www.sconul.ac.uk/sites/default/files/documents/Seven_pillars2.pdf.

UACJ (2017) *Eventos DHI, Desarrollo de Habilidades Informativas UACJ*, Internet Archive Wayback Machine, https://web.archive.org/web/20031230014352/http://bivir.uacj.mx/dhi/Eventos/Default.htm.

United Nations (2006) *Universal Declaration of Human Rights*, www.youthforhumanrights.org/what-are-human-rights/universal-declaration-of-human-rights/articles-1-15.html.

United Nations (2015) *Sustainable Development Goals*, www.un.org/sustainabledevelopment/sustainable-development-goals.

UNAOC (2018) 'Who We Are', United Nations Alliance of Civilizations (UNAOC), www.unaoc.org/who-we-are.

UNESCO (2003) *The Prague Declaration: towards an information literate society*, www.unesco.org/new/fileadmin/MULTIMEDIA/HQ/CI/CI/pdf/PragueDeclaration.pdf.

UNESCO (2017a) About Us, www.unesco.org/new/en/communication-and-information/about-us.

UNESCO (2017b) Media and Information Literacy and Intercultural Dialogue Yearbook 2017: call for papers, https://en.unesco.org/news/media-and-information-literacy-and-intercultural-dialogue-yearbook-2017-call-papers.

UNESCO (2017c) MIL as Composite Concept, www.unesco.org/new/en/communication-and-information/media-development/media-literacy/mil-as-composite-concept.

UNESCO (2018) *A Global Framework for Media and Information Literacy Cities (MIL Cities)*,
https://en.unesco.org/sites/default/files/gmw2018_draft_mil_cities_framework.pdf.

UNESCO (2019) GAPMIL Awards, https://en.unesco.org/themes/media-and-information-literacy/gapmil/awards.

Whitworth, A. (2009) Teaching Information Literacy within a Relational Frame: the Media and Information Literacy Course at Manchester, *Journal of Information Literacy*, 3 (2), 25–38. https://doi.org/http://dx.doi.org/10.11645/3.2.209.

Wilson, C. and Habermehl, C. (2016) Western Education Supports UN Effort to Improve Global Media Literacy, Faculty of Education, Western University, www.edu.uwo.ca/news-events/2016/unesco.html.

Wilson, C., Grizzle, A., Tuazon, R., Akyempong, K. and Cheung. C. K. (2011) *Media and Information Literacy Curriculum for Teachers*, UNESCO, www.unesco.org/webworld.

ZUMC (2014) About ZUMC, Zhejiang University of Media and Communications, https://en.wikipedia.org/wiki/Communication_University_of_Zhejiang.

Appendix 1: UNESCO MIL meetings and conferences integrated list

The acceptance of the concept by the IL and ML communities has made progress thanks to UNESCO's decade-old support, promoting and organising meetings and conferences. The major early meetings and conferences organised are listed here (UNESCO, 2017b).

2008 – International Expert Group to develop teacher training curricula for media and information literacy, UNESCO, Paris, France.

2010 – Expert group meeting on the development of a global framework of indicators to measure media and information literacy (MIL), Bangkok, Thailand.

2011 – The First International Forum on Media and Information Literacy (MIL), Faculty of Arts and Humanities, Sais-Fes; and Sidi Mohamed Ben Abdellah University, Fez, Morocco.

2011 – Media and Information Literacy Intercultural Dialogue Network (MILID), UNESCO and United Nations Alliance of Civilizations (UNAOC), Sidi Mohamed Ben Abdellah University, Fez, Morocco.

2012 – MILID Week Meeting, Barcelona, Spain.

2012 – International conference: 'Media and Information Literacy for

Knowledge Societies', UNESCO IFAP Russia National Office, Moscow, Russia.

2013 – Global Forum for Partnerships on Media and Information Literacy (GFPMIL), 'The Global Alliance for Partnerships on Media and Information Literacy' (GAPMIL) was established, Abuja, Nigeria.

2013 – Global Forum for Partnership on MIL (GFPMIL) 2013, Abuja, Nigeria.

2013 – MILID Week (2nd.), UNAOC and University of Cairo, Cairo, Egypt.

2014 – Media and Information Literacy and Intercultural Dialogue (MILID) Week, Tsinghua International Center of Communication (TICC), Beijing, China.

2014 – Latin American and Caribbean Media and Information Literacy Forum, UNAM, Public Broadcasting System of Mexico, and University of Barcelona; Mexico City, Mexico.

2015 – Regional Forum on Media and Information Literacy in MENA Region, Cairo, Egypt.

2015 – Media and Information Literacy Week 2015, and MILID Conference: 'Celebrating connectivity across cultures'. National Association of Media Literacy Education (NAMLE) and Temple University, Philadelphia, USA.

2016 – Second European Media and Information Literacy Forum, 'Media and Information Literacy in Europe: citizens' critical competencies for a rights-based, transparent, open, secure, inclusive information environment', National Library of Riga, Riga, Latvia.

2016 – International Conference on Media and Information Literacy for Building a Culture of Open Government, UNESCO IFAP Russia, Khanty-Mansiysk, Russian Federation.

2016 – Global MIL Week (GAPMIL, MILID), 'Media and Information Literacy: New Paradigms for Intercultural Dialogue', University of São Paulo, São Paulo, Brazil.

2017 – Global MIL Week (GAPMIL, MILID), 'Media and Information Literacy in Critical Times: Re-imagining Ways of Learning and Information Environments', University of the West Indies, Kingston, Jamaica.

2018 – Global MIL Week (GAPMIL, MILID), 'Media and Information Literate Cities: voices, powers, and change makers', Vytautas Magnus University and University of Latvia, Kaunas, Lithuania and Riga, Latvia.

Appendix 2: UNESCO media and information literacy main publications

(Published by UNESCO, Paris, unless otherwise stated.)

Banda, F. (2009) *Civic Education for Media Professionals: a training manual*.

Bokova, I. (2017) The Media: operation decontamination, *The UNESCO Courier*, 2, July–September.

Catts, R. and Lau, J. (2009) *Hacia unos Indicadores de Alfabetización Informacional*.

Frau-Meigs, D. (ed.) (2006) *Media Education: a kit for teachers, students, parents and professionals*.

Frau-Meigs, D. and Torrent, J. (eds) (2009) *Mapping Media Education Policies in the World: visions, programmes and challenges*.

Grizzle, A. and Wilson, C. (eds) (2011) *Media and Information Literacy Curriculum for Teachers*.

Horton, F. (2008) *Understanding Information Literacy: a primer*.

Horton, F. (2013) *Overview of Information Literacy Resources Worldwide*.

Lee, A., Lau, J., Carbo, T. and Gendina, N. (2013) *Conceptual Relationship of Information Literacy and Media Literacy in Knowledge Societies*. Series of Research Papers.

Moeller, S., Joseph, A., Lau, J. and Carbo, T. (2011) *Towards Media and Information Literacy Indicators*.

Pérez, J. and Pastor, L. (2011) *Guía para Radios y Televisiones sobre la Promoción del Contenido Generado por el Usuario y la Alfabetización Mediática e Informacional*, UOC.

Singh, J., Kerr, P. and Hamburger, E. (eds) (2016) *Media and Information Literacy: reinforcing human rights, countering radicalization and extremism*.

Skare K. and Rønning H. (2002) *Media in Development: an evaluation of UNESCO's International Programme for the Development of Communication (IPDC)*, University of Oslo.

UNESCO (2007) *Information for All Programme*.

UNESCO (2013a) *Global Media and Information Literacy Assessment Framework: country readiness and competencies*.

UNESCO (2013b) *Media and Information Literacy Policy and Strategy Guidelines*.

Appendix 3: Early meetings that shaped MIL

2008 – International Expert Group to develop teacher training curricula for media and information literacy, UNESCO – Paris.

2010 – UNESCO Expert group meeting on the development of a global framework of indicators to measure media and information literacy (MIL) – Bangkok, Thailand.

2011 – The First International Forum on Media and Information Literacy (MIL), UNESCO, in co-operation with the Faculty of Arts and Humanities, Sais-Fes; and Sidi Mohamed Ben Abdellah University, Fez, Morocco.

2012 – International Conference: 'Media and Information Literacy for Knowledge Societies', UNESCO IFAP Russia National Office, Moscow, Russian Federation.

2016 – International Conference on Media and Information Literacy for Building a Culture of Open Government, UNESCO IFAP Russia National Office – Khanty-Mansiysk, Russian Federation.

Appendix 4: MILID Yearbooks

Culver, S. H. and Kerr, P. (eds) (2014) *MILID Yearbook 2014: Global Citizenship in a Digital World.* Gothenburg, Sweden: UNESCO, UNITWIN, UNAOC, and International Clearinghouse on Children, Youth and Media NORDICOM, University of Gothenburg.

Grizzle, A, Singh, J., Culver, S. H. and Yee, S. J. (2015) *MILID Yearbook 2015: Media and Information Literacy for the Sustainable Development Goals.* Gothenburg, Sweden: UNESCO, UNITWIN, UNAOC, GAPMIL, and International Clearinghouse on Children, Youth and Media NORDICOM, University of Gothenburg, https://milunesco.unaoc.org/wp-content/uploads/2015/07/milid_yearbook_20151.pdf.

Singh, J., Kerr, P. and Hamburger, E. (eds) (2016) *MILID Yearbook 2016: Media and Information Literacy: Reinforcing Human Rights, Countering Radicalization and Extremism*, UNESCO, UNITWIN, UNAOC and GAPMIL, http://unesdoc.unesco.org/images/0024/002463/246371e.pdf.

[Editors to be named] *MILID Yearbook 2017: Media and Information Literacy in Critical Times: Re-imagining Ways of Learning.* In press at time of writing.

6

Information literacy and national policy making

John Crawford

Introduction

The relationship between information literacy (IL), national policy making and high-level national action has attracted surprisingly little attention in the wider world of information literacy research and development, given that it is reasonable to expect the production of an overarching strategy within which to situate specific aspects of information literacy. This chapter will explore the issues and problems in developing national IL strategies.

It is also the case that there is something of a backstory to IL and national policy making. The Prague Declaration (UNESCO, 2003) explicitly recognised IL as an all-encompassing phenomenon, a concern for all sectors of society and key to the social, cultural and economic development of nations, communities, institutions and individuals in the 21st century and beyond. The Alexandria Proclamation (Garner, 2005) reiterated some of these points, stating that IL provides the key to support economic development, education, health and human services. It also noted that IL encompasses learning, critical thinking and interpretative skills across professional boundaries and empowers individuals and communities, a point which will be returned to later. IL, therefore, can be interpreted as being about personal and civil rights, participative citizenship, lifelong learning, skills and financial well-being, education and critical thinking and the maintenance of a healthy lifestyle. Paul Zurkowski, who coined the term information literacy, emphasised the importance of the workplace (Bawden, 2001), describing information-literate people as 'People trained in the application of information resources to their work...'. But in the 1990s IL was taken up enthusiastically by academic librarians, who saw it as a natural progression from bibliographic instruction and who came to dominate the IL agenda. In higher education information came to be linked with the idea of a hierarchy or laddering of skills, as exemplified by the SCONUL *Seven Pillars of Information Literacy* (SCONUL, 2011). However, such a concept was less suited to IL activity in other sectors. Academics came to be concerned with learning outcomes and pedagogy which are susceptible to measurement, while public librarians were more concerned with social inclusion, which is less so (Crawford and Irving, 2013, 22–23).

Scoping national information literacy activities

Serious attention to sectors other than higher education is of more recent interest. In 2014 a study by Whitworth (2014) revealed that 60% of the IL literature relates to higher education. It is worth noting in this context that university graduates make up 6.5% of the world's population of over 7.6 billion, suggesting an imbalance of activity between higher education and other aspects of human activity. Battista et al. (2015) found unambiguous connections between social justice, human rights and IL and these point to areas which IL policies might address. In a helpful paper reviewing the literature of Everyday Life Information Seeking (ELIS), something which, as the authors point out, is still in its infancy, Martzoukou and Abdi (2017) address a variety of foci which explore demographic differences, e.g., older adults, fourth age/retired people, young people/men, early years/pre-school, nursery, aging women, diverse social roles (e.g. parents, retired persons, citizens) and everyday life situations that create information needs linked to learning, personal development and health and well-being. The authors situate civic participation as part of ELIS but note that the broad area of 'citizenship' has not attracted much interest, although citizenship is an important issue. In February 2015 the Right Information: Information Skills for a 21st century Scotland and the Scottish Library and Information Council (SLIC) jointly organised a conference which demonstrated that there is scope for extending the reach of IL to include information issues linked to claims and payments of Universal Credit (the UK Government's main social welfare benefit) and how housing associations contribute to information skills development among their tenants. It also covered issues previously referred to including health literacy and information skills development among young people. A key finding was that there is a wide range of organisations outside the information sector with information needs with which the information sector can work (Crawford, 2016). Bill Johnston (2016), who is not only an IL activist but also chairman of the Scottish Seniors' Alliance, argues that IL needs to become integral to many aspects of older people's lives but the bewildering variety of sources available represent a barrier to achieving this (this is explored more fully in Chapter 11 of this book). He notes that there is no single focus for addressing older people's issues within the Scottish Government and the lack of focus for government thinking on IL is a key policy issue. Hall, Cruickshank and Ryan (2017), in a study of information use by community councillors (these are the most local level of municipal elected representatives in Scotland), found that, for them, workplace experience is the main source of information skills, implying that citizens without a background in professional/information-based work are likely to be at a disadvantage. They also found that municipalities, not citizens, are the main source of information on local issues. Almost no community councillors obtain information about local issues from public libraries.

The issue of the civic political agenda has been reviewed by Smith and McMenemy (2017) in the context of the use of information to facilitate political decision making by young people. They found that the term 'political information' can be interpreted in different ways, and is often used synonymously with other terms such as 'political knowledge', 'civic literacy' and 'citizen competence'. Political information can be interpreted as knowledge about how the political system works, knowledge of the current political debate and everyday politics, and/or knowledge of political actors and their ideological differences. Smith has studied the use of information by young people and particularly how they use information for political decision making. This draws on the Scottish experience of the 2014 independence referendum, in which 16–17-year-olds were able to vote for the first time. The use of so many terms perhaps reflects uncertainty in the information world about what might be called political literacy and raises the question of whether civic or political literacy or whatever it might be called is linked to the emergence of devolved government, as has been the case in Scotland and Ireland (see below).

In Wales the Welsh Information Literacy Project developed accredited IL learning (Agored) units. At its concluding conference in March 2015 there was a series of presentations in which the presenters reported on how the Agored units had been used to develop skills among both young and older people as well as community groups (CILIP Information Literacy Group, 2015), thus extending IL into skills training for the wider community. Clearly the broad expectations of the Prague Declaration and Alexandra Proclamations are becoming a reality, albeit in a rather unstructured way. More recently the information needs of refugees have become a focus of interest. Work in this area is discussed by Konstantina Martzoukou in Chapter 10 of this book.

A recent contribution to the debate is the revised CILIP definition of IL (CILIP, 2018), which replaces a much shorter document prepared in 2004. There is a brief overview definition: 'Information literacy is the ability to think critically and make balanced judgements about the information we find and use'. The definition goes on to state that: 'Importantly, information literacy is empowering, and is an important contributor to democratic, inclusive, participatory societies'.

While previous documents might have focused mainly on education and in particular higher education, in the revised definition education is just one of a number of contexts, the others of which are: IL and everyday life, IL and citizenship, IL and education, IL in the workplace and IL and health. Each context provides a basis for advocacy among different groups of players. The definition draws from the Alexandria Proclamation and like all such documents is a compromise between comprehensiveness and conciseness.

Information literacy strategies and policies

Discussions and reviews of strategies and policies are mainly not recent but useful data can be harvested from previous work. Writing in 2011, Basili found that, in most countries, IL had not entered the policy agenda and it was still necessary to promote policy awareness about IL, a situation little changed today. She identified a total of 54 policy initiatives, although most of them did not focus specifically on IL and appeared mainly in ICT policy documents, some in reality being higher education course materials. Whitworth (2011), in a pioneering study, analysed six policy documents available in English, which are all, in some sense, national documents. The presence of small states in his analysis is a notable feature. Finland was found to be the only one with full state recognition, albeit concerned only with higher education. Hong Kong was found to provide the most comprehensive policy framework but did not consider the impact of IL on democracy and active citizenship.

Both Whitworth and Basili examine the situation in some detail and offer evaluative criteria for national policies but from the evidence available five elementary criteria emerge which should be met:

1 IL policy documents should be about IL and not something else.
2 They should have some form of government endorsement and support.
3 They should be genuinely cross-sectoral, covering all education levels from early years to PhD level, the workplace, health, lifelong learning, employability and skills development and citizenship and civil rights.

4 They should be at least informed and preferably led by the professional bodies of the countries concerned.
5 They should be collaborative, with input from all organisations in the countries concerned, such as skills development bodies, employers' organisations, trade unions, teaching and learning organisations and relevant NGOs.

The late Woody Horton, drawing on his own experience of many years of IL activity (Horton, 2011), noted the importance of patience and perseverance, a reminder that IL activity is not time-limited but has to be seen as a process which can take many years and which requires planning for the long haul, which has resourcing implications. He suggested aiming for the top, in other words engaging with politicians and policy-making civil servants. It is desirable to study pre-existing policy documents being produced by the countries concerned and link IL activity to them. It is also necessary to experiment and try a wide range of strategies.

In national IL policy making, working relationships are essential. Partnership and networking is crucial, using both personal and professional contacts. As the experience of the Scottish 2015 conference showed, it is essential to work cross-sectorally and not just with librarians and information specialists. Communities of practice with both regular face-to-face meetings and web-based communication are a good way to bring a diverse range of practitioners together, identify common problems and learn from a range of sectors. It is important to identify organisations to work with. There is a plethora of these:

• skills development agencies and other organisations involved in workplace training
• organisations concerned with promoting digital inclusion
• curriculum development bodies in education
• teachers and university lecturers' organisations
• professional organisations with an education and training role
• job centres and careers advisors
• community learning and development organisations
• telecommunications regulators (such as Ofcom in the UK)
• chambers of commerce
• employers' organisations
• trade unions.

All these can have an interest in IL outcomes. Again, this list raises resourcing implications, as keeping track of the activities of so many bodies is extremely time-consuming. Research into IL activity, whether at the level of individual institution or at a higher level, is strongly to be encouraged. Even at single institutional level worthwhile research can be done which can be replicated elsewhere. Research involving more than one organisation may well raise funding issues which, in turn, implies the deployment of expertise in obtaining funding. Reporting on research findings in appropriate journals is also to be recommended. This both increases the credibility of research and raises awareness more widely. Publication should not be restricted to library and information journals.

An interesting commentary on the repertoire of issues listed above is an article reviewing the situation in Canada in 2013 (Bradley, 2013) on the basis of a careful study of the literature. Topics discussed include the relationship with other literacies and an early discussion of the meaning of civic literacy and how this links to the concept of active citizenship. Responsibility for IL policy making is found to be too large and pervasive an issue to be the responsibility of only one profession. While the Canadian government was an early international leader in information technology policy development, with an emphasis on infrastructural developments, the same cannot be said of IL policy, although there are references in Canadian government policy documents to IL-like activity. Because education is a responsibility devolved to provinces and territories there is no central policy-making agency, a situation hardly confined to Canada. Somewhat surprisingly the Canadian Library Association has played little part in IL policy development.

In general terms the role of the state is limited, with participation usually being delegated to NGOs and quangos whose staff are willing to support IL but usually on a short-term basis.

Examples of practice

French-speaking Belgium

The francophone community of Belgium (Wallonia and Brussels) has no centralised policy for libraries. Public libraries are the only component under the auspices of a single authority. University libraries and schools libraries are responsible only to their own institutions (there are six universities and 19 higher education colleges). Collaborative initiatives come from libraries and institutions themselves.

Since 2013, ARES (Académie de Recherche et de l'Enseignement Supérieur, www.ares-ac.be/fr.) has brought together 127 higher education institutions in francophone Belgium. It set up a 'libraries' commission to carry out joint projects. In 2015, this commission created a working group, ILIB (http://ilib.be/Wordpress), specifically devoted to IL. Composed of 14 members, this working group is the successor to the association 'Groupe eduDOC' (1989–2010, http://infolit.be/edudoc), which was also an initiative led by librarians and information specialists.

The ILIB working group has already carried out several activities, with great success, over the past three years:

- an international conference. 'Training for Information Literacy in the time of Web 2.0 and discovery tools' (2015)
- an after-work evening for sharing experiences, methods and tools (2016)
- a training day on evaluation (2016)
- a day of 'How do I?' (2017).

At the time of writing, a survey of teachers' perceptions of information literacy and training needs is under way.

On the institutional side, there are also many achievements. The most emblematic are those of the three main universities that have set up IL working groups:

UCL (Université Catholique de Louvain): for several decades, the librarians of UCL and UQAM (Université du Québec à Montréal) have established a partnership to adapt its 'Infosphere' (https://bib.uclouvain.be/infosphere) to the Belgian context. The UCL library also offers eight humorous video capsules (https://uclouvain.be/fr/bibliotheques/bibliojack.html) to quickly train their users.

ULB (Université Libre de Bruxelles) has created a MOOC called 'What's up Doc – Documentary Training for All'. This is very successful both inside and outside the institution. The teaching team is composed of nine librarians.

ULiège (Université de Liège): while in other institutions librarians generally participate in existing courses, in Liège libraries have succeeded in creating 30 credited courses in the different faculties. In September 2017, they also published a specific IL framework: the 5PMIS (https://infolit.be/5PMIS). It is used to evaluate existing courses and create new courses, but mostly to communicate about IL.

Generally, thinking about IL has evolved considerably over the past 20 years. Training has become less technical, less tool-oriented and more methodological. Communication with teachers remains a priority to place IL at the centre of learning. Even if the situation improves, IL will remain the province of librarians rather than the wider community.

The Scottish Information Literacy Project 2004–2010

The Scottish Information Literacy Project, which was funded from a variety of sources, is notable for several reasons (Irving, 2011). It was the first national information literacy project within the UK and Ireland and its aims and objectives evolved from an initial focus on education to a much wider agenda embracing primary education, lifelong learning, employability, skills development, the workplace, health and adult literacies. The original concept, formulated in October 2004, was for a one-year innovative, national pilot to develop an information literacy framework with secondary and tertiary education partners which would produce secondary-school leavers in Scotland with a skill set which post-school education could recognise and develop or which could be applied to the world of work. However, such an aim takes many years to achieve and when the Project ended in the spring of 2010 much still remained to be achieved, especially in lifelong learning, health literacy and the workplace.

One of the Project's principal products was a framework of IL skills which used the Scottish Credit and Qualifications Framework (SCQF, which helps education and training providers of all kinds to identify the level that has been studied in a particular subject) and pre-existing models and definitions wherever possible, so that the Project could demonstrate a continuous learning process and 'peg' each information skill level to an appropriate learning level as specified by the SCQF Framework. Adopting SCQF lent authority to the planned IL framework. This was a key decision and one which was to be adopted by the Welsh Information Literacy Project which is described below.

Although the Framework is principally linked with formal education it also contains sections on definitions, IL and lifelong learning, IL education and how the Framework could be used. The outcome of the process, a 68-page document suitable for supporting implementation of the Framework and advocacy both to the education world and the wider community, was completed and evaluated in 2007–8.

Although the Project's initial aim was to link secondary and tertiary education it soon became apparent that to be 'effective, an IL policy must be firmly pegged to the information, lifelong learning, inclusion and digital policies of the state'

(Crawford and Irving, 2007, 40), a point which was subsequently taken up by the Welsh Information Literacy Project. The Project needed to engage in the wider world outside academia. This led to contacts with a wide range of organisations outside the information world, some of which were more successful than others, including Ofcom Scotland, the Confederation of Business and Industry (CBI) in Scotland, which represents employers, the Scottish Trades Union Congress which represents employees, the Glasgow Chamber of Commerce, which represents local business and industry, and Skills Development Scotland, the Scottish Government's skills development agency. This last agency proved to be the most successful contact, as its staff recognised the importance of information literacy as a skill for their staff, for career selection and for jobseekers. Some work was also done with adult literacies tutors and community learning and development staff to investigate the potential for developing IL as an employability and workplace skill in conjunction with public libraries, an area which has considerable developmental potential. However, some aspects of the Project were less successful. Although a meeting was held with a government minister this proved inconclusive, as the minister was primarily concerned with the digital inclusion agenda.

As with many IL initiatives and policies, the Project's impact on government was limited and it was most influential with non-governmental organisations (NGOs) and with direct education providers. It also set standards which have subsequently been followed in other areas. Although firmly based in Scotland and reflecting Scottish educational and socially inclusive values it aimed to be recognised both UK-wide and internationally. It received visitors from the USA, Finland and Australia and built up contacts with initiatives in other parts of the world, including the National Forum on Information Literacy in the USA. It directly inspired the Welsh Information Literacy Project and has received respectful attention in the Republic of Ireland. Five main lessons learned from the Project stand out:

- Develop strategies and advocacy from existing policies including, education, skills development, employability and social inclusion policies. Do not restrict yourself to information policies.
- Form partnerships and collaborate with a wide range of agencies, especially NGOs. Do not work only with fellow information professionals.
- Offer support to practitioners. They can benefit from your support, which they value, and you can use the findings from their work to inform policy development.

- Advocate and lobby tirelessly, especially outside the information world.
- IL policy must be firmly pegged to the information, lifelong learning, inclusion and digital policies of the state.

Although the Project concluded in 2010 it was reborn in 2012 as an online, cross-sectoral, IL community of practice 'Information skills for a 21st century Scotland', which is open to everyone who is interested in IL and associated skills and competencies, both within and outside the information profession, primarily in Scotland but also elsewhere. It still continues today.

The Welsh Information Literacy Project

The Welsh Information Literacy Project was initiated at the Gregynog conference in Powys in November/December 2009, where one of the speakers was the Director of the Scottish Information Literacy Project. As the Project document notes 'This project builds upon the work that was done in the National Information Literacy Framework Scotland'. It was managed by Welsh Information Literacy Steering Group and funded by CyMAL (Museums, Archives, Libraries Wales, a Welsh NGO). Although the Project shared some features in common with the Scottish Project it was administered differently and undertook some rather different work. The Project was divided into two phases. The first was led by Cardiff University (2009–2011) and from April 2012 until 2015 by Gr p Llandrillo Menai (a large FE college situated in North Wales). A notable feature of the framework was its basis on current Welsh Government educational and social welfare documents, notably the *One Wales* document, which outlined a vision of a prosperous, sustainable and better-educated Wales. The first phase of the Project mapped the IL landscape in Wales, supported by case studies and by the production of a Welsh Information Literacy Framework. The *Information Literacy Framework for Wales* takes inspiration from the Scottish Framework model. It draws on pre-existing work such as the SCONUL *Seven Pillars* and is structured as a sequential continuum matching IL skill levels against the Credit and Qualifications Framework for Wales (CQFW). The 'laddered' Framework extends from Entry Level 1 (lowest level) to Level 8 Doctoral.

Phase Two created accredited units of learning, undertook advocacy work and sought to develop IL through the digital inclusion agenda. The Welsh Information Literacy Project liaised closely with the National Institute of Adult and Continuing Education and Dysgu Cymru (Learning Wales) during the creation of the Framework, to ensure that the terminology used for the levels was appropriate to the CQFW. As a result of this partnership, the project was able to work with Agored Cymru, a CQFW-awarding organisation, to create seven units of learning to accredit lifelong learning in IL. These units range from Entry Level 1 through to Level 4 (Certificate of Higher Education, HNC (Higher National Certificate) or first-year undergraduate level). They could be delivered by librarians or adult and community learning trainers and were designed to recognise the learning achieved in IL. These are a notable feature of the Project and not one undertaken elsewhere.

A final phase involved work with schools and the curriculum and promoting IL in public libraries, which included the appointment of IL champions in several public library services. WILP project officers gave presentations to senior school staffs, which led to two schools participating in work to embed IL into the school curriculum (Eynon, 2013).

Although the Agored units remain they have been superseded by the Welsh Government's introduction of a digital competence framework and digital literacy essential skill, which include information literacy, and cover schools, colleges and work-based learners.

In Wales there are now three essential skills: application of number (literacy), comms (literacy) and digital literacy. The skills within the digital literacy framework – the Welsh Digital Competence Framework was developed in Welsh schools and focuses on developing digital skills which can be applied to a wide range of subjects and scenarios (Learning Wales, 2018) – are embedded in the Welsh Baccalaureate qualifications (which are effectively mandatory in secondary schools and widespread in academic and vocational provision in FE).

The Project concluded in 2015 with a closing conference which included five presentations by a range of professionals, some of whom had used the Agored units for a range of training initiatives (Welsh Information Literacy Group, 2015). This included a presentation by a youth worker for Denbighshire County Council, who had taken young people out of school and into the local public library to complete the Agored Cymru Information Literacy unit. Each individual chose a subject to research and concluded by producing a short film to showcase their results (Jones, 2015).

The Agored units in their new form seem to be the main legacy of the Project. Unfortunately the communities of practice set up after the Project finished did not long survive (Eynon, 2018). The Welsh Project was the most successful in the UK in obtaining government recognition and was notable for basing its work on wider policy documents.

Is it possible to evaluate national information literacy policies?

These examples of activity raise the question of whether it is possible objectively to assess national IL policies and activities.

In order to evaluate national IL policies and their activities it is necessary to devise performance indicators against which activity can be accurately measured. A performance indicator is a numerical or verbal expression derived from library statistics or other data used to characterise the performance of a library (Crawford, 2006, 15).

There are different types of indicator. For example:

- inputs – resources that are applied to providing a service, e.g. opening hours
- outputs – products and services created by the library, e.g. issue statistics
- outcomes – the contribution that a service makes to the activities of a user, whether they are related to work, learning or leisure
- quality – fitness for purpose
- value and impact – making a difference (Crawford, 2006, 16–17).

Of these, outcomes, quality and value and impact are the most informative. They are, however, the most difficult to assess, as they depend on the collection of evidence. The performance indicators derivable from the work of Horton (2011) and Whitworth (2011), might include the following:

- IL policy documents should be about IL and not something else.
- They should have some form of government endorsement and support.
- They should be genuinely cross-sectoral, covering all education levels from early years to PhD level, the workplace, health, lifelong learning, employability and skills development and citizenship and civil rights.
- They should be at least informed and preferably led by the professional bodies of the countries concerned.
- They should be collaborative, with input from all organisations in the countries concerned, such as skills development bodies, employers' organisations, trade unions, teaching and learning organisations and relevant NGOs.

Other useful points include the need for patience and perseverance, aiming for the top and finding in-house champions.

In Scotland the issue of champions has to some extent been addressed by attracting the support of professional bodies and also by engaging with other professions and activities which see the value of IL. Aiming for the top has been more problematic. While engaging with civil servants has not been a problem, a meeting with a government minister was less successful, with the emphasis being on digital literacy rather than IL. 'Linking IL to specific long standing goals and reforms' (Horton, 2011) has been key to Scottish activities. Objectively demonstrating the value and impact of activities is a continuing challenge (Horton, 2011). As for some of Whitworth's criteria, Scotland has from the beginning worked cross-sectorally both within and beyond the profession and has worked collaboratively with other relevant organisations. Although professional bodies have been supportive, they have not sought a leadership role. While it might seem obvious that IL policies should be about IL and not something else, this has in practice proved to be a particularly thorny issue, as separating out digital and IL skills in the minds of policy makers has proved challenging.

The Welsh project was funded by CyMAL. As in Scotland, the project worked cross-sectorally, involving schools and public libraries. Its success in developing training (Agored) units shows the need for at least an additional performance indicator. Professional bodies provided leadership and this was more structured and pervasive than any of the other projects. In-house champions were created by recruiting IL champions for public libraries. Both projects showed the need for a post-project strategy, another indicator which needs to be added.

In Belgium government involvement is lacking and activity emanates from the profession. Universities have set up useful initiatives but developments elsewhere are lacking. Making links with schools, however, is a useful innovation and one that all IL strategies should encompass.

This analysis suggests that any national IL project should be able to tick at least some of these boxes.

Problems and possibilities

The foregoing draws attention to a range of thorny problems in developing national IL policies and actions. The updated CILIP IL definition is a valuable contribution to the debate but much more could be said about IL in everyday life and what citizenship means in an IL context. Perhaps citizenship should be linked to the concept of the active citizen, someone who engages with society, a suggested measure of which is turnout in elections (Bradley, 2013). IL in higher education has benefited from many years of discussion and research and definitions and concepts are now well honed but this debate is still not complete in the context of wider society. There is a need for improved vocabulary and definitions to review such issues as the role of young people in information use and the politicisation of IL, which has led IL to be thrust into a spotlight of wider attention as never before. Another term in use is 'civic literacy'. The construct of 'civic literacy' means the capability and the willingness to listen to other people. Civic-literate persons establish informed and affective connections with other human beings. In other words, a social orientation is one of the qualities of a civic-literate person. Another quality that is mentioned is 'political knowledge and the skills to serve as active informed citizens'. Civic-literate persons are capable 'to make informed moral, economic, political and scientific judgements' and to participate in civil discourses. One can also say that civic literacy enables 'citizen empowerment and democracy'. Engagement with society is therefore linked to the concept of citizenship in IL (van Helvoort, 2018).

The above discussion has demonstrated that there are few areas of human activity in which IL does not have a role. The range of issues is truly vast and raises, *inter alia*, training issues and who should do it. Public libraries have long been recognised as having a key role in the training process, a good example being the training support offered by Scottish public librarians in the process of rolling out Universal Credit (the UK Government's main social welfare benefit), whose application processes require digital and information skills on the part of the claimants. The development of training units which can be delivered by public libraries was pioneered in Wales but there is much greater scope for such work. However, providing training is a large and complex issue and governments are reluctant to commit to the resources required.

The evidenced need to work with a wide range of organisations shows that the concept of IL as professional construct has to be abandoned and recognised as a right for everyone. This means interacting with a multiplicity of players. How is this to be done? How does one keep up to date with changing contacts, practices and policies within relevant organisations? This cannot be done in a serious way without dedicated staffing and this, in turn raises the question of public resources and organisation.

Working with governments has proved to be, in the Scottish context, a difficult issue and reflects wider experience. Judging by the experience of both Scotland and Wales it is easier to make progress in a small state where access to decision makers is easier. However, decision makers are always constrained by their policies and are reluctant to act outside them. While policies are widely in place to tackle digital inclusion issues this is not the case with IL and it is necessary to address different components of the decision-making structure in different IL contexts. Health literacy is a good example where a Scottish Government health literacy policy is in place which can be appealed to (Scottish Government, 2017). Unfortunately the same cannot be said of other specific contexts.

The experience of practitioners is that information literacy policy making and activity is a process, not an event and there is no discernible end to the process. Sustainability therefore becomes a key issue and any time-limited national activity should have an exit strategy in place. The Scottish Information Literacy Project did not have an exit strategy but key partners felt that the work was too valuable to abandon and this led to the setting up of a community of practice (Right Information, 2012) that has done useful work despite having virtually no resources other than the enthusiasm of its members. In Wales, although communities of practice were set up they did not long survive and training units is the project's principal legacy.

It is therefore easier to see the problems than the solutions. There is a fundamental paradox. There has never been greater scope for IL activity but the resources are not in place; funded public resources and organisation, with appropriate staffing is the only way forward but the required resources are nowhere available.

Acknowledgements

My thanks to Bernard Pochet for information about the situation in French-speaking Belgium.

References

Basili, C. (2011) A Framework for Analysing and Comparing Information Literacy Policies in European Countries, *Library Trends*, **60** (2), 395–418.

Battista, A., Ellenwood, D., Gregory, L., Higgins, S., Lilburn, J. et al. (2015) Seeking Social Justice in the ACRL Framework, *Communications in Information Literacy*, **9** (2), 111–25.

Bawden, D. (2001) Information and Digital Literacies: a review of concepts, *Journal of Documentation*, **57** (2), 218–59.

Bradley, C. (2013) Information Literacy Policy Development in Canada: is it time?, *Partnership: the Canada journal of library and information practice and research*, **8** (2), 1–28.

CILIP (2018) *CILIP Definition of Information Literacy 2018*, CILIP: the Library and Information Association, https://infolit.org.uk/ILdefinitionCILIP2018.pdf.

CILIP Information Literacy Group (2015) *Report on Welsh Information Literacy Project Closing Conference*, https://infolit.org.uk/report-on-welsh-information-literacy-project-closing-conference.

Crawford, J. (2006) *The Culture of Evaluation in Library and Information Services*, Chandos Publishing.

Crawford, J. (2016) Information Literacy Development in a Small Country: a practical proposition?, *Library and Information Research,* **40** (123), 47–68.

Crawford, J. and Irving C. (2007) IL and the Petition to the Scottish Parliament, *Library + Information Update*, **6** (3), 40–1.

Crawford, J. and Irving, C. (2013) *Information Literacy and Lifelong Learning*, Chandos Publishing.

Eynon, A. (2013) Welsh Information Literacy Project, *Library and Information Research*, **37** (114), 17–22.

Eynon, A. (2018) [Personal communication], 16 May.

Garner, S. D. (2005) *High-Level Colloquium on Information Literacy and Lifelong Learning*, www.ifla.org/publications/high-level-colloquium-on-information-literacy-and-lifelong-learning.

Hall, H., Cruickshank, P. and Ryan, B. M. (2017) *Information Literacy for Democratic Engagement*, Edinburgh Napier University, https://communityknectdotnet.files.wordpress.com/2017/10/lildem-stakeholder-report-october-2017.pdf.

Horton, F. W. (2011) Information Literacy Advocacy – Woody's Ten Commandments, *Library Trends*, **60** (2), 262–76.

Irving, C. (2011) National Information Literacy Framework (Scotland): pioneering work to influence policy making or tinkering at the edges, *Library Trends*, **60** (2), 419–39.

Johnston, B. (2016) Ageing and Information: the Scottish older people's movement, *Library and Information Research,* **40** (123), 4–13.

Jones, M. (2015) Welsh Information Literacy Project: closing conference, *Journal of Information Literacy,* **9** (1), 102–4.

Learning Wales (2018) *Digital Competence Framework*, http://learning.gov.wales/?lang=en.

Martzoukou, K. and Abdi, E. S. (2017) Towards an Everyday Information Literacy Mindset: a review of literature, *Journal of Documentation*, **73** (14), 634–65.

Right Information (2012) *Information Skills for a 21st Century Scotland*, www.therightinformation.org.

Scottish Government (2017) *Making it Easier: a health literacy action plan for Scotland 2017–2025*, www.gov.scot/Publications/2017/11/3510.

SCONUL (2011) *The SCONUL Seven Pillars of Information Literacy Core Model For Higher Education*, www.sconul.ac.uk/sites/default/files/documents/coremodel.pdf.

Smith, L. and McMenemy, D. (2017) Young people's conceptions of political information, *Journal of Documentation*, **73** (5), 877–902.

UNESCO (2003) *The Prague Declaration: towards an information literate society*, www.unesco.org/new/fileadmin/MULTIMEDIA/HQ/CI/CI/pdf/PragueDeclaration.pdf.

van Helvoort, J. (2018) Four Spaces of Civic Literacy Education: a literature review, European Conference on Information Literacy, Oulu, Finland, September 2018.

Welsh Information Literacy Group (2015) Closing conference, https://infolit.org.uk/report-on-welsh-information-literacy-project-closing-conference.

Whitworth, A. (2011) Empowerment or Instrumental Progressivism? Analyzing information literacy policies, *Library Trends*, **60** (2), 312–37.

Whitworth, A. (2014) *Radical Information Literacy: reclaiming the political heart of the ILMovement*, Chandos Publishing.

7

Information literacy as a growth pillar for a fledgling democracy

Reggie Raju, Glynnis Johnson and Zanele Majebe

Introduction

Almost a quarter of a century has gone by since political democracy[1] and the World Bank reported that South Africa is the most unequal society in the world, and that its poverty is the 'enduring legacy of apartheid'. The World Bank also reported that inequality has deepened since the dawn of this political democracy. This is contrary to the assertions made by successive national governments, which state that South Africa's transition from apartheid to democracy is a success. Keeton (2014) acknowledges that there have been significant attempts, through policy and legislation, to bring about economic and social democracy. He goes on to assert that poverty, lack of job creation, lack of public service delivery and so on are the root causes of inequality and not due to policy or political failure.

There is substantial commitment by the national government of South Africa to extend the political liberation to include socio-economic liberation; to bring into the democracy stable social inclusion. Buoyed by a progressive Constitution, complementary legislation and policy have been brought forward in support of a better future for the people of the country: a future in which no person lives in poverty, where no one goes hungry and where there is work for all. The elimination of poverty and reduction of inequality will accelerate the growth of the economy which will be of benefit to all South Africans. The National Development Plan (NDP) was constructed to serve as an action plan for securing the future of South Africans as advocated in the Constitution.

The NDP has, *inter alia*, the broad objectives of eliminating poverty and reducing inequality. Critical to achieving this and other objectives is the development of a citizenry that is skilled and has access to an infrastructure that will contribute to its growth and development. It is acknowledged that one of the most significant challenges that need to be overcome is that of illiteracy, which is viewed as a major cause of the poverty and failure of the nation. In order to overcome these challenges it is important that the country increases the literate base of the country to facilitate growth and development of the nation. The National Council for Library and Information Services, a legislated entity representing the LIS sector, advances the view that 'libraries have a critical role to play in nurturing democratic values by providing access to diverse views, encouraging critical thinking, and teaching information literacy' (National Council for Library and Information Services, 2014, 31). Unfortunately, at this point in the development of South Africa, the educational system from preschool to tertiary education is grappling with developing a citizenry with the necessary lifelong learning skills: citizens who are confident and independent, literate, numerate and multi-skilled, with the ability to participate in society as a critical and active citizen. This challenge of the poor educational system undermines the basic provisions in the Constitution.

The right of access to information, which is enshrined in the Constitution in its Bill of Rights, guarantees the freedom of expression and freedom of access to information.[2] However, the right of access to information is more than just the provision of information – it must include the capacity of the citizenry to absorb information in order to construct new knowledge with new interpretations.

Using the principle that information literacy is imperative to bring about national development and improve the conditions of society, this chapter will engage in a discussion on how information literacy can nurture and grow a fledgling democracy. There is significant evidence that there is willingness from the South African government to bring about socio-economic liberation. It is the view of the authors that, as a result of decades of apartheid on the back of centuries of colonialism, it will take two to three generations to bring about parity and socio-economic liberation.

At the epicentre of this transformation into an equitable and just society is a sound educational system that produces learners and students who can maximise opportunities to earn socio-economic liberation. Hence, this chapter focuses on the role of information literacy in growing the country against the backdrop of an efficient and effective school and public library system.

Characterisation of information literacy for a fledgling democracy

Information literacy in the global south must take on an additional responsibility beyond the 'classic' definitions articulated around the ability to identify, locate, evaluate, organise and effectively use information from a variety of sources. As posited by Tsaasan, Waite and Cheng (2015) information literacy has to 'empower people in the Global South, as information seekers decide *what* information they need, *when* they need it, and *which* information to use'.

In an era where there is a surfeit of information, the choice of information and its ethical use are significantly defining principles. However, in the global south, in countries such as South Africa where there is a relative dearth of information, choice is not that pivotal a principle. The lack of resources, especially indigenous knowledge and information in the vernacular, brings front and centre the principle of critical thinking. The authors submit that this is especially true in a fledgling democracy.

In Nielsen and Borlund (2011, 109), Facione states that critical thinking is a complex concept and can be defined as 'the process of purposeful, self-regulatory judgement which results in interpretation, analysis, evaluation, and inference as well as explanation of the evidential, conceptual and methodological considerations on which a judgement is based'. In an environment where there is a dearth of information and limited access to technology, information literacy is considered crucially important to enable people to deal with the challenge of making good use of limited access to information and limited communication technology. In this context, information literacy has become a new paradigm in the information and communication landscape. Within this information landscape, information literacy carries the purpose of empowering people to achieve their personal, social, occupational and educational goals.

In a fledgling democracy, information literacy forms the basis for lifelong learning. Lau states that:

> . . . information literacy and lifelong learning have a strategic, mutually reinforcing relationship with each other that is critical to the success of every individual, organisation, institution, and nation-state in the global information society. These two modern paradigms should ideally be harnessed to work symbiotically and synergistically with one another if people and institutions are to successfully survive and compete in the 21st century and beyond.

(Lau, 2006, 12)

In the global south, there is a greater urgency for learners to master content and extend their investigations, to become more self-directed, and to assume greater control over their own learning. As pointed out by Ranaweera:

> . . . information literacy encompasses knowledge of one's information concerns and needs, and the ability to identify, locate, evaluate, organise and effectively create, use and communicate information to address issues or problems at hand; it is a prerequisite for participating effectively in the information society, and is part of the basic human right of lifelong learning.
>
> (Ranaweera, 2010, 65)

As much as access to information is considered a basic human right in the global south, there is an added emphasis on growth and development. The slow growth of many African countries is attributed to the lack of access to information. Further, information that is accessible is a reflection of global needs and imperatives. The dearth of local African published content and limited access to indigenous knowledge must be juxtaposed to the relative abundance of global north content, as such a comparison is essential in developing strategies for the growth of a fledgling democracy.

Rights and information literacy

Former US President Barack Obama is cited as positing that information literacy is essential to the functioning of a modern democratic society (Demasson, Partridge and Bruce, 2017). Obama is not the only world leader who links information literacy to democracy – the late Kofi Annan (former Secretary-General of the United Nations) stated that:

> . . . in order to truly transform knowledge into power and to use information for liberation, users need to know what to search for, how to navigate potentially treacherous seas of information, and how to apply the new found knowledge in their everyday contexts . . .
>
> (Tsaasan, Waite and Cheng, 2015, 3)

The reality, though, is that information literacy is relatively low among most global south countries, hence negating basic rights and stunting growth and development.

There is no contestation that information literacy has moved into the realm of a basic human right, promoting social justice and social inclusion. This holds especially true within the South African context, as there are many legislative attempts for the inclusion of the previously disenfranchised into mainstream society. The right of access to information as a human right is an established component of South Africa's constitutional democracy. However, the legacy of apartheid presents the current government with unprecedented priorities to address which include, *inter alia*, basic health care, high unemployment, especially among blacks and high infant mortality rates. This long list of contradicting priorities has resulted in inappropriate allocations of funding from government in support of the eradication of information illiteracy. The South African government, which openly advocates the advancement of basic human rights, is in a Catch 22 situation, as it cannot provide all of its citizens with even a modestly defined right of access to information, because this will drain resources from other vital priorities. Therefore, the full enjoyment of the right of access to information is a long-term goal for millions of South Africans.

Despite South Africa's political and moral commitment to social cohesion and inclusion, the right of access to information is extremely important for redressing uneven distribution of power and status. At the centre of this redress is access to information, which has to be driven rather than relying simply on the goodness of others. This brings to the fore the distinction between the right of access to information and assistance in accessing information. Assistance maintains existing power structures, whereas to recognise another's right to access to information is to cede authority to them. Thus, the right of access to information argument is also more powerful in that, while the assistance argument typically addresses only temporarily urgent needs, the rights argument concerns itself with the broader structures of freedom and opportunities. In this debate of rights versus assistance, the former attempts to rebalance the power relationship with the goal of producing long-term, reliable structures that will remove the need for dependence in the future.

Adding to the debate on rights, Wijetung and Alahakoon (2005) draw attention to the correlation between information literacy, basic human rights and lifelong learning. They indicate that information itself is a transforming resource for emerging information societies. Without information literacy, the information society will not be able to achieve its full potential. Therefore, the concept and practice of information literacy must be promoted from an early age among school students. This early moulding of young minds through adoption of information literacy education and practices is the catalyst necessary to advance growth and development – to advance democracy. The authors posit that this is very much a case of the 'chicken or the egg first' – how can fledgling democracies such as South Africa make such investments in information literacy when there are other priorities – priorities that are directly linked to life and death?

Ubuntu, democracy and information literacy

South Africa's democracy was founded on the principles of Ubuntu. This African philosophy limits individualism and stresses that social interrelations and responsibilities are a precondition for human life: that is, the individual has meaning only in relation to an experience of the community. It places emphasis on fostering a strong connection with others in the community, lending a helping hand wherever possible, sharing individual challenges and difficulties, enabling societies to strive for equality, freedom and access to basic human rights (Msengana, 2006).

As a philosophy, it can be adapted to serve the universal right of access to basic education and literacy. However, in order for this concept to possess any true meaning, it requires a resurgence of unity and rekindling of the human spirit amongst people from all walks of life, to unite in advocating for the rights of nations across the globe. Societies and communities must strive to uphold the basic right to education and literacy. This is the stepping stone for individuals to gain true independence and freedom from all human and social ills (Msengana, 2006).

Ubuntu is a form of human engagement that allows for critical thinking, non-domination and the optimal development of human relationships. It nurtures unity in supporting those who continue to lack access to education and literacy – thereby developing an educated voice and empowering a nation in a manner that not only enriches oneself, but has the leverage to empower the lives of all people across the globe.

The communalism foundation of Ubuntu highlights the interdependence of the extended family: everyone is a learner and a contributor to the growth of the village. Letseka (2013) asserts that critical thinking is perhaps the most important skill a student can learn in school and college, because critical thinking is associated with 'philosophical inquiry'. In an Ubuntu environment, this philosophical inquiry begins prior to formal schooling. The concepts of 'thinking', 'reflective thinking', and 'critical thinking' underscore the importance of Ubuntu teaching and learning.

Waghid (2004) posits that the communal element of Ubuntu accentuates the importance of being reasonable. Ubuntu, in advancing critical thinking, promotes on the one hand the ability of people to articulate clear, logical and defensible arguments, and on the other hand to demonstrate a willingness to listen carefully to others (Waghid, 2004, 57). In corroborating Waghid's posit, Bodunrin (1981) points out that critical thinking is guided by the power of reason and insight rather than by authority of the communal consensus and Ubuntu promotes the engagement in discussions in a critical and meaningful way.

Quan-Baffour and Romm (2015) posit that Ubuntu in education is considered to be African cultural capital that provides indigenous knowledge that is important for the integration of the African conception of inclusion, which in turn promotes inclusivity, equality and social justice in our education system. This assertion is corroborated by Lefa (2015), who states that the purpose of education is to free the minds of the oppressed in order to destroy social classes. The authors propose that a strong educational system, underpinned by strong information literacy skills to support lifelong learning from preschool to tertiary education, is the golden thread necessary to eliminate years of indoctrination and colonisation: this is the route for economic and social emancipation. Education and information literacy, in the African Ubuntu context, is driven by the principle that the community is the beneficiary of education as the individual is a significant part of the core of the community.

Education and information literacy is the mechanism driving liberation and opportunity for change in life not only for the individual but for the community as a whole (Quan-Baffour and Romm, 2015). The better the education, the better the chance of having a successful life and the more positive the impact on the community. The growth of the community creates opportunities for the growth of other individuals and this snowball effect will strengthen the growth trajectory of the community and the democracy of the country.

The viciousness of South Africa's low literacy circle

There is significant empirical evidence demonstrating that the benefits in the transition to democracy will be negated by the low levels of literacy. South Africa's fledgling democracy is fraught with a number of contradictions – at this point in the history of the country it is a vicious circle.

South Africa is almost 25 years into a new democracy and there are many who believe sufficient time has passed for the playing field to be regarded as level. There is an expectation that there should have been significant change and the vestiges of apartheid should no longer exist. There seems to be an underestimation of the full extent of the devastation that the system of apartheid has caused and it will take another two to three generations, in the view of the authors, before there is equality and equity. To expand on this assertion, a child from a parentless household, living in poverty in a township or rural area, needs to overcome these major challenges. At best, this person with almost no support would have to obtain a quality education (unfortunately, the current public educational system is extremely poor) to release him or her from this state of poverty – this generation is about survival. Assuming that there is some level of success, the generation following will have a slightly greater chance of success – hopefully the next generation will end up with better job prospects, which will aid in creating the opportunity for their children to attain some higher education qualification. The contribution of education to economic growth is acknowledged by the HSBC report of 2014. Currently, the education system is so skewed that breaking out of this apartheid mould is going to take a monumental effort.

As pointed out by van der Berg et al. (2011), the rate of grade progression by the previously disenfranchised into secondary education is generally low. Much of this is attributed to poor quality of schooling, resulting in substantial drop-out prior to matric (South Africa's equivalent to what is commonly referred to as Grade 12). Failure to pass matric and the prospect of not achieving a university entrance qualification are factors that significantly contribute to the high drop-out rate. The low prospects of academic success must be viewed against the backdrop of the poor home support in the foundational years of a child's education and literacy. The system of apartheid has destroyed the learning fabric of society. This poor learning system is compounded by the sparse availability of pre-literacy training at home or exposure to books, as parents are often illiterate. This is exacerbated by the fact that there are not enough books in African languages to initiate and nurture a culture of reading. It must also be noted that reading in the conventional sense is foreign to African culture, which is steeped in the oral tradition (Jiyane and Onyancha, 2010).

As indicated, it will take a monumental effort for someone from a disadvantaged background to break out of this mould. South Africa's low literacy levels and poor school system is a vicious circle and to break out of it requires literacy, which is essential to grow further literacy, and there is a need for education to grow the next generation of successful learners – literacy begets literacy and education begets education. The absence of literacy and poor education at home is a road to nowhere.

Indigenous knowledge and information literacy

Indigenous knowledge, as posited by Quan-Baffour and Romm (2015), is important for an integrated African educational system that promotes inclusivity, equality and social justice. It brings into the educational system familiar, unique and local contextual knowledge that originates from the people who are native to a particular geographic area (Dorner and Gorman, 2008). This unique body of knowledge, abilities and skills of local people accumulated through many years of experience, learning, development and transmission cannot be marginalised, as it is this which makes the African educational system relevant.

However, as pointed out by Kateregga (2016), indigenous knowledge is poorly linked to the current content in the school curriculum, resulting in education being irrelevant to the needs of the country, let alone its contribution to mediocre performance. This assertion is corroborated by Srikantaiah (2005), who states that if indigenous knowledge is brought into the learning environment, learners will connect better to taught material and it can become a major knowledge source for their community's sustainable development. The marginalisation of indigenous knowledge has a negative impact on information literacy. Nomlomo and Sosibo (2016) assert that research has shown that indigenous knowledge is often marginalised in formal learning, despite the fact that it is central to early literacy development, as young learners are exposed to oral language in their natural or social environments. They go on to state that folktales and traditional children's songs are a rich reservoir for empowering learners with different kinds of knowledge, such as social and ethical values. The kinds of knowledge are shaped by the learners' socio-cultural environment and they reflect the children's social identity. In other words, folktales and traditional children's songs are not only indigenous forms of knowledge that enhance learners' cognitive, linguistic and social skills, but are also a valuable pedagogical tool in literacy instruction. The values and skills acquired from folktales and traditional songs are relevant in the workplace, and they prepare the children for adult life.

Dorner and Gorman (2008, 4–5) bring to the fore the indigenous knowledge component in their definition of information literacy. They define information literacy as the ability of individuals or groups:

- to be aware of why, how and by whom information is created, communicated and controlled, and how it contributes to the construction of knowledge
- to understand when information can be used to improve their daily living or to contribute to the resolution of needs related to specific situations, such as at work or school
- to know how to locate information and to critique its relevance and appropriateness to their context

- and to understand how to integrate relevant and appropriate information with what they already know to new construct knowledge that increases their capacity to improve their daily living or to resolve needs related to specific situations that have arisen.

School libraries and information literacy

As much as the authors would advocate the adoption of Dorner and Gorman's (2008) definition of information literacy, the South African education landscape needs to be taken into consideration. As indicated earlier, the focus of this chapter is on the role of school and public libraries in supporting information literacy. The efforts of the higher-education sector represent a much greater challenge because the foundation of information literacy is missing. This exercise at higher-education institutions becomes far more complex and energy-draining. In going back to the school system, Hart (2006b) points out that there is a general sense of agreement that the state of public schools is failing society and the relatively recent democracy. It is proposed that the restructuring of the education system is probably the most critical construct in order to liberate society and its struggle for survival. Integration of information literacy into the curriculum is viewed by Ranaweera (2010) as the best way to implement information literacy programmes. Curriculum integration is the best approach for developing information literacy because it supports student-centred learning at the point of need. Integration into the curriculum provides all students with equal opportunities to become information literate (Ranaweera, 2010).

Curriculum reform, although not uncontroversial, represented a strong break from previous arrangements and sought to advance critical thinking and problem solving. Public spending on education has gone from being highly unequal on the basis of race under apartheid to being well targeted towards poor children. Despite some positive trends, a far more resilient legacy from the past has been the low quality of education within the historically disadvantaged parts of the school system. The repercussions of a skewed educational system are phenomenal and it may take another generation or two to restore balance. The effects of decades of a poor educational system have to be countered before equity can be achieved, as information literacy is very dependent on family circumstances and other communal support systems which include, amongst others, well-resourced libraries and qualified librarians.

Within South Africa, the quality of education varies widely: there are effectively two functioning schooling systems. In one system, the majority of children are located in a historically disadvantaged system, which still serves mainly black and coloured children. The result is that learners in these schools typically demonstrate low proficiency in reading, writing and numeracy, and learners carry an educational backlog equivalent to well over two years (van der Berg et al., 2011). The other system mostly concerns schools that historically served white children and produces educational achievement closer to the norms of developed countries.

Hart (2006a) states that fewer than 30% of South African schools have libraries and of this small percentage a very large proportion is at historically advantaged schools (previously white schools). Educational reform in post-apartheid South Africa has resulted in a shift from textbook-based rote-learning towards resource-based learning and continuous assessment by means of portfolios and projects. In confirming this pedagogical shift, Fraser (2013) posits that the shift from the teacher being the 'the expert', imparting knowledge with the aid of textbooks and notes, to a constructivist approach demands sufficient facilities. In this constructivist model where learning is in terms of active discovery, problem solving and knowledge construction, the library is a critical resource. However, there is a dire lack of school libraries, resulting in extensive demands on public libraries, whose resources are exponentially stretched as learners seek information for their projects and assignments. The relationship between school and public libraries is considered below.

Curriculum 2005

As part of the strategy to strengthen South Africa's democracy, the national government introduced legislation to support the growth in education, as this was viewed as critical in reinforcing the new earned democracy. Curriculum 2005 was one of the pieces of legislation aimed at strengthening primary and secondary education.

Curriculum 2005 requires learners to be able to identify, discover and use new knowledge along with basic ability to solve problems. The authors posit that the introduction of Curriculum 2005 was prematurely implemented without first addressing challenges such as ICT infrastructure, the upskilling of teachers and integration of ICT pedagogies in the training of school teachers. Hence teachers' response to Curriculum 2005 was apathetic. Teachers were unable to incorporate teaching pedagogies with information technology which serve as a tool to access information. Dlamini and Brown (2010) draw attention to the implementers of Curriculum 2005's constricted vision that does not reflect on black disadvantaged classroom realities and the demands that it makes on accessing information.

Curriculum 2005, exacerbated by the shortage of school libraries, has brought an increase in learners' use of public libraries. Hart (2006a) states rural libraries might well be experiencing the most intense pressure, since rural schools are the least equipped in terms of libraries and learning support materials whilst being even more underfunded than either school or public libraries.

The end of apartheid education has meant that black children now have the same demands made of them as white children. Unfortunately, schools in townships do not have libraries nor do they have access to adequate resources. Further, most black families cannot afford to buy books or have access to the internet (Hart, 2006b). In addition to this, many black children are first-generation school-goers who cannot be supported properly by parents who have themselves not been able to complete school.

This unequal education system feeds an unequal society. Apartheid has had such devastating consequences that it is going to take some brave decision making by national government to build an educational system that is going to contribute positively to a hard-earned political democracy. The authors are of the opinion that it is far more beneficial for learners to leave the schooling system at earlier grades with sound literacy and numeracy skills and with the ability to contribute to the country's socio-economic life than for them to go through to matric, only to become a burden to the economy of the country and thereby perpetuate an unequal society.

Public libraries and formal school education

Several studies have examined the impact of public libraries in communities. Kerslake and Kinnel (1998, 159 and 164–5) point out that the impact of public libraries on skills is authenticated by their efforts to support literacy and information competence, lifelong learning and a reading culture for long-term benefits. The immediate effect of this is that public libraries take on the role of school libraries by assisting learners with their homework and finding relevant information for their tasks.

This expanded role is added to their basic mission of providing collections and services to meet the developmental needs of local communities. The public library is traditionally viewed as the local gateway to knowledge and information, and makes provision for lifelong learning, community development and independent decision-making by individuals. However, in countries where a large section of the population lives in rural areas where new technologies are not within the reach of people (as is the case in most global south countries), the gap between information-rich and information-deprived communities becomes alarmingly larger. This growing information gap is contrary to the *UNESCO Public Library Manifesto*, which advocates for the public library to promote democracy, equity and equality (UNESCO, 1994).

The expansion of the role of the public libraries is corroborated by Hart (2006a), who suggests that South African public libraries are in a state of transition – leaving behind the inherited Western models of service. In this transition, public libraries have taken on a much wider role. Given that the majority of schools in South Africa do not have libraries, public libraries have to double up as joint school/public libraries. More than a source of information and support from qualified librarians (when they are available), libraries serve as safe spaces with required amenities, including electricity. Librarians have to serve the role of information specialists as well as aftercare mothers, fathers and nurses. Public libraries must be viewed against the backdrop of South African society, where the parent leaves home when it is dark and returns when it is dark. A large number of households are headed by children, owing to the scourge of HIV and other illnesses.

This multiplicity of roles must be incorporated into the government's endeavours to make education add value to democracy. Unfortunately, all Curriculum 2005 has done is increase the use of public libraries by school learners. There has been only little acknowledgement of the educational role of public libraries. The lack of school libraries and the increase in numbers of school learners heighten pressure on public libraries. South African public librarians have to now take on the enhanced responsibility for information literacy education, and indeed, for formal education in general, which in some other countries might be assumed to be the specific mission of school librarians.

In supporting Curriculum 2005, the strain on public libraries is exacerbated by the generalised criticism that there is a lack of communication between them and schools. This lack of communication has forced public libraries to 'embrace their role in the educational process to the extent that there is a shift from how the curriculum impacts libraries to how libraries impact the curriculum' (Raju and Raju, 2010, 8).

Despite the generalised criticism, there is evidence of growing collaboration between schools and public libraries. Hart and Nassimbeni assert that throughout South Africa:

> . . . there are scattered instances of successful collaboration which can
> provide the scaffolding for new configurations. These might range from

formal agreements with schools for regular programmes of homework and information literacy support through scheduled visits to the establishment of joint use of libraries.

(Hart and Nassimbeni, 2013, 20–1)

In terms of collaboration, public libraries support school learning through learning and information resources such as the provision of books, photocopies, pamphlets and pages copied from the world wide web. Many libraries maintain what is commonly referred to as 'project shelves' for materials set aside for current projects. These collaborative initiatives support learning via portfolios and projects as well as literacy. There is also direct support for information literacy. Public libraries offer library orientation to groups of school learners, usually at the beginning of the school year or during South Africa's annual Library Week. The core of the orientation programme is instruction in library layout and procedures with demonstrations on the use of reference tools (Hart and Nassimbeni, 2013). These orientation programmes are delivered to support the constructivist curriculum and project-based learning.

However, Hart and Nassimbeni (2013) and Hart (2006b) assert that there is little awareness of the evolution of information literacy education from the 'book education' that prevailed in South African schools in the 1980s. It is suggested that information literacy education must be embedded in the classroom learning programme, as the acquisition of information skills is most effective when it is linked to assignments and projects: hence the desperate need for improved communication between school educators and public librarians to stimulate information literacy among learners and support the new constructivist curriculum. Curriculum 2005 is very dependent on access to well-resourced school libraries which, unfortunately, is not available in the majority of black schools.

Public libraries, education and information literacy

Skov (2004) asserts that the information-seeking processes are an integral part of the learning process, in which individuals engage in a constructive process of finding meaning. In essence, the information-literate person is one who has learned how to learn. The emphasis on the use of information and information seeking is integral with the learning process being the linkage to formal education. It is in the educational system, from preschool and onwards, that the foundation for information literacy and lifelong learning should be laid. As it is, too much energy and time are being used in institutions of higher education in teaching students' skills and attitudes they should have learned at an earlier stage (Skov, 2004).

The challenge for public libraries is to develop their capacity to become involved in the knowledge construction process of schoolchildren, in collaboration with schoolteachers and school librarians. In South Africa, a number of public libraries have ventured into joint projects with the formal education system. Public libraries and local schools have developed a shared and common set of values regarding learning processes and project work.

Hart (2004) posits that owing to a lack of resources in schools, learners make use of public libraries, obliging them to manage large numbers of school learners. A typical example of a collaborative relationship between schools and public libraries is the development of a policy by the Nelson Mandela Bay Municipality. The policy calls on public libraries to support the school educational system. The policy states that:

> . . . the 'Municipality's Library Services will strive to achieve the following goals:

> (a) Supplement and partner with schools to include awareness-building of the value of libraries and reading, inculcating a culture of lifelong learning, and providing access to resources that are complementary to the formal educational sector. This includes building up a collection of career-oriented resources, both printed and electronic.
> (b) Printed and electronic resources will include items that allow the users to optimise informal educational opportunities. In supplementing and partnering with educational services, the Municipality's Library Services will endeavour to:
> 　(i)　Coordinate and facilitate opportunities to expose young library users to a wide range of fields and subjects.
> 　(ii)　Coordinate and facilitate opportunities for students to discover career interests and aptitudes.
> 　(iii)　Introduce materials and library experiences that begin to prepare students for future learning.

> (Nelson Mandela Bay Municipality, 2017, 19–20)

The public library is one type of library in a continuum of libraries concerned with information literacy and lifelong learning. It has a major part to play – deciding not only to provide ready-made answers and access to resources, but also to take on an educational role by being actively involved in the knowledge construction processes of its target community groups in collaboration with other stakeholders.

Conclusion

South Africa's fledgling democracy is haunted by the legacy of apartheid. Almost 25 years since political democracy was established, the vestiges of apartheid are still very much a challenge. The multiplicity of priorities has done very little to alleviate the burden of the socio-economic enslavement despite the 'good-willed' interventions of the government of South Africa. One of those interventions is Curriculum 2005 for primary and secondary schools, which has placed a significant burden on public libraries to deliver a number of traditional services as well as take on the role and responsibility of school libraries. The remit of public libraries has been expanded so much that roles have become blurred and critical responsibilities such as consolidating information literacy are being neglected. This means that, since information literacy is one of several critical literacies which are routes to socio-economic liberation, the growth of democracy has consequently been neglected, too. The citizenry is still left vulnerable because the building blocks for engagement are absent: information literacy is not a priority, *not* because it is *not* recognised as a priority, but because there are other priorities that have life-or-death implications.

The surge to consolidate South Africa's democracy triggered the NCLIS directive to develop and nurture democratic values by providing access to diverse views, encouraging critical thinking and teaching information literacy. Unfortunately, the infrastructure is inadequate to fulfil the mandate of developing a citizenry that is confident and independent, literate, numerate and multi-skilled, with the ability to participate in society as critical and active citizens. Hence, the citizenry is denied a strong foundation for information literacy, which leads some to question the assertion that information literacy is critical for the growth of South Africa's fledgling democracy.

South Africa's Constitution is focused on ensuring that the bondages of apartheid are totally wiped out, that the basic human rights of the citizenry are protected. The right of access to information is guaranteed in the Constitution: how can this right be exercised when the citizenry is not sufficiently literate to convert this access to basic knowledge for survival? The issue of redress and social cohesion is but a concept in the Constitution – there is very little evidence of redress and social cohesion to support a fledgling democracy. Poverty is rampant, as the citizenry is not literate enough to be gainfully employed.

As much as there are significant barriers, public libraries are making efforts to deliver on information literacy. Schools that have libraries are also making their contributions to information literacy, albeit not to the extent that the authors would have expected. Those that are delivering must ensure that indigenous knowledge is incorporated into information literacy programmes, as it is viewed by the authors as the 'entry' level of information literacy. There is no denying that South Africa's fledgling democracy would benefit massively from a radical injection of information literacy programmes by school and public libraries. The challenges that have to be picked up at tertiary level will become that much more manageable. An information-literate citizenry can only consolidate South Africa's democracy if there is enough will on the part of all stakeholders. It will happen – the question is, how fast?

Notes

1 In 1994 South Africa had its first democratic elections which is now commonly referred to as the start of South Africa's political democracy.
2 Access to information 32. (1) Everyone has the right of access to – (a) any information held by the state; and (b) any information that is held by another person and that is required for the exercise or protection of any rights (Republic of South Africa, 1996).

References

Bodunrin, P. O. (1981) The Question of African Philosophy, *Philosophy*, **56** (216), 161–79.

Demasson, A., Partridge, H. and Bruce, C. (2017) How do Public Librarians Constitute Information Literacy?, *Journal of Librarianship and Information Science*, 1–15, doi: 10.1177/0961000617726126.

Dlamini, B. and Brown, A. (2010) *The Provision of School Library Resources in a Changing Environment: a case study from Gauteng Province, South Africa*, Diversity Challenge Resilience: School Libraries in Action – The 12th Biennial School Library Association of Queensland.

Dorner, D. and Gorman, G. (2008) *Indigenous Knowledge and the Role of Information Literacy Education*, World Library and Information Congress: 74th IFLA General

Conference and Council, 10–14 August, Quebec, Canada, https://archive.ifla.org/IV/ifla74/papers/090-Dorner-en.pdf.

Fraser, H. (2013) Dual-use School/Community Libraries in South Africa: a new focal point, *Cape Librarian*, January/February, 50–2, www.westerncape.gov.za/text/2013/January/19_jf2013-research.pdf.

Hart, G. (2004) Public Libraries in South Africa – Agents or Victims of Educational Change?, *South African Journal of Libraries and Information Science*, **70** (2), 110–20.

Hart, G. (2006a) Public Librarians and Information Literacy Education: views from Mpumalanga Province, *South African Journal of Libraries and Information Science*, **72** (3), 172–84, http://sajlis.journals.ac.za/pub/article/view/1114/1050.

Hart, G. (2006b) Educators and Public Librarians: unwitting partners in the information literacy education of South African youth?, *Innovation*, **32** (June), 74–93.

Hart, G. and Nassimbeni, M. (2013) From Borders and Landscape to Ecosystem: reconfiguring library services to meet the needs of South African youth, *South African Journal of Libraries and Information Science*, **79** (1), 13–21, http://sajlis.journals.ac.za, doi: 10.7553/79-1-106.

HSBC (2014) *The Value of Education Springboard for success: Canada report*, www.hsbc.ca/1/PA_ES_Content_Mgmt/content/canada4/pdfs/personal/HSBC_Childrens_Education_Canada_Report.pdf.

Jiyane, V. and Onyancha, B. (2010) Information Literacy Education and Instruction in Academic Libraries and LIS Schools in Institutions of Higher Education in South Africa, *South African Journal of Libraries and Information Science*, **76** (1), 11–23, http://sajlis.journals.ac.za/pub/article/view/82/74.

Kateregga, A. (2016) Using Indigenous Knowledge to Develop Rwanda's Language Curriculum, *Journal of Linguistics and Language in Education*, **10** (1), 37–54, http://journals.udsm.ac.tz/index.php/jlle/article/view/1289.

Keeton, G. (2014) Inequality in South Africa, *The Journal of the Helen Suzman Foundation*, **74**, https://hsf.org.za/publications/focus/state-and-nation/5.inequality-in-south-africa-g-keeton.pdf/view.

Kerslake, E. and Kinnel, M. (1998) Public Libraries, Public Interest and the Information Society: theoretical issues in the social impact of public libraries, *Journal of Librarianship and Information Science*, **30** (3), 159–67, doi: 10.1177/096100069803000302.

Lau, J. (2006) *Guidelines on Information Literacy for Lifelong Learning* [final draft], International Federation of Library Associations and Institutions, http://libcmass.unibit.bg/ifla-guidelines-en.pdf.

Lefa, B. (2015) The African Philosophy of Ubuntu in South African Education, *Studies in Philosophy and Education*,

https://www.researchgate.net/publication/274374017_The_African_
Philosophy_of_Ubuntu_in_South_African_Education.

Letseka, M. (2013) Understanding of African Philosophy Through Philosophy for
Children (P4C), *Mediterranean Journal of Social Sciences,* **4** (14), 746–53, doi:
10.5901/mjss.2013.v4n14p745.

Msengana, N. (2006) *The Significance of the Concept 'Ubuntu' for Educational
Management and Leadership During Democratic Transformation in South Africa,*
PhD thesis, Education and Policy Studies, University of Stellenbosch,
http://scholar.sun.ac.za/handle/10019.1/1192.

National Council for Library and Information Services (NCLIS) and Department of
Arts and Culture (2014) *The Library and Information Services (LIS) Transformation
Charter,* www.liasa-new.org.za/wp-content/uploads/2016/04/2014-Final-Edited-
Transformation-charter-DocumentTABEdit-2.pdf.

Nelson Mandela Bay Municipality (2017) *Nelson Mandela Bay Municipality Library
Services Policy,* www.nelsonmandelabay.gov.za/datarepository/documents/
library-services-policy-adopted-30-nov-2017.pdf.

Nielsen, B. and Borlund, P. (2011) Information Literacy, Learning, and the Public
Library: a study of Danish high school students, *Journal of Librarianship and
Information Science,* **43** (2), 106–19, doi: 10.1177/0961000611408643.

Nomlomo, V. and Sosibo, Z. (2016) Indigenous Knowledge Systems and Early
Literacy Development: an analysis of IsiXhosa and IsiZulu traditional children's
folktales and songs, *Studies of Tribes and Tribals,* **14** (2),110–20,
doi: 10.1080/0972639X.2016.11886738.

Quan-Baffour, K. and Romm, N. (2015) Ubuntu-inspired Training of Adult Literacy
Teachers as a Route to Generating 'Community' Enterprises, *Journal of Literacy
Research,* **46** (4), 455–74, doi: 10.1177/1086296X15568927.

Raju, R. and Raju, J. (2010) The Public Library as a Critical Institution in South
Africa's Democracy: a reflection', *Libris,* **20** (1), 1–12,
https://www.libres-ejournal.info/536.

Ranaweera, P. (2010) Information Literacy Programmes Conducted by the Universities
in Sri Lanka, *Journal of the University Association of Sri Lanka,* **14** (1), 61–75,
https://jula.sljol.info/articles/abstract/10.4038/jula.v14i1.2688.

Republic of South Africa (1996) *Constitution of the Republic of South Africa: Chapter 2:
Bill of Rights,*
www.justice.gov.za/legislation/constitution/SAConstitution-web-eng-02.pdf.

Skov, A. (2004) Information Literacy and the Role of Public Libraries, *Scandinavian
Library Quarterly,* **37** (3), http://slq.nu/?article=information-literacy-and-the-
role-of-public-libraries.

Srikantaiah, D. (2005) Education: building on indigenous knowledge, *Indigenous Knowledge (IK) Notes*, **87**, World Bank, https://openknowledge.worldbank.org/handle/10986/10747.

Tsaasan, A. M., Waite, P. and Cheng, K. G. (2015) *A New Model for Increasing Information Access and Literacy in the Global South*, www.ideals.illinois.edu/bitstream/handle/2142/73724/396_ready.pdf?sequence=2.

UNESCO (1994) *UNESCO Public Library Manifesto*, http://unesdoc.unesco.org/images/0011/001121/112122eo.pdf.

van der Berg, S., Taylor, S., Gustafsson, M., Spaull, N. and Armstrong, P. (2011) *Improving Education Quality in South Africa: report for the National Planning Commission*, Department of Economics, University of Stellenbosch, http://resep.sun.ac.za/wp-content/uploads/2012/10/2011-Report-for-NPC.pdf.

Waghid, Y. (2004) African Philosophy of Education: implications for teaching and learning, *South African Journal of Higher Education*, **18** (3), 56–64.

Wijetung, P. and Alahakoon, U. P. (2005) Empowering 8: the information literacy model developed in Sri Lanka to underpin changing education paradigms of Sri Lanka, *Sri Lankan Journal of Librarianship & Information Management*, **1** (1), 31–41,. doi: 10.4038/sllim.v1i1.430.

8

Information literacy and the societal imperative of information discernment

Geoff Walton, Jamie Barker, Matthew Pointon,
Martin Turner and Andrew Wilkinson

Introduction

This chapter explores current research on how young people make judgements about the information they encounter. There will be a discussion on why some young people appear to trust, without question, online information whilst others show remarkable powers of insight and critique. Evidence on how this might affect their physical and mental well-being will be provided. Why this is important both in educational and political terms is discussed. There will then be an exploration of the approaches that can be employed to help young people develop a more discerning approach to engaging with the information they see, hear and read in any context.

The discussion put forward here is based upon a synthesis of research findings involving three groups of young people from the UK – 16–17-year-olds, at a secondary school, 18–19-year-old university students in their first undergraduate year and finally 18–24-year-old men recruited for an experiment, mostly undergraduates – all carried out in the UK. For the first two groups there was a concern voiced by teachers and academic tutors respectively that their students exhibited a noticeable lack of the necessary capabilities to make well-calibrated judgements in order to select good-quality information to support their work for assignments. The 16–17-year-olds were working towards gaining their Extended Project Qualification (EPQ)[1] – a mini-dissertation in addition to their A-level study. Walton et al. (2018a) provide a comprehensive reflection of these studies. The 18–19-year-olds were working towards completing their first assignment and had to find good quality information about a sporting issue of their choice (see Walton and Hepworth, 2011; 2013 for a more detailed account). These two groups are quite similar in their context and we will see that their comments and experiences and our analyses align in an encouraging way. How? They both appear to indicate that most (but by no means all) students present with remarkably poor capabilities in making judgements about information, which prevent them from making the most suitable choices. The third group were recruited to find out whether the cognitive process of information discernment has a physiological component. Why? We wanted to find out whether being good at information discernment is related to positive responses to stress. Conversely, whether being poor at information discernment was related to negative responses to stress. Given our findings, we argue that it is an educational imperative that information discernment (or indeed information literacy) should be taught as part of the school, college and university curriculum. We base this on the knowledge that, with the right kind of information literacy teaching, people can move from being poor to good information discerners. Also, making poor judgements about information could have far-reaching consequences for their education, health, political engagement and everyday life.

Why is this an important issue?

This is especially critical in our current context, which has been described as one of a 'democratic crisis' (BBC, 2018a) where misinformation, fake news and conspiracy theories are in danger of becoming accepted knowledge. We use the term misinformation to mean inaccurate information of any kind, either intentional or unintentional. We are aware that some writers use the term disinformation to describe deliberately misleading information, in contrast to misinformation, describing unintentionally misleading or inaccurate information. The intent is not an issue for us, as it is the effect of such information on individual cognition that interests us, and so we use misinformation to describe both types. In short misinformation is 'any piece of information that is initially processed as valid but that is subsequently retracted or corrected' (Lewandowsky et al., 2012, 124–5).

The misinformation carried by social media has been identified by the Department for Digital, Culture, Media and Sport (DCMS, which is the relevant government ministry in the UK), the European Union and the US Congress as a vehicle that represents an existential threat to the very foundations of our democratic order. Alex Jones and his poisonous InfoWars platform are a particular case in point (BBC, 2018b). Interference in the 2016 US Presidential election and the 2016 Brexit referendum in the UK by the Russian government, and the manipulation of voters by Cambridge Analytica, are instances of the ease with which unscrupulous organisations are able to attempt to affect people's behaviour for political ends. This is so much more prevalent because digital technologies and communications are everywhere, and the blizzard of online information challenges our ability to make sense of the world. This is particularly so for young people. Although many in the UK, but by no means all, have smartphones (95% of 16–34-year-olds in 2018 according to Statista, 2018), when confronted with a plethora of information of hugely varying quality, young people tend not to possess the skills or discernment to understand this variability. The variability in quality of information — from blogs run by 'spiritual healers' that expound the cancer-curing virtues of crystals to carefully curated health information provided by the NHS – is just one example of a phenomenon that renders young people particularly vulnerable to being misinformed and confused. Recent research (Brazier, Walton and Harvey, 2018) confirms what we have known for some time: that young people are poor at searching for information and cannot tell the difference between the good- and the poor-quality information that they find. In essence, what we need to be able to do is instil resistance to the effects of misinformation such as fake news and dubious health information (see Chapter 4 of this book for more about 'inoculating' against misinformation). This is not just about digital information however. It is about information of any kind, whether hard-copy or digital. It is also about the spectrum of information, ranging from high-quality information such as, but not exclusively, peer-reviewed journal articles, to the deliberate misinformation spread by highly motivated individuals or organisations. It is becoming clear from the Brexit vote that people were misled on a number of issues (Carter, 2016; Watson, 2018). What is not clear is the actual economic, political and social significance of this vote. Only time will tell. If people had been taught how to be more information-discerning (Walton et al., 2018a) perhaps the voting outcome may have been different. Either way, peoples' voting intentions may have been more informed and based on more accurate and balanced assessment of the information presented to them.

However, we also need to take care, because there is a danger. Encouraging people to question absolutely everything can lead them to become cynical rather than critical. Consequently, a situation where people trust nothing could, in certain circumstances, collapse into, at best, unproductive relativism or at worst, anti-science and anti-intellectualism. It remains essential to make the argument that authoritative and credible sources of scientific and other information are out there to be found. We recognise that *all knowledge is provisional* (Thornton, 2018), but this is based on the notion that good-quality evidence exists which is to be built upon and extended. In short, facts do exist, but questions such as who is stating them, when they were published, with what foundations (i.e. the research, the recognised practice and the evidence which underpins them) and what motivated their publication, all need to be taken into account. It does require more cognitive effort, but will help to begin to address the issue of what some believe is a looming 'democratic crisis' (BBC, 2018a).

What is information discernment?

Information discernment is a sub-set of information literacy and is primarily concerned with how people make judgements about information, well-calibrated or otherwise. Often expressed as 'evaluating information' in all of the major information literacy models (ACRL, 1989; Big Blue, 2002; ACRL, 2016; SCONUL, 2011; Secker and Coonan, 2011; CILIP, 2018), it is included as an important capability which CILIP has restated in its new definition of information literacy:

> The ability to think critically and *make balanced judgements* about any information we find and use. It empowers us as citizens to reach and express informed views and to engage fully with society.
>
> (CILIP, 2018; italics added)

We have made several attempts at defining information discernment over the years (see Walton, 2017, for a summary of these endeavours) and each time it seems to become an ever-more complex and challenging notion to pin down. Our latest iteration moves away from a normative to a more exploratory version. It can be thought of as a process which describes and analyses:

> the ways in which social, psychological, behavioural and information source factors influence peoples' judgements about information
>
> (Walton, 2017, 151)

A number of identifiable factors can help to understand the process of making judgements about information. First of all, people generally are more inclined to trust information such as a TV news bulletin, a newspaper article or a blog post because it takes more cognitive effort to be sceptical than to believe (Lewandowsky et al., 2012). There is a very good reason for this. As children we are looked after by our parents or other significant adults; they tell us what we need to know and we trust them. We develop a cognitive default position of trust which it takes effort to undo. Our work with 16–17-year-old schoolchildren confirmed this. A survey we carried out revealed that they were more inclined to trust their parents than teachers, peers or the media (Walton et al., 2018a).

Context is a central factor in how we make judgements about information, particularly the social situation in which we find ourselves, the roles we have, the norms expected and the tasks associated with it. These are such strong influences that young people find it challenging to transfer information literacy capabilities from one context (for example school, where they are students (role) studying for a qualification (norm) and completing an assignment (task)), to home, where they are say, shopping (role) for a tee-shirt (task) to wear at a music concert (norm). Our research indicated that young people did not think at all about using their newly found capabilities outside the educational context. They did not for instance, think about questioning the reputation or security of a website from which they were purchasing items. Walton et al. (2018a) noted that:

> One student in particular displayed a curious disparity in their information-seeking behaviour, observing there was a difference between what they did at home compared to at school. Whilst they clearly displayed that they knew how to recognise 'good' information (e.g. citations), they observed that this was a behaviour they only used at school. In essence, they knew how to identify 'good' information but did not always choose to apply this knowledge in other contexts. In other words they experienced difficulty in transferring their skills from one context to another.
>
> Walton et al. (2018a, 305–6)

This may be another reason why otherwise high information discerners can be less so outside the educational context. We believe that this can be overcome by ensuring that information learning and teaching interventions include a range of contexts in their content. We also need to ensure that we explain to learners that these are transferable capabilities that have an everyday application.

What has also come into sharper focus recently is the effect that the psychological factor of prior knowledge has on the ways in which we make judgements about information. It is not just about expertise, it is about the way we view the world. It appears that there are four major factors which shape prior knowledge and underpin the way people make judgements about the information they encounter: worldview, confirmation bias, epistemic beliefs and motivated reasoning. The underpinning factor is worldview; our political leanings appear to determine everything else in this process. Worldview is a person's deep-seated personal ideology (Lewandowsky et al., 2012). Confirmation bias (Campbell et al.,

1960) is the behaviour we exhibit as a result of our worldview and of the social and political culture characterising that worldview. For example, people who are left-leaning will read a particular newspaper which shares their beliefs whilst those who are right-leaning will read another. It also causes us to seek out people with similar views and preferences to ourselves and can contribute to the echo chamber effect experienced in social media, which can eventually lead to extremism. Worldview also shapes motivated reasoning. Kahan et al. (2012) has shown that expert scientists' beliefs are shaped by their political leanings, with right-wing scientists tending to be climate-change sceptics whilst left-leaning scientists tends to recognise climate change as a phenomenon driven by human activity. This is because of a conflict between personal interests, where a person's beliefs are matched with those held by others with whom they have close ties, which are in tension with a collective interest of making use of science to promote common welfare. Personal ties and allegiances come first every time and consequently drive motivated reasoning. This is where very able scientists will cherry-pick the data to support their beliefs; those who are adept at using numerical information are more able to confirm their own biases and ignore inconvenient evidence (Jones, 2016). Finally, Trevors et al. (2017) noted that when people are presented with conflicting information, reading it can have an emotional effect leading them either towards resisting new ideas or viewing it as a chance to learn. Participants in their study who believed that knowledge is about comparing and contrasting many sources showed more surprise and curiosity when reading conflicting texts. This affective state appeared to motivate them to comprehend new information and recognise multiple viewpoints. In contrast, those participants subscribing to the idea that information is fact-based, from authoritative sources and should be digested like food, felt confused when dealing with a range of authorities. This feeling of confusion caused them to remember less information and ignore any controversial information. The belief that knowledge is certain caused participants to feel less surprise, and more anxiety, when dealing with these contradictions. This phenomenon is known as 'epistemic beliefs' and can have a bearing on a person's level of information discernment.

Other important psychological factors which influence information discernment include: the cognitive processes which we employ to analyse, apply and synthesise information; how we reflect on these processes via metacognition and how we feel whilst engaged in these activities. Metacognition, or how we think about our own thinking and learning, plays a particularly important role in enabling us to become more aware of how we make judgements about information. Emotion, or affect, has been shown to be a critical component in information seeking (Kuhlthau, 1991) and also forms part of the information discernment process. This also ties in with epistemic beliefs discussed above. We will see later in this chapter that our most recent research confirms this view regarding the importance of emotions.

Where information originates from is also a critical factor in how we judge the information we encounter. These information source factors are important and it does not matter whether it is a search engine, database, newspaper or a person. People, for example, are more likely to believe President Trump if they are a Republican than if they are a Democrat (Lewandowsky, Swire and Ecker, 2018) – further demonstrating the very strong influence of worldview on how people make judgements about information. By the same token, because Google is, for all practical purposes *the* search engine to use, some people believe that the results they find, especially the first page of an organic search, are the most reliable information sources to use. For some, no further checking is necessary. Clearly, this is unsatisfactory and I (with various colleagues) have spent some time attempting to understand how people make judgements about information with a view to enabling them to improve their capabilities where such an improvement is necessary.

How young people make judgements about information

Our studies show that young people are not one homogenous group of either 'digital natives', capable of expert navigation through the online environment, nor are they completely bereft of any information literacy capabilities, like the young people characterised in the CIBER report (UCL, 2008). After conducting many studies, both qualitative and quantitative, we have concluded that there is a spectrum of information literacy capabilities within those aged between 16–24. Our research shows that high information discerners exhibit a number of defining characteristics. We found that they are more curious about the world than low information discerners and this difference is statistically significant. This echoes the work of Trevors et al. (2017) and shows that high information discerners have a different epistemological compass to those who exhibit low information discernment. Their epistemic beliefs are more flexible and they appear to be open to different ideas, even if they contradict their own. They use multiple sources to verify information and tend to include conflicting information which is in line with the 'curiosity' characteristic mentioned earlier. They are more likely to be sceptical about information on search engines such as Google. High information discerners do not believe that everything on search engines is true or of the highest quality. In tandem with this they do not regard the first page of results found by a search engine to be the most trustworthy information. They are also aware of the importance of authority and will check an author's background. Conversely, low information discerners are statistically significantly less likely to be aware of these issues and are generally less attentive to the content put in front of them (Walton et al., 2018b).

We believe that the in-built curiosity exhibited by high information discerners leads them to readily question the information they read. This 'cognitive questioning state' tends to manifest itself as people questioning such things as where the information was from (e.g. who wrote it and why?) and its credibility (for example, was it well-researched with many references or an opinion piece without recourse to credible evidence?). It also leads them to use a wide variety of information to explore more than one side of an argument. We know from previous research that this cognitive questioning state can be operationalised in young people by employing the appropriate learning and teaching intervention (Walton and Hepworth, 2011; 2013; Walton, 2017; Walton et al., 2018a). This is discussed more fully in the next section.

Eye-tracking research that we conducted during 2018 suggests that there appears to be a relationship between eye fixation (as of attention) when reading an online article and participants' level of information discernment. In short, high information discernment corresponds with high attention and low information discernment corresponds with low attention. The data from our research indicates that low levels of information discernment can affect reading behaviour, as characterised by the number of fixations and durations spent on areas of interests within the article. Areas of interests are drawn around key areas within an article (including headers, author, text and images or graphics) to determine levels of fixation and gaze. Eye-tracking data show that there appears to be a level of disengagement with the content, particularly for participants with a low level of information discernment. Based upon gaze data gathered during our research, participants with low information discernment did not show a high level of fixation or concentration (measured by duration). It was also very apparent that low information discerners ignored factual information such as graphs and tables and tended to concentrate on emotive content. The behaviour shown by low information discerners displayed fixations that do not follow a logical order or seem to engage fully with the article. This type of unintentional or unordered fixation behaviour indicates that participants are scanning and looking for keywords rather than engaging with the text (Schmar-Dobler, 2003; Liu, 2005). Conversely, high information discerners tended to interrogate the whole document, text, graphs and images in a structured way, a process of information behaviour resonating with 'working memory capacity' (Gere et al., 2017), where working time was applied to the more complex areas of the article.

What was perhaps most interesting about our recent research findings is the different physiological reactions to misinformation between high and low information discerners. Overall, our results suggest that information discernment can affect our physical and psychological health in several ways. First, information discernment levels affect the way in which we approach stressful tasks. Individuals are challenged if they believe that their resources (i.e., self-efficacy, perceptions of control and goal orientation) outweigh the perceived demands of a task, whereas they feel threatened if these resources are not sufficient to meet the perceived demands. Challenge and threat theory maintains that individuals respond to stressful situations with either an adaptive (challenge) or maladaptive (threat) response, dependent upon the evaluation of the situation (Blascovich and Mendes, 2000). When presented with misinformation, higher-discerning individuals viewed the stressful situation as more of a challenge than a threat to their well-being. Second, when presented with misinformation, higher information discernment levels resulted in more favourable (i.e., adaptive and healthy), physiological outcomes. Specifically, individuals with high discernment responded to stress with a more efficient blood flow, equating to a healthier heart response. Third, when given misinformation, higher information-discerning individuals responded with more positive emotions before and after the stressful task, in comparison to lower information-discerning individuals. It seems apparent that having a high level of information discernment is not only intellectually and socially useful but may actually have a beneficial physiological effect. Given these finding we argue that it is imperative that we attempt to enable all people to gain higher information discernment capabilities. Previous research (for example Walton and Hepworth, 2011 and 2013; Shenton and Pickard, 2014; Pickard, Shenton and Johnson, 2014; Walton and Cleland, 2017; Walton et al., 2018a) has shown that this is achievable. The next section outlines a possible way of delivering effective information discernment teaching and learning.

How can we enable young people to develop a discerning approach to information?

This can be achieved in many different ways. However, there are a few underlying principles which underpin the most successful approaches. We suggest that any learning and teaching intervention should follow closely the factors that impinge on information discernment. Therefore, the context for the situation that participants find themselves in should be fully recognised. Thus, for learners finding out about a subject such as sociology, make the session as specific as possible, find out what their assignment brief contains. For learners finding out about job opportunities, find out what specific roles they are interested in beforehand and tailor the session accordingly. Should this not be possible, make the subject a topical or controversial one. Generic information literacy teaching does not work. Information literacy capabilities are enacted in a context, as we have seen from the discussion set out above.

Spend as little time as possible telling learners things and more on getting them to do things for themselves – whether that be searching for information or making judgements about what they have found. Learning by doing works best. This should not preclude the scaffolding of learning and teaching intervention, that is, give the learners more help at the beginning and gradually let them do more and more by themselves until they can search and make well-calibrated judgements without help from facilitators. In particular, it is recommended that learners have a discussion regarding what constitutes high-quality evidence in support of an argument. An interesting example could be the extent to which the stance taken say by Donald Trump (or any other prominent figure with a similar view) is supported, or not, by the evidence. Below is our recommendation based upon the workshop approach we took with 16–17-year-olds at a school in the UK and reported in Walton et al. (2018a):

- Develop a series of participatory research workshops, in order to gain a rich understanding of the current information behaviour of school students.
- Use results to create an enhanced pedagogy to teach information discernment to school students.
- Involve school students and teachers in designing and improving the method.

Our approach relies on Participatory Action Research and Action (PAR), which places an emphasis on the participants' perceptions and interpretations of their own information needs and treats people as experts in their own experience to promote adolescent health and well-being (see Tavares, Hepworth and De Souza Costa, 2011; Walton et al., 2018a) for more information on specific PAR techniques).

This approach boosts learners' skills of searching, discerning and selecting information. Participatory methods ensure that all voices are heard. Monitoring and evaluating activities by seeking immediate feedback from participants is essential. A final evaluation employing individual in-depth interviews with stakeholders is recommended. This approach will ensure that the strengths and weaknesses of the proposed methodology are evaluated and modified as necessary.

We recommend that the learning and teaching intervention be carried out by employing two two-hour workshops delivered on separate days at least one day apart. The desired outcome is to empower learners to be able to make well-calibrated judgements about information and misinformation. Initially, learners should be invited to explore and discuss how they currently evaluate information, using examples provided, and describe what criteria they use in that process, if any, to foreground their current practice.

Day 1 – Two-hour workshop: This workshop can be delivered to up to 50 learners (following Walton et al.'s framework reported in 2018a). For the teaching element, learners should be given the information discernment toolkit (based on previous research by Shenton and Pickard, 2014). Elements of the previous toolkit to be used as learning and teaching resources are: the Source Evaluation Model, which provides a set of 10 information evaluation criteria which maps the criteria young people use when they place their trust in digital information. These criteria are grouped into various categories such as 'objectivity and motivation': for instance, 'why was the information published?' Learners should be given this model and asked to compare their own current practice against these 10 criteria. The next task is to use the Meta-Evaluation Pro Forma, which provides a means for learners to think about their own thinking to assist them in reflecting on the value of each criterion (from the Source Evaluation Model and their own practice) and how they might synthesise these to evaluate new information. These two resources are designed to encourage learners to develop their own 'personal' models of information discernment. Group work is encouraged in order to foster a collaborative approach to evaluating information. This encourages meanings to be negotiated and shared between learners.

For the workshop element, learners are directed to brainstorm in small groups and create posters to record their thoughts about how they make judgements about information. What is written on these sheets may not necessarily be structured but captures the topics and ideas learners will discuss throughout the sessions. These posters are to be collected at the end of each session to triangulate data and gain a rich picture of participant contribution.

Day 2 – Two-hour workshop (one day apart): Learners are given a range of specially selected information sources of varying quality, including misinformation. We found that information sources that were controversial were most useful in promoting discussion. They are asked to use their Meta-Evaluation Pro Forma which they completed in Day 1 to judge the quality of a new set of information in Day 2.

It is recommended that follow-up interviews are carried out with a small sample of students 14 weeks after the workshops to establish whether learning has taken place. In addition, a sample of directly involved other stakeholders, such as teachers, academics and other facilitators, should be interviewed separately for approximately one hour, and on an individual basis six weeks after the workshops have been delivered.

Authority is contextual and contested but the most reliable information sources share particular characteristics.

Recommended data collection tools

- pre-delivery quantitative information discernment questionnaires based on Walton et al. (2018a) to garner baseline data
- workshop outputs – flip-chart group work posters
- Source Evaluation Model
- Meta-Evaluation Pro Forma
- post-delivery quantitative questionnaire (after six weeks to measure 'stickiness' of recently learnt information discernment capabilities)
- group interview with student focus group (14 weeks after workshop)
- individual interviews with teachers (six weeks after workshop) to triangulate with student data.

The workshops have been shown to work with 16–17-year-olds in a school setting and with 18–21-year-olds in higher education settings. We argue that by combining the learning and teaching elements in this way there is a greater likelihood, although it is by no means guaranteed, that learners' information literacy capabilities will be improved.

Conclusion

In summary, we feel that the need for people to be high information discerners is a critical part of being a member of civic society and could also be a factor of a person's well-being. Why? It is essential because people are constantly encountering information and misinformation. Some individuals are very good at making well-calibrated judgements and probably do not need any extra help.

However, on the basis of estimates drawn from our varied datasets, at least half of the population, and possibly more, need additional assistance to develop their ability to resist the effects of misinformation, whether this be for example, political, financial, scientific, commercial or health-related. What we cannot expect is for information discernment to lead people to think that one form of worldview (e.g., left- or right-leaning) is superior to another. What we can expect is that when high levels of information discernment are engendered, people are able to sort the factual wheat from the polemical, toxic and misinformational chaff. In so doing they can begin to make judgements based on a well-calibrated, balanced and detailed consideration of all points of view before making a decision or choosing to believe what they read in newspaper articles, blog posts, political exhortations or pieces of academic research. When a genuinely cognitive questioning state is instilled, people may begin to interrogate what they see and hear more effectively and act accordingly. Additionally, when presented with misinformation, those with higher levels of information discernment experience more positive heart and emotional responses and exhibit a greater degree of concentration, which ultimately contributes to healthier psychological and physiological responses to misinformation.

Note

1 The Extended Project Qualification or EPQ is for students studying at A-level stage in the UK – usually towards the end of their first year and is not compulsory. It involves a project chosen in agreement with the student's supervisor and includes structured reflection. The EPQ can enhance the chances of students gaining a place at university.

References

ACRL (Association of College and Research Libraries) (1989) American Library Association (ALA) (1989). *Presidential Committee on Information Literacy: Final Report*, www.ala.org/acrl/publications/whitepapers/presidential.

ACRL (Association of College and Research Libraries) (2016) *Framework for Information Literacy for Higher Education*, www.ala.org/acrl/standards/ilframework.

BBC (2018a) *Fake News a Democratic Crisis for UK, MPs warn*, 28 July, www.bbc.co.uk/news/technology-44967650.

BBC (2018b) *InfoWars Publisher Alex Jones Sues PayPal*, 2 October, www.bbc.co.uk/news/technology-45719245.

Big Blue Project (2002) *The Big Blue: information skills for students: final report*, www.icyte.com/system/snapshots/fs1/2/8/9/7/2897dd42d34f59739cd8809e48c4bfd3 2e2aa12f/index.html.

Blascovich, J. and Mendes, W. B. (2000) Challenge and Threat Appraisals: The role of affective cues. In J. Forgas (ed.) *Feeling and Thinking: The role of affect in social cognition,* 59–82. Paris: Cambridge University Press.

Brazier, D., Walton, G. and Harvey. M. (2018) An Investigation into Scottish Teenagers' Information Literacy and Search Skills, Information Seeking In Context (ISIC) Conference, Krakow, 8–11 October.

Campbell, A., Converse, P. E., Warren, E., Miller, W. E. and Stokes, D. E. (1960) *The American Voter*, John Wiley.

Carter, M. (2016) The Brexit Broadcast that Stoked Fears over the NHS's Future, *British Medical Journal*, **354**, doi:10.1136/bmj.i4342.

CILIP (2018) *CILIP Definition of Information Literacy 2018*, CILIP: the Library and Information Association, https://infolit.org.uk/ILdefinitionCILIP2018.pdf.

Gere, A., Kókai, Z. and Sipos, L. (2017) Influence of Mood on Gazing Behavior: Preliminary evidences from an eye-tracking study, *Food Quality and Preference*, **61**, 1–5.

Jones, D. (2016) Seeing Reason: human brains skew facts. How can we change our minds, asks Dan Jones. *New Scientist*, **232** (3102), 29–32.

Kahan, D. M., Peters, E., Wittlin, M., Slovic, P., Ouellette, L. L., Braman, D. and Mandel, G. (2012) The Polarizing Impact of Science Literacy and Numeracy on Perceived Climate Change Risks, *Nature Climate Change*, **2**, 732–5, doi:10.1038/nclimate1547.

Kuhlthau, C. C. (1991) Inside the Search Process: information seeking from the user's perspective, *Journal of the American Society for Information Science*, **42** (5), 361–71.

Lewandowsky, S., Ecker, U. K. H., Seifert, C. M., Schwartz, N. and Cook, J. et al. (2012) 'Misinformation and its Correction, Continued Influence and Successful Debiasing, *Psychological Science in the Public Interest,* **13** (3), 106–31.

Lewandowsky, S., Swire, B. and Ecker, U. K. H. (2018) Are We 'Post-Truth' or 'Post-Caring'? When political affect becomes decoupled from truth, International Meeting of the Psychonomic Society, Amsterdam, 10–12 May.

Liu, Z. (2005) Reading Behavior in the Digital Environment: Changes in reading behavior over the past ten years, *Journal of Documentation*, **61** (6), 700–12.

Pickard, A. J., Shenton, A. K. and Johnson, A. (2014) Young People and the Evaluation of Information on the Web: principles, practice and beliefs, *Journal of Library and Information Science*, **46** (1), 3–20, doi: 10.1177/0961000612467813.

Schmar-Dobler, E. (2003) Reading on the Internet: The link between literacy and technology, *Journal of Adolescent & Adult Literacy*, **47** (1), 80–5.

SCONUL (2011) *The SCONUL Seven Pillars of Information Literacy Core Model For Higher Education*, www.sconul.ac.uk/sites/default/files/documents/coremodel.pdf.

Secker, J. and Coonan, E. (2011) *A New Curriculum for Information Literacy (ANCIL)*, Cambridge University Library, http://openaccess.city.ac.uk/17370.

Shenton, A. K. and Pickard, A. J. (2014) *Evaluating Online Information and Sources*, Minibook Series, UK Literacy Agency.

Statista (2018) *UK: smartphone ownership by age from 2012–2018*, www.statista.com/statistics/271851/smartphone-owners-in-the-united-kingdom-uk-by-age.

Tavares, R. B., Hepworth, M. and De Souza Costa, S. M. (2011) Investigating Citizens' Information Needs Through Participative Research: a pilot study in Candangolândia, Brazil, *Information Development*, **27** (2), 125–38.

Thornton, S. (2018) Karl Popper. In Zalta, E. N. (ed.) *The Stanford Encyclopedia of Philosophy*, https://plato.stanford.edu/entries/popper.

Trevors, G. J., Muis, K. R., Pekrun, R., Sinatra, G. M. and Muijselaar, M. M. L. (2017) Exploring the Relations Between Epistemic Beliefs, Emotions, and Learning from Texts, *Contemporary Educational Psychology*, **48**, 116–32, http://dx.doi.org/10.1016/j.cedpsych.2016.10.001.

UCL (University College London) (2008) *Information Behaviour of the Researcher of the Future: a CIBER briefing paper, executive summary*, www.webarchive.org.uk/wayback/archive/20140614113419/http://www.jisc.ac.uk/media/documents/programmes/reppres/gg_final_keynote_11012008.pdf.

Walton, G. (2017) Information Literacy is a Subversive Activity: developing a research-based theory of information discernment, *Journal of information Literacy*, **11** (1), 137–55, http://dx.doi.org/10.11645/11.1.2188.

Walton, G. and Cleland, J. (2017) Information Literacy – Empowerment or Reproduction in Practice? A discourse analysis approach, *Journal of Documentation*, **73** (4), 582–94, https://doi.org/10.1108/JD-04-2015-0048.

Walton, G. and Hepworth, M. (2011) A Longitudinal Study of Changes in Learners' Cognitive States During and Following an Information Literacy Teaching Intervention, *Journal of Documentation*, **67** (3), 449–79.

Walton, G. and Hepworth, M. (2013) Using Assignment Data to Analyse a Blended Information Literacy Intervention: a quantitative approach, *Journal of Librarianship and Information Science*, **45** (1), 53–63.

Walton, G., Pickard, A. and Dodd, L. (2018a) Information Discernment, Misinformation and Pro-active Scepticism, *Journal of Librarianship & Information Science,* **50** (3), 296–309, http://journals.sagepub.com/doi/abs/10.1177/0961000618769980.

Walton, G., Barker, J., Pointon, M., Turner, M. and Wilkinson, A. (2018b) *Measuring the Psychophysiology of Information Literacy*, European Conference on Information Literacy (ECIL) Oulu, Finland, 24–27 September 2018.

Watson, L. (2018) Systematic Epistemic Rights Violations in the Media: a Brexit case study, *Social Epistemology – A Journal of Knowledge, Culture and Policy*, **32** (2), 88–102, https://doi.org/10.1080/02691728.2018.1440022.

9

Libraries and democracy: complementarity in a regime of truth

Hilary Yerbury and Maureen Henninger

Introduction

Traditionally, libraries and librarians have played an important part in the provision of information to support democracy and the democratic processes. In this context, this chapter reports on a study conducted in 2017 which explores and compares the respective contributions of public libraries and university libraries in Sydney, Australia, to supporting democratic processes. It concludes that in spite of a shift from an institutionally based view of truth to one focusing on an individual, librarians are still concerned with principles that underpin the understanding of quality in information.

Democracy and library services

Western culture has developed based on notions that truth, by overcoming falsehood, underpins democracy. However, Rose and Barros (2017) claim we are no longer concerned with creating a consensus of knowledge, and Harsin (2015) asserts that we are undergoing a shift from a regime of truth to a regime of post-truth, where citizens acknowledge that they cannot easily verify a truth claim. Foucault – whose influence on thinking on the relationship between information, knowledge and authority is described by Andrew Whitworth in Chapter 2 of this book – wrote that 'each society has its regime of truth, its general politics of truth: that is the type of discourse which it accepts and makes function as true, the mechanisms and instances which enables one to distinguish true and false statements' (Foucault, 1980, 131). Foucault's regimes of truth are produced by institutions in which there are relatively clear processes for identifying the authority of the source of a message and therefore the credibility of that message, control over channels of communication is understood, the processes for validation of the content of messages are recognised, mechanisms for addressing audiences are regulated and competing messages can be categorised so that the flow of information is not overwhelming.

For Harsin (2015), key factors in a regime of post-truth include fragmentation of sources of information leading to a dilution of authority, the creation of social groups bounded by the use of technology, content targeted to these bounded groups, along with shifts in journalistic practices, political communication and the speed of communication. Lewandowsky, Cook and Ecker (2017, 420) identified seven societal trends indicating 'the emergence of a post-truth world', although they acknowledge that this list may not be exhaustive. These included declining trust in institutions and civic engagement, as well as in science and research findings, fragmentation in sources and audiences, growing inequality in society, polarisation in politics and a rise in individualism.

Libraries work within an institutional regime of truth, and have been considered a 'trusted forum', evaluating information and playing a role in increasing civic literacy (Rettig, 2010). They are representative of an institutional regime of truth that has democratic processes inherent in it, as reflected in statements of their professional associations, for example:

> A thriving national and global culture, economy and democracy will best be advanced by people who are empowered in all walks of life to seek, evaluate, use and create information effectively to achieve their personal, social, occupational and educational goals. It is a basic human right in a digital world and promotes social inclusion within a range of cultural contexts.
> (Alexandria Proclamation 2005)
> (Australian Library and Information Association, 2006)

To understand how libraries support democratic processes, it is important to recognise what democracy is. Rivano Eckerdal (2017, 1012) notes the existence of two traditions, the liberal tradition and the democratic or deliberative tradition. The liberal tradition is concerned with rights and the respect for individual freedoms, valuing the individual's ability to make well-founded decisions which contribute to society. The democratic or deliberative tradition is concerned with equality and active citizenship (Touraine, 2000), and values open discussion in which the conflict in points of view can be made public, even if they cannot be resolved (in a similar vein, Chapter 1 of this book outlines four different 'models' for modern democracies). Budd (2007) echoes the well-recognised view in the literature of librarianship that fundamental to the democratic tradition are deliberation and reflection among people in a community and that for these to be possible, 'informing sources' are a fundamental requirement. These elements, which are the roles that public libraries have traditionally been seen to play in a community, and which lead to well-informed local communities being able to play an active part in shaping these communities, can be seen as significant factors in a regime of truth.

Lor, on the other hand, acknowledges that libraries are confronted by a discourse of post-truth, and states that libraries and librarians need to revise their understanding of the relationship between libraries, information and democracy (Lor, 2018, 317), because, in his view, the issues go beyond the world of libraries into society at large and thus information literacy frequently developed through single sessions is no longer an adequate solution. Librarians need to partner with educators, journalists and the media to rework this relationship, using their trusted position (Rettig, 2010) as soft power, and maintain a focus on a longer-term goal of remaining a constant in a context of 'ephemeral messages and constantly shifting attention' (Lor, 2018, 317).

Public libraries are in a focal position in the development and maintenance of a democratic society. Not only do professional associations give them a specific responsibility for supporting the development of a democratic society (Australian Library and Information Association, 2009), but in New South Wales these libraries may also provide services for the employees of local government, engaged in setting and implementing the policy which, at the local level, affect people's everyday lives. An earlier study of the practices of public librarians in providing information services, including information literacy services, to these employees found that the belief that the employees were information-literate, because of their post-secondary education and the availability of access to Google, meant there was no longer such a pressing need for information literacy programmes or for targeted reference services (Yerbury and Henninger, 2018). Thus, the study reported in this chapter sought to explore the complementarity of the information literacy services provided in these public libraries and in university libraries, as well as considering the extent to which a new regime of truth might be developing in the view of the information literacy services provided by those librarians.

Information literacy

Information literacy is often linked to the ability to use information for effective decision making and the support for a regime of truth. Public libraries may be involved in programmes intended to develop information literacy (Kranich, 2005), an activity perhaps more commonly linked to schools and universities; Gibson and Jacobson (2018, 184) argue that all librarians are engaged in a teaching and learning process with their communities. Their own professional education, which has provided them with a range of skills, including understandings of the authority of information, the development of search strategies intended to retrieve relevant and appropriate resources, methods for understanding the needs and expectations of groups of information users and of individual enquirers and principles for assuring the quality of information and information resources, fits librarians for this role in supporting a regime of truth. An approach to information literacy and to the identification of 'fake news' which relies on the use of checklists is criticised by Whitworth (2014) as having too narrow a focus (see also Chapter 2 of this book) and Lor (2018, 315) considers such tools as the IFLA checklist on how to spot fake news 'naïve'.

Librarians may be able to engage in the kinds of dialogue that can promote critical scrutiny of sources leading to conversations on how information is created and used, going beyond a limiting application of a checklist of evaluation criteria (Rivano Eckerdal, 2017, 1026). Academic librarians may develop in students 'habits of mind' (Bourdieu and Passeron, 1977), through carefully designed learning experiences. Tran and Yerbury (2015) showed how recent graduates used the information skills they had learned to assert their own criteria on the outputs of searches conducted in their workplace; they were able to demonstrate and articulate their thinking, that is, their 'habits of mind' in the face of Google's so-called filter bubble. These 'habits of mind', while at one level belonging to an individual, can be seen as shared knowledge 'within the community', whether of students, employees or citizens (Rivano Eckerdal, 2017, 1011). Marsh and Yang (2017, 402) go further, asserting that someone who is information literate should not only be able to find and evaluate information, they should be able to 'recognise weak arguments', which may be developed from credible sources of information.

This literature, mostly, takes a normative approach to the roles that librarians 'ought' to play in developing and maintaining a well-informed community, whose members are able to contribute to the development of a democratic society. This study aims to provide empirical evidence by exploring the practices of public librarians who provide programmes and services for the employees of local government and those of the academic librarians who may have supported the development of information literacy in these people when they were students.

Methodology

Using a practice theory approach, this study has collected data from the small number of specialist public librarians in Sydney whose specific role is to provide information services to employees of local government, elected representatives in local government and the general public and from librarians in university libraries with some level of responsibility for the provision of information literacy services and programmes. Six public librarians were interviewed and two more provided written responses (L1–L8). These participants, all women with at least 20 years' professional experience, came from six local government areas, ranging in size from a population of just over 36,000 to over 218,000. Eighteen librarians (L9–L26) employed in seven university libraries with a significant presence in Sydney were interviewed, ranging from subject librarians to senior managers responsible for policy development, including information literacy. They included men and women who had a range of experience, with some having only two years of professional experience and others having more than 20. Interviews, which lasted on average 45 minutes, were audio-recorded and transcribed verbatim. To identify key features of the practice of these librarians, transcripts were analysed using thematic analysis, with a focus on democratic processes and information literacy. Both phases of the study were approved through the Human Research Ethics Committee of the University of Technology Sydney with the condition that no participant was to be named, the employing university, similarly, was not to be named and the local government area in which the public library was situated was to be anonymised. Contiguous numbering of participants should not be taken to mean that participants are from the same library.

The context of the libraries

The metropolitan area of Sydney in New South Wales (NSW) currently covers 30 local government areas, generally referred to as councils. Local government was in a state of flux when interviews were carried out in 2017 following the NSW State Government's proposal to reduce the number of councils through amalgamations. This proposal was hotly contested, and although some mergers went ahead, others were eventually dropped. Each council employs a number of staff with a wide range of responsibilities. A key factor about council workforces is that local government employees are generally more highly educated than the general workforce (Hastings et al., 2015, 9), with more than 30% having studied at university and more than 40% have a qualification from the technical and further education sector. The public libraries included in this study have established services, known as corporate library services, especially for council employees, although all would provide services on request. In New South Wales, corporate librarians were appointed by a number of councils from the early 2000s, some responsible for collections of materials and others not. The introduction of these services came at a time when public libraries had access to online databases whereas the council employees did not necessarily have easy access to the internet. Over time, the number of corporate librarians appointed has decreased, for a variety reasons, including universal access to the internet for council employees with Google seen to remove the need for specialist assistance in searching; changes in organisational structure; shifts in local priorities; and the non-replacement of retiring staff. In councils where amalgamations had taken place, a review of library services was being undertaken and some librarians interviewed were unsure about the future of the services they offered to council employees.

The seven university libraries represented in this study included the five universities traditionally based in Sydney and the two national universities with campuses in the city. The universities of which these libraries are a part vary in size, and fall into three groups by enrolment numbers, two having over 50,000 students, three around 40,000 and two below 35,000 students. All universities have seen a significant increase in student numbers in the past ten years, with an increase of 43.7% nationally across the sector (Australia Department of Education and Training, 2017). The university libraries provide information literacy services and programmes in a range of ways: one provides only online programmes with no face-to-face interactions with students, while another only provides face-to-face programmes for coursework postgraduate students. Some require completion of an information literacy programme (a hurdle task); some include statements about information literacy in the list of attributes a graduate is expected to have; all have online materials, but for some these are in no way linked to specific education programmes. Universities have also seen an increase in the number of casual academic staff, with more than 50% of teaching now being carried out by staff employed on a semester-by-semester basis, meaning that librarians need to renegotiate links for teaching into subjects each semester.

Explaining the work

Without exception, the public librarians were clear that their work involved providing information and informational resources to council employees, to verify information within the context of council decision making and to support council employees in 'sorting quality from dross'. Their work was easy to summarise. This was not the case with the academic librarians, all of whom described the provision of different programmes and services to different parts of the university community. The academic librarians, including those whose titles indicated that they were subject specialists, noted that it was rare for them to provide information services to administrative staff or to the executive of the university, although they assumed that requests came at senior management level or through the university librarian. However, everyone spoke of conducting 'consultations', one-to-one sessions aimed at helping researchers to understand the databases and conduct a useful search.

As a group, the academic librarians tended to make a distinction between their responsibilities in providing services to coursework students and their roles in supporting teaching staff, researchers and the administrative staff, placing much more emphasis on the former. For coursework students, they did not see themselves as providing information resources, but rather as working in collaboration with academic staff and sometimes with learning support staff in the university to develop an understanding of the process of finding and evaluating resources. The way they expressed this role differed; some (L9, L10, L12, L14, L16, L17, L19, L26) saw themselves developing skills of critical thinking; some (L11, L12, L14, L15, L16, L18, L23) thought their role as 'teacher' was focused on helping students to be successful in their assessment tasks; a third group (L18, L20, L21, L22, L24, L25, L26) focused on encouraging the understanding of evidence-based practice; and a fourth on the embedding of information literacy in the education programme of the university (L12, L13, L14, L19). Although several librarians assumed that critical thinking subsumed the notion of rational argument (L9, L10, L13, L19) only L10 emphasised the importance of being able to develop an argument: 'You [an engineering student] have got the skills to put up a building, you don't have the skills to put up an argument'. Several participants expressed their view of their role differently in different parts of the interview and thus appear in more than one group.

Complementarity of approach

For graduate employees working in local government, the question of whether the services provided by public librarians and university librarians were complementary was the starting point for interpreting data gathered in this study. Respondent L25 expressed the view that the relationship between a public library's services and democratic processes was straightforward and could be openly discussed in the local government context, whereas any focus on these processes in the university would have to be a 'deep game', a phrase from gaming, indicating greater complexity, including a number of options accessible through a range of skills. Most academic librarians acknowledged that their university had statements of graduate attributes which included the skills of information literacy, yet few (L11, L12, L13, L14, L15 and L24) recognised the contributions of their programmes of information literacy to 'take into their professional lives' (L15) because 'the priority is with current students' (L12). University libraries do provide services to alumni graduates, sometimes at no additional cost to the individual, but these are restricted to access to the collection and to open-access databases. Only L18 mentioned interviewing graduates and their employers as a way to make information literacy programmes more relevant. As will be explored in more detail below, there is a focus on quality in both types of library: in public libraries, the focus is on the quality of the answers provided to users and enquirers, whereas in the university setting, the focus is on the quality of the resource and the way that the content of the resource is used to present an answer.

Understanding library contributions to democratic processes

There is no common understanding between the public librarians and the academic librarians of how their professional practice contributes to democratic processes. From the perspective of Lloyd's (2005) information literacy landscapes, this is perhaps not surprising. Whereas all the public librarians (L1–L8) thought that the way they raised awareness of information resources contributed to the processes of deliberation and decision making in their community, not all of the academic librarians expressed the importance of information and its relationship to democratic processes. Indeed, six of them (L9, L11, L15, L17, L24, L25) expressed surprise at the question of how their professional practice might contribute to democratic processes: 'That's a big question!' 'That's a really tough one!' L14 considered that information literacy programmes 'enhance awareness . . . in a professional sense . . . so it is an oblique contribution to democratic processes'. L9 thought that the work of the librarian should be 'apolitical', but at the same time acknowledged that 'we can make people harder to fool and we can make people better at fooling'.

A second key difference between the public librarians and the academic librarians is that the public librarians saw themselves as being reactive rather than proactive (L5, L7), answering questions from council employees and elected representatives, although some (L1, L2, L4, L5) acknowledged that the work of the public library helped to empower the local community because of its involvement in the consultative processes for local policy making and its work in helping community members to understand the decision-making processes of local government. The academic librarians who did acknowledge that their work might enhance democratic processes saw themselves in a more proactive role, for example engaged in 'creating more information-savvy citizens [who were] . . . more aware of information sources' (L19), 'equipping our students for life' (L24) or 'empowering the students to use information responsibly and critically' (L25). L17 also took an active, future-oriented perspective, explaining that developing skills in evaluating information was important because 'if you don't have reliable information, then I guess it can't be a true democracy'. This distinction between reactive and proactive approaches can obscure a more fundamental distinction. The public librarians were concerned with the identification of content to be used in deliberative processes, whereas the academic librarians emphasised the importance of skilled individuals able to use information.

Understanding a regime of truth

Implicit in the responses of these librarians was the assumption that changes in the world around them could signal changes in a regime of truth, but that they believed that an information-literate populace could moderate the effects of some of these changes.

To a large extent, the public librarians asserted that 'things haven't changed' (L5), their focus here being on the principles of evaluating quality in information, even though they described significant changes to their work context. L8 stated the view that one of the reasons for there being less emphasis on information literacy, and fewer opportunities to do the 'meatier searches', was because most staff were tertiary educated (a point made also by L1), and because of their experiences at university, were better able to do their own searching. As already noted, this ability for employees to do their own searching was also facilitated by the introduction of desktop access to the internet. However, these changes did not mean that the librarians did not provide information literacy services; they provided them in different ways, for example through induction programmes for new staff with information posted on the relevant intranet page (L4), and through special workshop sessions, where 'we can teach them how to access the information themselves or how to use the databases' (L3) and other events (L1).

On the other hand, the academic librarians were aware they were doing things differently. The disruptions to their work processes have arisen from the increase in student numbers and through the casualisation of the teaching staff. Whereas technology had been seen as disruptive to the relationship between the specialist public librarians and council employees, in the university setting, it permitted academic librarians to maintain and even extend the services they provided to students and in some universities, the requirement for students to complete online information literacy programmes outside the constraints of a programme of study meant that the need to liaise with teaching staff, who may change every semester, was removed. Some academic librarians noted that unlike in the past, their expertise was not always used directly in interactions with students and staff, but was sometimes mediated through others, for example with skills in the use of educational technologies (e.g. L14, L22) or with expertise in learning support (L14, L25). Others noted the continuing importance of establishing partnerships with academic staff in developing information literacy programmes, as this meant that the particular requirements of a field of study or practice (L10, L11, L13, L15, L18, L20, L21, L22, L24) were emphasised to students, although 'there's real struggle in that way to try and cover some of the stuff that maybe academics don't see as much value in' (L25).

The championing of open access, similarly, is a feature of a longstanding regime of truth, where scholarly knowledge is expected to be able to flow freely, rather than being constrained by economic and legal factors, such as cost and the licensing of access to scholarly work. Many of the academic librarians (L12, L13, L14, L15, L16, L18, L21, L25, L26) expressed themselves as strong supporters of the open access movement. Some considered it an important step in the democratisation of scholarly knowledge, pointing to the benefits to the wider community in gaining access to peer-reviewed content outside the licensing conditions which constrained so much of the literature describing innovations relevant to professional practice. Those with involvement in the health sciences spoke of open-access research materials as an important contribution to the global field of health care. This topic was touched on by only one public librarian (L1), when she reported on a conversation with a professional in the community who championed open access as a way to maintain currency with new methods and research findings in his field.

Open access is an important aspect of a regime of truth, since those who are no longer affiliated to a university may lose access to the key resources they have relied on during their professional education. The licensing conditions of these commercial databases preclude alumni of a university in most cases. The impact of this is that graduates educated through the use of specialist materials relevant to their professional training often lose access to the very materials necessary for continuing development as professionals. In other words, they may know how to access authoritative resources, but they are unable to do so; thus, where open-access materials are not available, they are left to use what they can find through a Google search or through social media.

Providing authoritative information or ensuring that users understood how to identify authoritative sources of information was common to all participants. L3, a public librarian, emphasised the importance of focusing on local matters and 'hav[ing] the facts right'. All public librarians made a distinction between the kind of search a librarian might do and one done by a staff member using Google: 'It's not like quality, is it?' (L4), although it might sometimes be 'fit for purpose' (L8). The search done by the librarian would not use sources lacking in 'authority' (L5). All the public librarians acknowledged that from time to time a key part of their work is verifying information, while no academic librarian reported having been asked to do fact-checking. However, understanding how to identify appropriate databases, peer-reviewed resources and the standing of journals was central to the work of many of the academic librarians. In other words, the focus was on authority, but within the context of scholarship, where peer review was taken as the surrogate for authority. One respondent (L11) applied the principles of authority and trusted sources to the social media resources commonly used globally in the health sciences area. She explained: 'I want people, right from the beginning, to recognise the authoritative sources of information, so [we set up a Twitter feed in the teaching software and included], the World Health Organisation . . . PLOS ONE . . . that sort of thing . . . so they really start to think, well, the World Health Organisation, they're good. They recognise PLOS ONE as a trusted source.'

Librarians in both phases of the study identified what they saw as 'key trusted partnerships' (L2) or 'natural allies' (L12, L24) in the development of a well-informed information-literate community and in helping to support of a regime of truth. For public librarians, partners were most likely to be identified as the local newspaper (L1, L4, L5), local chambers of commerce (L1, L3, L7), key community groups and non-government organisations (L1, L5, L6). Partners for academic librarians were most likely to be identified as staff in schools, both teachers and teacher librarians (L5, L6, L12, L16, L17, L18, L19, L22, L24, L25) or librarians in other kinds of library, especially public libraries (L10, L15, L18, L24, L26). Others were seen as 'natural allies' because of the professional area related to field of study, so local businesses and industry (L18), community groups (L14), professional associations (L14, L24) and health professionals (L12, L26) were all considered important potential partners, often emphasising the strategic direction of the university. The media, so important for a local community, and local organisations which are part of a community were mostly not mentioned by academic librarians.

While all the public librarians took for granted that they, as public librarians, had a responsibility for contributing towards a well-informed and information-literate community, that is, to habits of mind in the community, the responses of academic librarians did not take a uniform approach. That libraries, the media and education (i.e. schools and universities) had responsibility for this essential aspect of democratic processes were stock responses, but one respondent quipped: 'If I had the answer, I'd be President of the World' (L10). Others recognised that identifying a single institution, or even several, as having responsibility was problematic: 'Librarians might think they [have the responsibility] but they don't. A cop-out answer is "everybody".' (L17); 'rather than have that bystander effect where everyone says it's someone else's [responsibility], it's actually all of our [responsibility]' (L12); Who IS responsible? . . . in a free society, how do you tell people what they should think?' (L23). Nonetheless, there was a strong sense among some academic librarians (including L16 and L18), that 'as always in life, the ultimate responsibility remains with the first person' (L22); or 'everyone in a community should be an autonomous individual . . . so it's a bit paternalistic to say who's responsible' (L24).

Similar but different

At a superficial level, these findings suggest that the services and programmes provided to university students and to graduate employees in local government are complementary, supporting the assertions from employees in local government, who claimed to have developed skills in information literacy as part of their university education. At a more complex level, an analysis of these findings to shed light on the regime of truth within which the two sets of librarians operate will be instructive.

A similar regime of truth emerges from the practices of the librarians who participated in this study. Firstly, the ability to know how to 'sort quality from dross' (L8) is seen as essential to the practices of both public librarians and academic librarians. Secondly, recognition of a societal engagement with a regime of truth was evident in the use of the phrase 'natural allies' (L12, L24) and in the commonality in the listing of those with whom a library, whether public or university, might partner to ensure a well-informed and information-literate community. The unhesitating inclusion of teachers and teacher librarians, and other educators, journalists and the media as potential partners in the development of democratic practices matches one of Lor's four suggestions for ways to revise the understanding of the relationship between libraries and democracy (Lor, 2018, 317). Thirdly, the participants in this study are, in one way or another, engaged in a teaching and learning process within their communities, as Gibson and Jacobson (2018) argue, in order to strengthen across that community a key aspect of a regime of truth, the ability to use the skills of information literacy (Rivano Eckerdal, 2017, 1011). An example of the institutionalisation of the importance of the skills of information literacy was to be found in the statements of graduate attributes or graduate capabilities issued by the universities.

There are also strong indications of the potential for differences in the expression of regimes of truth. Harsin (2015) and Lewandowsky, Cook and Ecker (2017) identified a range of factors which could indicate that a regime of truth is shifting towards a regime of post-truth. These include fragmentation of content and audience, digitisation, individualisation and the use of social media. Each of these is evident in the descriptions the librarians give of their practices and their perceptions of them, although the concern for political polarisation was missing. While some academic librarians clearly value the provision of identical online materials in different degree programmes, where all new students have to complete a so-called 'hurdle task', others emphasise the importance of understanding the differences in fields of study, leading to a range of different content. L15, aware that the ways the big database providers present their products and searching capabilities impacts skills development in information literacy programmes in a university context, proposed that it was important to incorporate the materials produced by companies such as Clarivate and Scopus in those programs. As already noted, only one academic librarian discussed how she incorporated the use of social media by authoritative organisations in the education programme she had developed. The public librarians were all sceptical of the value of content found through Google, and of the use of social media, although one acknowledged almost grudgingly that such content could be 'fit for purpose'. Online access to scholarly materials was taken for granted, and although only one librarian (L22) specifically mentioned predatory journals, most discussed the importance of understanding how to identify peer-reviewed material.

A major difference between the public librarians and the academic librarians is in the emphasis that the latter seem to give to the individual. The linking of information literacy to academic success brings the focus to the individual student, as does the emphasis on critical thinking, which in the educational context is often considered the skill of an individual, rather than a habit of mind that could form an expectation of society. The emphasis on the individual is also apparent in the assertion that it was important to avoid the bystander effect and to recognise that we each have a responsibility to ensure that the information we find and use is reliable, so that the responsibility for contributing to a well-informed and information-literate community rests with individuals.

Yet, this significant emphasis on the individual does not need to be seen as evidence of a move to a regime of post-truth. Instead, following Rivano Eckerdal (2017, 1012), it can be seen as a difference in an understanding of what democracy entails. It would seem that most of the academic librarians, with their emphasis on individual skills and responsibilities, are working with the liberal tradition of democracy, emphasising the individual, whereas all of the public librarians can be seen to work with the democratic tradition of democracy, acknowledging an emphasis on a shared acceptance of how society should work. There is no easy explanation for this difference in understanding of what democracy entails; here, as there is no evidence, there can only be speculation. Two possible explanations come to mind. The first is that the public librarians, all of whom have more than 20 years of professional experience, have a worldview which differs from their younger counterparts in the university libraries, bringing to mind Bennett's claims (2007) about generational differences in notions of civic engagement. The second is that the culture of the universities more overtly reflects values of individualism than does the culture of local government, and although equity and inclusiveness were stressed by several participants from academic libraries, and others acknowledged that students were also citizens and members of society, the overriding emphasis was on students who are individuals needing to be educated and trained to succeed as students and in the workplace.

Conclusion

The level of information literacy of local government employees, developed during their post-secondary education, and their familiarity with online searching, are shifting the focus of the specialist public librarians from the process of developing information literacy skills to the quality of the outcome of searches conducted by the employees. Whether they are from a public library or a university, the librarians who participated in this study see the regime of truth within which they provide information services in similar ways, with the emphasis on the quality and authority of the information provided and the development of skills in students and local government employees to determine these. Yet, the conceptualisation of democracy within which these practices take place appear to be different, although it is unclear whether this arises from the librarians themselves or from the culture of the organisations in which they work. This is a topic for further research.

References

Australia, Department of Education and Training (2017) *Selected Higher Education Statistics – 2017 Student Data*, www.education.gov.au/selected-higher-education-statistics-2017–student-data.

Australian Library and Information Association (2006) *Statement on Information Literacy for All Australians*, www.alia.org.au/about-alia/policies-standards-and-guidelines/statement-information-literacy-all-australians.

Australian Library and Information Association (2009) *Statement on Public Library Services*, www.alia.org.au/about-alia/policies-standards-and-guidelines/statement-public-library-services.

Bennett, W. L. (2007) Challenges for Citizenship and Civic Education. In Dahlgren, P. (ed.) *Young Citizens and New Media: learning for democratic participation*, Routledge, 59–78.

Bourdieu, P. and Passeron, J. C. (1977) *Reproduction in Education, Society and Culture*, translated R. Nice, Sage.

Budd, J. (2007) Public Library Leaders and Changing Society, *Public Library Quarterly*, **26** (3–4), 1–14.

Foucault, M. (1980) *Power/Knowledge: selected interviews and other writings, 1972–1977*, translated C. Gordon, Pantheon Books.

Gibson, C. and Jacobson, T. E. (2018) Habits of Mind in an Uncertain Information World, *Reference & User Services Quarterly*, **57** (3), 183–92.

Harsin, J. (2015) Regimes of Posttruth, Postpolitics, and Attention Economies', *Communication, Culture & Critique*, **8** (2), 327–33.

Hastings, C., Ryan, R., Gibbs, M. and Lawrie, A. (2015) *Profile of the Local Government Workforce 2015 Report*, Sydney Australian Centre of Excellence for Local Government, University of Technology Sydney.

Kranich, N. (2005) Civic Partnerships: the role of libraries in promoting civic engagement, *Resource Sharing & Information Networks*, **18** (1–2), 89–103.

Lewandowsky, S., Cook, J. and Ecker, U. K. (2017) Letting the Gorilla Emerge from the Mist: getting past post-truth, *Journal of Applied Research in Memory and Cognition*, **6** (4), 418–24.

Lloyd, A. (2005) Information Literacy Landscapes: an emerging picture, *Journal of Documentation*, **62** (5), 570–83.

Lor, P. (2018) Democracy, Information and Libraries in a Time of Post-truth Discourse, *Library Management*, **39** (5), 307–21.

Marsh, E. and Yang B. (2017) A Call to Think Broadly About Information Literacy, *Journal of Applied Research in Memory and Cognition*, **6**, 401–4.

Rettig, J. (2010) New Technologies, Citizen Empowerment, and Civic Life. In *Proceedings of the International Conference Qualitative and Quantitative Methods in Libraries: theory and applications*, Chania, Crete, 26–29 May 2009, World Scientific Publishing, 191–7.

Rivano Eckerdal, J. (2017) Libraries, Democracy, Information Literacy, and Citizenship: an agonistic reading of central library and information studies' concepts, *Journal of Documentation*, **73** (5), 1010–33.

Rose, J. and Barros, M. (2017) Scientists Have a Word for Studying the Post-truth World: agnotology, *The Conversation*, 20 January 2017.

Touraine, A. (2000) *Can We Live Together? Equality and difference*, Stanford University Press.

Tran, T. and Yerbury, H. (2015) New Perspectives on Personalised Search Results: expertise and institutionalisation, *Australian Academic & Research Libraries*, **46** (4), 277–90.

Whitworth, A. (2014) *Radical Information Literacy: reclaiming the political heart of the IL movement*, Chandos Publishing.

Yerbury, H. and Henninger, M. (2018) Civil Commitment and the Role of Public Librarians. In Kurbanoğlu, S. et al. (ed.), *Proceedings of the Fifth European Conference on Information Literacy*, St Malo, France, 18–21 September 2017, *Communications in Computer and Information Science*, **810**, 376–85.

10

Scottish public libraries welcome Syrian new Scots: a transition from being a refugee to becoming an active part of the community

Konstantina Martzoukou

Introduction

This chapter offers an overview of the information needs and experiences of Syrian refugees in Scotland, drawing from data collected as part of 'Lost in Information: Syrian new Scots' information literacy way-finding practices', a research project which was funded by the CILIP Information Literacy Group (ILG) in the UK. The aim of the research was to explore the information needs of Syrian refugees, their habitual and adaptive information literacy practices and the barriers and enablers they encountered within their new socio-cultural setting via their interaction with people, tools and processes. The chapter begins by discussing the Scottish government strategy for welcoming Syrian refugees and by exploring the fundamental everyday life needs of Syrian refugees during the first few months after relocating to Scotland. These included learning English, reuniting with family members, securing employment and achieving financial security. In view of this focus and based on the emphasis of this book on the role of information for democracy, civic rights and participation, the chapter discusses Scottish public libraries' vision of supporting vulnerable communities and helping to build capacity for the active contribution of refugees to their host society, enabling information support and activities that create a sense of belonging for all. The chapter concludes with presenting a number of Scottish public libraries' case studies from the northeast of Scotland, showcasing how they have responded to the social needs of Syrian refugees, offering information-related services, organising specific integration related activities and programmes and making library space a place for learning. Public libraries in Scotland have developed impactful work to support Syrian refugees in their local communities, which could be further empowered by creating close partnerships with refugee support services and organisations. There is potential for public libraries to make a sustainable difference to the lives of Syrian new Scots and the communities which have welcomed them supporting civic participation and inclusion for all.

Syrian new Scots: Syrian refugees in Scotland

On 7 September 2015 the UK Prime Minister (at that time David Cameron) announced an expansion of the existing 'Syrian Vulnerable Persons Relocation Scheme (VPRS)' to resettle over five years (by 2020) an additional 20,000 Syrians drawn from established refugee camps. A second resettlement route to the UK was also announced on 21 April 2016 for 3,000 vulnerable 'children at risk' (as defined by the United Nations High Commissioner for Refugees (UNHCR)) from the Middle East and North Africa (MENA) region. This broad category includes unaccompanied, separated from their families and vulnerable children (e.g. child carers and those at risk of child labour, child marriage or other forms of neglect, abuse or exploitation) (Brokenshire, 2016).

Following the UK government's announcement of the arrival of Syrian refugees, the Chartered Institute of Library and Information Professionals (CILIP) outlined the important role of public and school libraries in the country, as key sources of information, as welcoming places and as access points to information about refugees, helping to inform local communities about the realities of forced migration (Vincent, 2015). In addition, on 25 September 2015, the Society of Chief Librarians (which leads and manages public libraries in England, Wales and Northern Ireland and is made up of the head of service of every library authority) and ASCEL (the Association of Senior Children's and Education Librarians, which is a national network of senior managers in children's public and schools library services) produced a statement setting out the role that public libraries play in welcoming refugees. A number of areas where library leaders across England and Wales expressed their commitment to offer support included the following areas (Society of Chief Librarians, 2015):

- free access to computers and Wi-Fi
- free access to materials to learn English, and access to physical and online resources in other languages (including Welsh in Wales)
- free activities and reading resources for children and families
- trained workforce who can help with access to information and resources
- community space to use for learning and networking
- signposting to local education, health and well-being services

- signposting to other council services
- signposting to community organisations and resources
- tours of the library and all services offered

In Scotland, the target number of Syrian refugees accepted via the Syrian VPRS programme was set to 2,000 (10% of the total number in the UK) by 2020. However, Scotland reached that target by the end of 2017, accepting one in five Syrians brought to the UK through the resettlement scheme. The new Scots (this is the preferred name for refugees in Scotland) integration strategy (2014–17), which was developed as a partnership of the Scottish Government, the Convention of Scottish Local Authorities (COSLA, which is the voice of local government in Scotland) and the Scottish Refugee Council, addressed the needs of refugees as well as those seeking asylum, using the 1951 UN Convention relating to the Status of Refugees (Refugee Convention) and the supporting 1967 Protocol which defines a refugee as a person who:

> . . . owing to well-founded fear of being persecuted for reasons of race, religion, nationality, membership of a particular social group or political opinion, is outside the country of his nationality and is unable, or, owing to such fear, is unwilling to avail himself of the protection of that country; or who, not having a nationality and being outside the country of his former habitual residence as a result of such events, is unable or, owing to such fear, is unwilling to return to it.
>
> (Scottish Government, 2017, 2)

The purpose of the strategy was to co-ordinate the work of different organisations in this area in Scotland, creating active partnerships and ensuring that Scotland is a welcoming and supporting place for people who have experienced persecution and human rights abuses. This meant close communication and consultation with the refugee community and aligning strategic objectives with their direct needs, addressing health, housing, welfare rights, employability, education, community integration and social connections. Under this umbrella, the Scottish Refugee Council (SRC) offered the 'refugee integration' (RIS) programme which focused on supporting vulnerable Syrian families to address their initial critical needs. The *New Scots: integrating refugees in Scotland's communities 2014–2017 Final Report* (Scottish Government, 2017) highlights a number of key achievements, including collating best practice approaches to supporting Syrian new Scots and establishing partnerships with a wide range of support groups. The Scottish Government also took the position that integration should commence not from when refugee status has been granted but from day one of an asylum seeker's journey. Therefore this effort also concentrated on mapping the services and support required during the asylum application process, leading to informed and focused action (this was addressed via creating an Asylum Dispersal thematic group). There was also emphasis in the scheme on helping new Scots to become active members of Scottish communities, building their confidence and resilience and supporting them to gradually develop strong social relationships, considering that Syrian new Scot families encounter multiple challenges and family members have diverse needs (e.g. pregnant women, children, people with disabilities).

A second new Scots strategy 2018–22 was published recently (Scottish Government, 2018), which aims to further support refugees and asylum seekers in Scotland's communities. The vision of the strategy is 'For a welcoming Scotland where refugees and asylum seekers are able to rebuild their lives from the day they arrive' and where Scotland:

- is a place of safety for everyone, where people are able to live free from persecution as valued members of communities
- enables everyone to pursue their ambitions through education, employment, culture and leisure activities;
- has strong, inclusive and resilient communities, where everyone is able to access the support and services they need and is able to exercise their rights
- is a country that values diversity, where people are able to use and share their culture, skills and experiences, as they build strong relationships and connections (Scottish Government, 2018).

COSLA provided a supporting and co-ordinating role to all 32 local authorities in Scotland in the Syrian VPRS. The main indicators of integration included employment, housing, education, health, making social bridges, bonds and links in the communities, helping Syrian new Scots to develop language and cultural knowledge of their host country, ensuring their safety and stability and that they were aware of and were exercising their rights as citizens (COSLA, 2016).

The COSLA resettlement strategy included specific actions and milestones which addressed key points in the migration and resettlement experience of Syrian new Scots:

(a) at pre-arrival

(b) at the point of arrival

(c) up to the first month after arrival

(d) up to the first year of resettlement (COSLA, 2016).

Research with Syrian new Scots

The research project 'Lost in Information: Syrian new Scots' information literacy way-finding practices' was funded by the CILIP Information Literacy Group (ILG). The aim of the project was to explore the information needs of 'Syrian new Scots', their habitual and adaptive information-literacy practices and the barriers and enablers they encountered within their new socio-cultural setting via their interaction with people, tools and processes. The project ran from September 2016 to June 2017 and was conducted via interviews with three Local Authority Leads for Syrian Resettlement and focus groups with 38 Syrian new Scots in three geographical locations in Scotland (which represented a mix of urban and rural locations). A drawing exercise that helped Syrian new Scots to discuss/elaborate on their main needs for information was used to enable creative communication about the participants' information world, and their experiences around seeking, receiving and communicating information. This approach helped to elaborate how and from where they received information, ways in which they shared information and how different people, things and circumstances could be presented as barriers or enablers in that process.

The progress and outputs of the research project during its different stages have been documented via the project blog (Martzoukou, 2016). In addition, some of the key findings addressing information needs, barriers and the role of information in the newcomers' socio-cultural adaptation have been published in Martzoukou and Burnett (2018). The research found that the everyday-life information needs of Syrian new Scots and the socio-cultural adaptation barriers they encounter are diverse. Some of these barriers are discussed below.

Lack of English-language skills

One of the most significant barriers that the community of Syrian new Scots encountered was learning English. English language acquisition was a key to the integration of Syrian new Scots and the Home Office had addressed a number of requirements in relation to the provision of English for Speakers of Other Languages (ESOL) classes, recognising the centrality of English-language support. For example, English-language classes would be provided no later than a month after arrival, they would be at a level that was appropriate for the needs of individual people and they would be offered by an accredited provider. English-language support would be provided in different ways, delivered by Community and Development (CLDS), local colleges, voluntary sector partners and depending upon local differences and circumstances. There was also the recognition that developing a peer education pilot programme with the help of volunteers who supported learning was important (COSLA, 2016).

However, the research found that although ESOL classes were provided, there were evident differences in the progress made by Syrian new Scots, with some progressing more slowly than others. This was for a number of different reasons:

(a)   *Age differences:* Learning English was perceived to be particularly difficult for senior learners, who required additional support to help maximise their learning potential.

(b)   *Education:* Syrian new Scots had varying levels of education. Some had basic school education, whereas others lacked basic Arabic-language reading or writing skills.

(c)   *Diverse previous life experiences:* Some people had been exposed to richer life experiences back in Syria (e.g. travelling, socialising, working abroad, and living in a large city as opposed to living within an isolated rural community) which made the process of developing new connections with people easier.

(d)   *Different learning preferences/cultural differences:* Some people preferred more structured, traditional learning approaches within the class, whereas others perceived peer-learning and involvement with the local English-speaking community as the most effective ways of learning conversational English, which made them more confident in everyday-life encounters with other local people.

Thus some Syrian families were learning faster and this also meant a faster integration into their host communities and gaining a sense of confidence, managing their family's matters independently. On the other hand, there were families who, despite being in Scotland for several months, still lacked confidence and were reluctant to attempt to communicate in English, progressing at a much slower pace and relying more on the support of their key workers. However, learning English was a significant priority for Syrian new Scots, as it was directly linked to enabling progress with community integration and reducing feelings of isolation (Figure 10.1 opposite). English language was also important for securing employment opportunities and ensuring financial security, overall, helping them to address proactively and independently their own information needs and to solve everyday life problems.

Figure 10.1 *Female participant demonstrating the importance of learning English quickly (translation by interpreter)*

Lack of financial security

In line with the COSLA resettlement strategy, the local authority resettlement support service ensured that a bank account was opened for each Syrian new Scot family, when they arrived, and that they could withdraw money immediately. The Syrian new Scot families could access welfare benefits, social housing, health care and education services on the same basis as other citizens. However, the Syrian new Scots had financial concerns which were linked to longer-term considerations. Male research participants, in particular, highlighted concerns which revolved around receiving support from the government in the future: 'If that stopped we would not know what we would do' (Syrian new Scots focus group discussion). The slow transition from being a recipient of welfare services and benefits to an independent, self-reliant employee was an important ongoing worry and a source of stress which became a barrier to integrating to their receiving society:

> We are always thinking, we are very stressed, very worried. We are not enjoying life because of our worries, being stressed, always being stressed about this. . .this makes it hard to integrate. It's all an ongoing worry.
> (Syrian new Scots focus group discussion. All unattributed quotes in what follows are from these discussions)

A 'big obstacle', as put by Syrian new Scots, was the lack of English language and the lack of fast progress with learning, as explained earlier. In addition, many were not in a position to work because of serious health issues (which impacted them or a member of their family directly) or because of their previous experiences of severe violence and psychological trauma (Home Office, 2015).

The research participants had varied careers before the war. Some examples included car mechanic, joiner, electrician, decorator, art teacher, salesman, hotel owner and teacher of Arabic. A few participants had managed to find volunteering positions (e.g. working as a gardener, helping at a bakery). However, they were looking to be occupied with something they knew 'how to do, their career', utilising their previous expertise and knowledge.

In addition, Syrian families, who relied on benefits, experienced difficulties on the basis of addressing everyday additional expenses (e.g. the council tax, building maintenance expenses, the costs of electricity and other household bills). One problem that was mentioned particularly by people living within a rural area was transportation. Some of the basic needs of the families (e.g. hospital/job centre appointments and ethnic food shopping/halal food) were expensive activities, as they required travelling regularly from a small town into the city. Because of the expenses of moving around, people were also less inclined to explore the local area, an issue which could have been addressed with a suitable transportation option or a fee reduction in the initial months of the resettlement process. As one of the research participants put it: 'The transportation for us is even more important than food. It's very, *very* important.'

Challenges with internet connectivity and ICT skills

One of the most important priorities concerning technology when the Syrian new Scot families had first arrived in Scotland was internet connectivity. There was a lot of support provided by the local community to ensure that the Syrian new Scots families had the basic means to connect to the internet. For example, in one of the locations of the study, the local church had donated dongles and the university had donated PCs, which meant that every family had a computer in the house and could get on the internet immediately. The Local Council Authority Leads for Resettlement had placed priority on internet connectivity, which was the only means the families could get in touch with their families displaced in other countries, such as Lebanon and Turkey. However, broadband or internet connection could not be organised straightaway, as the families did not have e-mail addresses (which was also a barrier to paying utility bills, setting up bank accounts and receiving health services such as repeat prescriptions). In addition, for some, e-mail communication was considered to be a tool for business rather than a necessity for everyday life purposes.

Nevertheless, the local mosque had provided mobile phones with pay-as-you-go mobile SIM cards and these were used frequently for internet connectivity, especially in the first few days. Syrian new Scots used their phones as the basic means of communication locally and externally with their displaced families. In one of the locations of the study, a WhatsApp group had been set up for the families with the support of six or seven Arabic-language volunteers who would help with translating. This was a helpful tool when it came to quickly translating important information, such as hospital appointments and, as most of that communication was kept in English, it offered opportunities for practising conversational English. WhatsApp was also used by their families to communicate with displaced family members in different parts of the world. Although younger Syrians used additional apps on their mobile phones for navigating in town, for train and bus schedules and for translation activities, different age demographics were not a barrier to the basic use of mobile phones. A characteristic example was an older female who used different apps to communicate with other Syrians, to get information from her peers and her teacher around English-language lessons and to find answers for things she did not understand. She also often communicated with digital images, for example, the image of a rose to express gratitude when progressing with the English-language class. Her 12-year-old daughter was proactive in educating her in the use of technology. However, there was need for further support with classes for ICT literacy around the use of mobile apps and other useful online tools that would help the Syrian new Scots to effectively communicate, entertain their families, organise their everyday life needs (e.g. utility bills, hospital appointments), learn English and keep in touch with their families and friends.

Family separation

As explained earlier, the COSLA resettlement strategy included specific plans for addressing everyday life needs in different stages of the integration process during the first year of Syrian new Scots' resettlement. Therefore, the local authority service had put together family integration plans, with a checklist of key milestones that were to be addressed with the families; for example, registering with doctors' surgeries, for English-language classes and with the job centre. However, emphasis was placed on understanding the families and catering for their individual needs as they had to deal with different and complex needs, ranging from addressing a disability or a terminal illness to reuniting with their families and children who still resided in another country, overcoming previous negative resettlement experiences in other host countries and addressing war-related depression and post-traumatic stress after being a victim of torture or violence. An important issue was separation from their family members. Although most of the participants had extended families, some of their children, their parents or siblings were displaced in different countries (e.g. Syria, Lebanon and Egypt) and in some cases they had not seen them for years. These separation worries were illustrated via the drawings of participants (Figures 10.2 to 10.6) and in the participants' verbalisations: 'I hope we can all be together in one place. I miss my two girls' (focus group discussion, female participant). In Figure 10.2, the participant drew on the left her two daughters, one in Lebanon and one in Egypt (names removed).

Figure 10.2 *A drawing depicting a female participant's family back in Syria*

One of the other female participants had not seen her family and her son who was in Lebanon for two years. Another participant had not seen her family in Jordan for the past five years, nor had she ever met her grandchildren, who were born in Egypt. Referring to two explosions in Lebanon, very close to where some of their families lived, they expressed how they felt that nowhere was safe: 'it is not safe in Beirut, it's not safe at all. Everywhere, it happened in Istanbul. It's not safe anywhere to be honest. Even here.'

The Syrian families had complex information needs around issues that concerned the possibility of being reunited with their displaced family members – for example, what information they needed to know and what they should do for bringing them to Scotland, or their own eligibility for travelling to the countries to which they have been relocated. Out of the six children of one of the male participants, only his younger son was with him in Scotland and as he was experiencing health problems he was worried that he would not be in a position to take care of himself as his son was still very young:

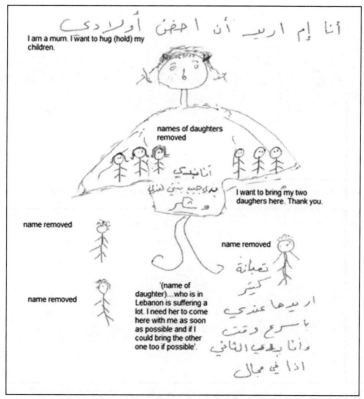

Figure 10.3 *A Syrian mother drawing herself holding her daughters and sons (names of children have been removed)*

Figure 10.4 *A female participant drawing herself separated from her three children*

Figure 10.5 *A female participant drawing herself separated from her child*

Figure 10.6 *A female participant drawing herself separated from her son*

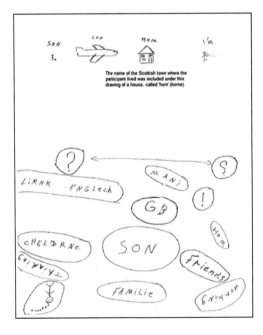

. . . what worries me is the future; what is going to happen. Okay, we are adapting but what's next? . . . Because we all have families elsewhere. Will we be able to have citizenship here? Will we be able to travel to visit our families elsewhere? Our families, will they be able to visit us here?

Figure 10.7 *Male participant's drawing depicting himself crying on the basis of concerns around family reunion, English language, financial security and integration*

There were different levels of vulnerability and family and health-related needs (Figure 10.7), which meant that there could not be a single approach for a homogenous group. Support, at least in the initial months of adaptation, needed to be tailored to individual family needs. This required building up capacities of knowledge and understanding and working closely with other partners (Local Authority Lead for Syrian Resettlement).

Scottish public libraries support for Syrian new Scots

The National Strategy for Public Libraries in Scotland 2015–20 encompasses a vision and mission which sees Scotland's public libraries as 'trusted guides connecting all of our people to the worlds' possibilities and opportunities' and as 'part of a shared civic ambition to fulfil the potential of individuals and communities' (Scottish Library and Information Council, 2015, 3). Public libraries have the ability and potential to 'play a key role in improving access to opportunities for all of us including the most vulnerable' (11). Strategic aim 4, particularly, relates to the role of public libraries in Scotland 'contributing to social well-being, tackling social isolation, inequality, disadvantage, fractured communities and ill health'. According to this strategic aim, there are five main ways in which libraries can contribute to social well-being. These are (Scottish Library and Information Council, 2015, 25):

1 responding to the social needs of individuals and groups in their communities and developing activities and programmes to respond to particular needs
2 making library space and support available for community interest groups and members of the community looking to support one another
3 contributing to the ability of individuals to become involved in their local communities and take part in local and national life
4 strengthening the identity and sense of community
5 creating a public service hub for the delivery of a range of public services.

Therefore public libraries in Scotland encompass the vision of welcoming and helping vulnerable communities, such as refugees, embracing an ethos of social inclusion, nurturing their needs for learning, social well-being, community integration, helping to build capacity for active contribution of refugees to their host society and enabling activities that create a sense of belonging for all. Public libraries are safe and welcoming spaces that are the heart and the central hub of the community as centres of readily accessible, free and useful information services to all members of society. This inclusive ethos means that libraries are ideally placed to contribute to improving the quality of life of vulnerable or excluded groups such as asylum seekers and refugees and help them to integrate into existing communities.

As part of the Syrian new Scots' research project, the role of the local public libraries and their existing support were explored, placing emphasis on the potential of transforming the library into a trusted 'third' place for Syrian new Scots, 'a place where people choose to go that is outside of their work or home'. In that way 'the library can become the "third place" giving them a place to meet and create a sense of community' (Montgomery and Miller, 2011, 232). Two areas specifically were addressed: public libraries' role in helping Syrian new Scots to develop English language and ICT skills, and their emerging role as community centres helping in the social integration of Syrian refugees, supporting them to address everyday life information needs (e.g. health, housing, rights and entitlements, job seeking).

In one of the locations of the research study, it was clear that during the first few days in Scotland almost no one had considered the library as a place for connecting to the internet or for borrowing resources for learning English. When the Syrian new Scots had initially arrived, they felt that the public library was not the right place to visit. Women in particular felt that they were visibly differently dressed and, at the initial phase of resettlement, 'things were a little too intense so it wasn't a priority' (Local Authority Lead for Syrian Resettlement). In addition, neither the Syrian families nor their local support services used the word 'refugee'. The families were Syrian new Scots and 'refugee' was perceived as a process they were going through: 'it's part of their identity but it's not something they want to be associated with':

> On the first day some of the people were really keen to talk about how people see us. They've obviously following the media, they are following the thing about the UK, understood a lot about how things were changing in Europe and how they are going to be perceived . . . they didn't want to be refugees.
>
> (Local Authority Leads for Syrian Resettlement)

However, after the first few months, Syrian new Scots were more open to using the library. For example, one of the female participants from the urban location had a library card she used to borrow books, mainly in Arabic language (and she indicated that she could find quite a lot of variety). She also borrowed books to help her with English although she found that learning that way was 'very difficult and complicated'. On the other hand, other people felt that there were not sufficient Arabic resources available (for example there were more in other languages, such as Polish). One of the Local Authority Leads for resettlement felt that if there was a specific Arabic resource and if every library had guaranteed a hub and the families had received that information, they would have been more likely to use the library more extensively. In addition, the presence of Arabic speakers in the library would motivate people to visit it more.

Overall, access to the library differed locally. For example, Syrian new Scot families who had been placed in the urban location found it difficult to gain the confidence required to use the bus to visit the city centre, especially in the first months and until they felt more able to communicate in English. As explained earlier, the use of transportation was also an important financial consideration. On the other hand, the families who had been placed in the rural location had easier access to local facilities including the library, as these were closer and within walking distance. A distinctively different approach was also followed for the rural component of the study, where the library was situated within the community building and where local services to the Syrian new Scots families were offered together with a range of social activities. Access to the library was easier for the families. The library worked in partnership with the ESOL service and the English-language classes were held in the rear of the library, so the families familiarised themselves with everything that happened in the library area. The Local Authority Leads had worked in partnership with the library as part of the strategic and operational plan before the families had arrived. The library had invested money in dual-language story books for children and had ordered them before the families arrived (although they did not know the ages of the children, so they had tried to address needs at various levels).

The library also organised mother-and-toddler groups (put together with the help of a volunteer who brought books for the children) to encourage parents to take their children into the library at an early age. There were a small number of the mothers who were going to these weekly sessions. Participants in that location mentioned using the library for a number of different purposes, e.g. borrowing books in both English and Arabic, using the internet and attending the toddlers' rhyme-time group at the library. One female participant had been referred to early years' sessions by her midwife (demonstrating how that partnership had extended beyond the council, ESOL and the library to the NHS).

The library was also keen to attract new potential volunteers to see the work with the existing volunteers and the Syrian new Scots families. This was very valuable, as it encouraged other Syrian families to come forward as potential volunteers themselves. This was a crucial emerging role for the public library on the basis not only of offering library space where activities for learning English and other classes could be organised, but also for increasing awareness in the local community. Having already been through the initial phases of the integration process and becoming increasingly more confident and independent, Syrian new Scots themselves could play a significant role in the integration of new arriving families. All the Syrian participants were positive about helping others, communicating with them and sharing their experiences as much as possible: 'whatever we could do, we would do anything'. However, they would not just offer new families their experiences; they would 'relate' their experiences, 'show them around the town, the shopping, the centres. Show them the basics, how to get by, how to deal with the health centre and transportation'.

One of the Syrian new Scots had already offered to become a volunteer co-ordinator, offering support to the next arriving families; he was expected to have a recognised role and be a formal part of the team offering an insight into what is important and what will be challenging for the integration of the families. The importance of this contribution was beyond a simple information-provider role. It would offer value to community development, as the families would not just 'become a guide to information but they become part of the social integration' (Local Authority Lead for Syrian Resettlement). Similarly, another participant, who was an Arabic-language teacher, was very interested in helping with the integration of Syrian refugees who were illiterate in Arabic and with overcoming the initial communication barriers. A few months after the focus-group interviews, a young Syrian new Scot had already set up a local group which aimed to help with the integration of new arriving families. The group had plans to organise a number of events that would bring people together (e.g. coffee mornings). One of the first more formal support activities which the group had started to get involved with was also a peer English-language-learning programme which had been developed in response to the Resettlement Programme (of Syrian refugees to Scotland). The programme had put together a working group of peer educators selected from refugee families and local community volunteers with the aims of learning English, building social connection and exchanging cultural experiences via a number of formal or informal social activities that would be organised in the local community (e.g. women's walking, smoking cessation, making new memories). Therefore, there were important roles for Syrian new Scots who had already been through the first phase of integration (i.e. they had been in Scotland for several months and felt more familiar with how their new environments were structured and what support they could provide to the new families).

Case studies of public libraries in Scotland supporting Syrian new Scots

Some of the work that public libraries have developed to support refugees in Scotland has been documented via The Network website (www.seapn.org.uk/about), which is a network of local authorities (public libraries, archives and museums) in England, Wales, Scotland and Northern Ireland, national museums, archives and libraries, university departments, professional bodies (such as CILIP), heritage organisations (including English Heritage and the Heritage Lottery Fund), charities, voluntary sector organisations (including the National Literacy Trust) and individuals committed to tackling social exclusion.

However, the majority of the projects reported on The Network have been based in England and with a focus on refugees in general. A systematic effort to put together information on Scottish public libraries' contribution to Syrian new Scots in particular is not readily available and this means that a lot of the excellent work that public libraries do in this area is not formally documented. The 'Lost in Information: Syrian new Scots' information literacy way-finding practices' project sought to initiate this process by collating examples of good practice in selected local communities, via a call to showcase public library support, resources, projects and activities aimed at Syrian new Scots. Although the examples presented below from different Scottish geographical areas, who responded to the call, are not representative or necessarily typical of the present picture, they offer a starting point for further information sharing and exchange of ideas.

North Ayrshire Council Libraries

Prior to the arrival of Syrian new Scots in North Ayrshire, North Ayrshire Council libraries met with housing, education and community learning colleagues to establish how many Syrian new Scots were expected, where they would be housed, and find out more about the demographic characteristics of the expected families (e.g. children of school age). Based on these discussions, the libraries bought a collection of Arabic books (e.g. children's books, short stories collections and dual Arabic/English-language resources) and placed them in the library nearest to where the new families had been housed. The libraries are also considering offering meeting spaces in the libraries and recruiting Arabic-speaking computer buddies and BookBug leaders.

Rothesay Library, Isle of Bute

In September 2015 Argyll and Bute agreed to resettle 20 Syrian refugee families through the Home Office's Syrian Vulnerable Persons Relocation Scheme. Since then additional families have been resettled:

> The Refugee Resettlement Group was formed under the banner of the Community Planning Partnership with membership from both Council services and partner agencies. Members included housing, education, adult learning, health and social work, benefits, Business Gateway, communications, ACHA, Fyne Homes, Police Scotland, Scottish Fire and Rescue, DWP and from the third sector Bute Advice Centre, Carr Gomm and Argyll and Bute Third Sector Interface (TSI).
>
> (Argyll and Bute Council Community Services, 2017)

The library extended a warm welcome to the Syrian new Scots who arrived to the island and has several Syrian library members. The library holds Arabic leaflets in its MCISS (Macmillan Cancer Information and Support Service). Popular services with the Syrian new Scots families, when they first arrived, were the library's guest free internet Wi-Fi access offered via the 'People's Network' programme, before gaining access to these facilities at home. The Adult Learning team invited female Syrian new Scots to the library to introduce Community-based Adult Learning services and classes which include how to keep up with new technology, take the first steps into learning, enjoy community life more fully, progress into further learning and gain skills to find work. The library has a collection of children's and young adults' books in Arabic and several Syrian children come to the library during school visits. The library also offers a venue for English Language Classes in the Adult Learning office or in the Greet Tree Room (Moat Centre).

Aberdeenshire Libraries

The first Syrian new Scots families arrived in Aberdeenshire in February 2016. Since then additional families were resettled via the Home Office's Syrian Vulnerable Persons Relocation Scheme undergoing a programme of integration. An initial meeting was held in Inverurie Library on how Aberdeenshire Libraries could support the Syrian new Scots Aberdeenshire classes. Following that meeting, a number of community and learning events were organised for Syrian new Scots in close collaboration with a local charity organisation, 'Al Amal', set up by a group of young Syrian new Scots to raise awareness about the

Syrian new Scots in the local community; and help new families gradually integrate into their new society with the help of Syrian new Scots who have already been via the process of initial integration, putting emphasis on the value of peer support. The mission and vision of 'Al Amal' (which means 'hope') is set on the following priorities:

- to improve resettlement experiences by enabling Syrian families to contribute to the planning, operational and evaluative process
- to reduce isolation, low mental health, boredom and frustration by encouraging active community participation
- to develop community projects that build on the skills, knowledge and expertise of Syrian new Scots
- to co-ordinate and work with other groups with similar objectives
- to develop employability skills and learning
- to raise funds for cultural trips and experiences
- to enable Syrian new Scots to support community events and projects locally
- to develop the use of social media to aid communication
- to advocate for the unmet needs of Syrian new Scots locally.

The Syrian families resettled in Aberdeenshire were keen to have ICT classes within the library to help with their resettlement within the area. They were also interested in having BookBug sessions solely for Syrian families to allow women to come along without fear of being in the company of men. The Information Literacy and Learning Librarian for Aberdeenshire Libraries, Ms Jacqueline Geekie, was tasked with appointing an ICT volunteer from the group of young Syrians. Although the library normally provides one-to-one support, the Syrian new Scots were keen to have a class for several students; this worked better than the usual format and could be taught by the Syrian volunteer in a self-sufficient way. The introduction of these classes caused a huge interest on the Al Amal WhatsApp group, with 15 participants signing up to attend the classes. The class took place in the library on a Saturday afternoon when the computers were booked for the group to use. The most suitable topics selected were computer basics; e-mail; shopping online including an overview and how to shop from Amazon, eBay and some of the sites. The tutor was open to adding in anything else they would like to learn. However, soon after the classes began it became apparent that, as well as ICT help, the group required their English to be improved. The library was asked to purchase Arabic keyboards to allow the students to pick out the English letters on the keyboard. These are now available in the Inverurie Library and can be requested when required.

As part of Book Week Scotland 2017, Aberdeenshire Libraries organised an event in Inverurie Library with the 'Al Amal' group to share the culture of the Syrians and a little of their story coming to Scotland. The theme of Book Week Scotland 2017 was 'Nourish' and one of the strands was called 'Breaking Bread' and was about sharing culture. The 'Al Amal' group created a film which they shared with the community to explain about their homeland. It was a very powerful evening which was fully booked and helped to integrate the Syrians even more into their community. There was a definite feeling of wanting to help and encourage, and the 'Al Amal' group thanked the communities for the welcome they received.

Future Plans of Aberdeenshire Libraries involve continuing using the format they have already used during Book Week Scotland and organise similar events in the libraries in each of the communities where Syrian families have settled. These events will include Syrian food, which will be supplied by 'Al Amal'.

Aberdeen City Libraries

A pop-up Learning Space was created in Aberdeen Central Library in 2017, to accommodate up to 10 Syrian learners and a tutor for ESOL classes. The classes ran twice weekly, a men-only class and a women-only class, hosting approximately seven learners in each. This was set up to help solve issues surrounding childcare. Due to the success of the classes the bookings were extended into 2017/18, consisting of four classes per week, two classes for men and two for women, each lasting for 1½ hours.

Additionally, Aberdeen City Libraries developed digital support for Syrian new Scots, working closely with the Adult Learning Team. A computing class was established in the Central Library in 2017 which is open to all ESOL learners and the people in the Syrian learner groups were invited to attend. ESOL tutors working with the Syrian learners classes are now also making use of these computer facilities, adjacent to the Learning Space, to support both their language skills and their everyday-life skills, for example, using software such as the learner driver, Theory Test Pro.

Aberdeen City Libraries have offered support with reading and learning and Syrian new Scots have been given tours of the Central Library. Many of them (both female and male) have now joined the library and are active members, borrowing both English and dual-language books to read individually and/or with their children. Library staff are working closely with the ESOL tutors as part of the stock selection process to ensure there are appropriate resources available to the learners at the correct levels to support and encourage progression in their reading and learning.

Feedback from the ESOL tutor has expressed thanks for creating an 'effective learning space in the library, for my Syrian classes'. For example, following the tour of the library by the men's class, the tutor contacted the library staff to say: 'What a joy to see learners walking out with armfuls of books!' As the tutor put it, 'It's about confidence and breaking down barriers, opening up access for them where before things were inaccessible simply because they didn't know all the fabulous stuff that was available to them or had no idea what they had to do to get it, or insufficient confidence to try in case they got it wrong or misunderstood something crucial.'

Discussion and conclusion

Public libraries have been actively developing projects and activities to support the needs of refugees (and asylum seekers). They have long been connecting to their refugee and asylum-seeker communities coming from diverse ethnic backgrounds. For example, 'Welcome to your Library' (WTYL) was a project which took place from 2003 to 2007, funded by the Paul Hamlyn Foundation and co-ordinated through London Libraries Development Agency, with the aim of connecting public libraries with refugees and asylum seekers (ADP Consultancy, 2007). The foreword by the Chair of London Libraries Development Agency places emphasis on public libraries as 'one of the very few services that anyone can access freely, irrespective of status or money. And because libraries act as gateways to civic presence, with the library card as an easily accessible symbol of citizenship' (ADP Consultancy, 2007, v). The project case studies demonstrated examples of library services beyond the provision of information to actively involving the refugee communities in practical activities (such as discussion groups and 'conversational clubs', citizenship activities) emphasising the need for moving 'from delivering services to people and towards delivering services with people'. Public libraries play a significant role as central spaces for accessing information and resources for diverse learning, recreational and creative activities, bringing the community together, encouraging people to engage and interact with each other on a local level. Designing active programmes which help the refugee communities to develop and enhance their existing skills and make a more direct contribution to their local community, through engaging them in service delivery locally is vital (for example, by means of engaging refugees and the local community in local events that celebrate different cultures and encourage cultural heritage exchange, or by sourcing support to newly relocated refugees from the local refugee community). In addition, raising awareness of the issues that refugees are facing as well as an understanding of social inclusion barriers, in general, is crucial and this could be enabled via staff development programmes. Finally, the project stressed the importance of promoting the contribution and role of public libraries to the wider policy context and contributing to cross-sectoral agendas via diverse partnership development beyond the library sector.

In our research, we, similarly, found that supporting Syrian new Scots to become more independent and proactively involved with the community helped them increase their confidence in navigating their new information environments, interact with the local community and regain a sense of normality. Organising social activities helped Syrian families to build social and emotional bonds with other local Scottish families more directly, and helped them to create reciprocal contributions on the basis of their already existing knowledge and skills. However, with lack of English, in the first year, the provision of bilingual resources on their own was not sufficient. There was the need for ongoing commitment of bilingual support either from the volunteering or the Syrian community which was fundamental for building trust and bridging communication barriers in a more direct and purposeful way. Based on the research findings of the 'Syrian new Scots' information literacy way-finding practices' and via additional consultation with a number of other key stakeholders, a number of key recommendations on ways in which public libraries could further support and enable Syrian new Scots to adapt to their local communities, feel a sense of belongingness and successfully establish their identity into the Scottish society have been put forward as follows:

- establishing a single library card for Syrian new Scots and automatically signing families as members
- setting up a community hub with volunteering and working opportunities for Syrian new Scots
- providing health information in accessible pictorial formats
- helping Syrian new Scots to develop their health and digital literacy (via the provision of additional classes)
- offering source material in Arabic (including newspapers and material for children) and Arabic speaker volunteers based in local public libraries
- setting up family sessions and getting Syrian new Scots to engage additionally with the early years programme

- creating a friendly, welcoming and trusted 'third place' for families to learn, socialise and feel part of the community (e.g. by introducing induction sessions and a short film on what public libraries could offer).

Public libraries in Scotland have already put some of the above plans into action. However, greater and more systematic visibility of their contribution is required to showcase their impact and additional collaboration within the library sector that will enable greater capacities. For example, one of the recommendations of the 'Welcome to Your Library' project was for creating a central, nationally co-ordinated 'information hub' for sharing resources across the entire library sector for the purpose of developing engagement activities. These may include volunteering and working opportunities for Syrian new Scots, which may create social capital for their hosting communities. Staton (2017) has described how the movement of refugees into cities 'could become a positive part of urban life . . . spurring population growth and economic development' if the bureaucracy 'which often hampers efforts to get refugees into work' is reduced. For example, in Sweden the government has encouraged new arrivals into work, via a fast-track to employment programme, called *Snabbspåret* – the programme matches refugees with jobs in sectors where there is a shortage of workers, offering training and mentoring. Another example includes a group of Syrian refugees in the Netherlands who have joined efforts, with the support of a social inclusion programme, to recycle thousands of lifejackets abandoned on Greek beaches into commercial items (e.g. laptop bags and flags) (Holligan, 2018). The 'Makers Unite' organisation explores participants' talents, supports them to develop entrepreneurial skills and introduces them to educational training, internships and employment opportunities.

Libraries in Scotland could play a key role in their local communities by enabling capacities in partnership with other external organisations and the voluntary sector via diverse partnership projects related to support for health, everyday life, citizenship, skills and employability. For example, for supporting Syrian new Scots with their employability, public libraries could join forces with a number of services, e.g. Careers Scotland (part of Skills Development Scotland) offering career guidance and advice about becoming more employable; Job Centre Plus (the UK Government website with links to Universal Jobmatch Service and employment advice); Volunteer Scotland (the national website for finding volunteering opportunities across Scotland); and Bridges Programmes (www.bridgesprogrammes.org.uk), which is a specialist agency in Glasgow supporting the social, educational and economic integration of refugees, asylum seekers, migrants, and anyone for whom English is a second language. Scottish libraries could also work in partnership with key local organisations that offer volunteering opportunities, such as Volunteer Glasgow (www.volunteerglasgow. org), Volunteer Edinburgh (www.volunteeredinburgh.org.uk), The Wise Group (www.thewisegroup.co.uk), as well as work closely with local colleges and universities to offer employability and skills training.

As eloquently put by Amina Shah, Director of Programme at The Scottish Book Trust, during the 'Scotland's Libraries: inspiration for the nation' campaign:

> Those of us who work in libraries and with books . . . should shout as loudly as we can about the fact that libraries are not just nice to have – not a peripheral luxury, but the absolute bedrock of a democratic society; of one that believes in investment in preventative measures and in giving everyone equal access to information, books, space and time to live an empowered and informed life and a real answer to reducing poverty, inequality and the attainment gap.
>
> (Shah, 2016)

Scotland's public libraries are developing into 'trusted guides', connecting Syrian new Scots to the possibilities and opportunities created within their new communities, and their role in welcoming refugees can be further empowered by maintaining close partnerships with key organisations that directly support refugees' social well-being, health, employment opportunities and overall societal integration. The European Bureau of Library, Information, and Documentation Associations (EBLIDA) (an independent umbrella association of library, information, documentation, and archive associations and institutions in Europe), supports the notion that 'libraries all over Europe should act as a platform for democratic and open-minded values, and be a safe place where social inclusiveness for all is a priority' (EBLIDA, 2015). Public libraries in Scotland have embraced this strategic agenda with impactful work to support Syrian refugees in their local communities and are developing further services which, with close partnerships, could make a real difference in the lives of Syrian new Scots and the communities which have welcomed them.

References

ADP Consultancy (2007) *Welcome To Your Library: connecting public libraries and refugee communities*, Evaluation Report, November, www.seapn.org.uk/uploads/files/WTYLEvaluationReportrevisedversion.pdf.

Argyll and Bute Council Community Services (2017) *Year 2 Evaluation of The Argyll and Bute Refugee Resettlement Programme*, 30 November, www.argyll-bute.gov.uk/moderngov/documents/s121810/Year%202%20Report.pdf.

Brokenshire, J. (2016) Refugees and Resettlement: written statement, HCWS687, 21 April, www.parliament.uk/written-questions-answers-statements/written-statement/Commons/2016-04-21/HCWS687.

COSLA (2016) Scottish Local Authorities and the Syrian Vulnerable Person Resettlement Scheme, Teaching ESOL to Refugees Event, Glasgow, Monday 29 February, https://education.gov.scot/improvement/documents/cld17-cosla-esol-event.pptx.

EBLIDA (2015) *Public Libraries in Europe Welcome Refugees*, press release, 21 September, www.eblida.org/news/press-release-public-libraries-in-europe-welcome-refugees.html.

Holligan, A. (2018) Refugees in Amsterdam Giving Lifejackets a New Life, *BBC News*, 12 May, www.bbc.co.uk/news/av/world-44086942/refugees-in-amsterdam-giving-lifejackets-a-new-life.

Home Office (2015) *Syrian Vulnerable Person Resettlement (VPR) Programme*, www.gov.uk/government/uploads/system/uploads/attachment_data/file/472020/Syrian_Resettlement_Fact_Sheet_gov_uk.pdf.

Martzoukou, K. (2016) *Lost in Information? Syrian new Scots' information literacy way-finding practices*, 24 September 2016, https://syrian-information-literacy.blogspot.co.uk/2016/09.

Martzoukou, K. and Burnett, S. (2018) Exploring the everyday life information needs and the sociocultural adaptation barriers of Syrian refugees in Scotland, *Journal of Documentation,* **74** (5), 1104–32, https://doi.org/10.1108/JD-10-2017-0142.

Montgomery, S. E. and Miller, J. (2011) The Third Place: the library as collaborative and community space in a time of fiscal restraint, *College & Undergraduate Libraries*, **11** (2–3), 228–38, www.tandfonline.com/doi/full/10.1080/10691316.2011.577683?scroll=top&needAccess=true.

Scottish Government (2017) *New Scots: integrating refugees in Scotland's Communities 2014–2017, Final Report*, www.gov.scot/Publications/2017/03/5825.

Scottish Government (2018) *New Scots Refugee Integration Strategy 2018–2022*, www.gov.scot/Resource/0053/00530097.pdf.

Scottish Library and Information Council (SLIC) (2015) *Ambition & Opportunity: a strategy for public libraries in Scotland 2015–2020*, https://scottishlibraries.org/media/1133/ambition-opportunity-scotlands-national-public-library-strategy.pdf.

Shah, A. (2016) *Scotland's Libraries – Promoting the Value of Literacy and Learning: Inspiration for the Nation 2016*, CILIPS: Scotland's Library and Information Professionals, www.cilips.org.uk/scotlands-libraries-promoting-value-literacy-learning.

Society of Chief Librarians (2015) *Library Leaders Across England and Wales Confirm the Welcome Offered to Refugees and Asylum Seekers from Public Libraries*, 25 September, https://ascel.org.uk/sites/default/files/uploads/public/Libraries%20extend%20welcome%20to%20refugees%20and%20migrants.pdf.

Staton, B. (2017) How Sweden is Fast Tracking Refugees into the Workforce, *Fast Company*, 28 July 2017, www.fastcompany.com/40446055/how-sweden-is-fast-tracking-refugees-into-the-workforce.

Vincent, J. (2015) Welcoming Refugees to the UK (and to Libraries), CILIP, 30 September, https://archive.cilip.org.uk/blog/welcoming-refugees-uk-libraries.

11

Information literacy, lifelong learning and the needs of an ageing population

Bill Johnston

Introduction: the ageing population – a contested demographic

This chapter will focus on the civic possibilities of information literacy in relation to the needs and issues of an ageing population. This is a global question and it will be addressed from that perspective, but also using insights from: (i) the author's experience in Scotland's civic spaces – principally influencing government and political parties through Third Sector activism; and (ii) his interest in lifelong learning strategies as a useful conceptual lens – particularly those derived from the work of Paulo Freire.

The UK population has undergone a fundamental demographic shift in age structure, including falling birth rates, longer life expectancy and increase in the average age (HM Government Office for Science, 2016), which will require substantial changes across most areas of civic life, democracy and politics. In effect we are living in a society where the majority of people are in older age groups and this trend is set to continue. Significant change in age structures is a global experience shared with other nations and regions (Zimmer and McDaniel, 2013; UN Department of Economic and Social Affairs, 2017). Clearly forecasting population change is fundamental to anticipating and making the various provisions required to adapt to change and maintain society.

In response, key concepts about the age structure of society like 'old age', 'retirement' and 'state pension age' are being systematically reframed in a public narrative, shaped by a dominant neoliberal political economy, as entailing unsustainable pension costs with equally unsustainable associated health and care costs (Macnicol, 2015). This narrow framing is contradicted by an alternative view of such socio-cultural features which views retirement and pension costs as essential features of the lifecourse, to be managed constructively by developed nations in order to sustain themselves as cohesive civic spaces.

Concepts like retirement, the state pension and the nature of social care arrangements have implications for everybody in society and are therefore important practical aspects to consider whenever demographic ageing is discussed as a public policy issue (Harper, 2016). Of equal importance is the challenge of linking demographic ageing to other macro-level global dynamics such as climate change, technological change and the economic environment, which are currently treated as separate issues (British-Irish Council, 2016; Lawrence, 2016).

The premise of this chapter is that an ageing population is a dynamic social force for participative democracy, with its older members acting in their own interest around specific needs and issues arising from those needs, but also playing their part in the wider agenda of democratic dialogue about population ageing. Those immediate needs are typically associated with the changes impacting on social, economic and personal circumstances triggered by retirement from the workforce and related to the state-funded support structures enjoyed in later life, such as pension provision, health and social care services. Need in this sense relates to the circumstances of a specific constituency within democratic society defined by age as older, or retired, people. It includes a variety of associated sociocultural assumptions about the nature of age and ageing in addition to government analysis and interpretation of population data in relation to public policy for an ageing population.

The concept of 'retirement' and its consequences is one such cultural assumption with definite political and policy implications. Questions of when retirement occurs, what triggers retirement, how diversity and inequality shapes the experience of retirement, what are the labour market consequences of changing retirement practices, how retirement aligns with State Pension Age (SPA), and how retired people are perceived and treated arise in all nations, and are answered differently in different countries with different histories and social structures. The answers can quickly become contested political questions about the funding and management of pension systems within the wider welfare and healthcare budgets (Macnicol, 2015; Department for Work and Pensions, 2017).

In effect, retirement in developed countries is closely linked with the concept of pensioner dependency on economically active age groups i.e. the ratio of older 'dependents' to those of working age. Social attitudes based on a dependency construct of ageing, retirement and old age are significant political forces within democracy, influencing debate on specific policies and potentially creating intergenerational tensions.

Age, ageism and agency: the politics of population change

By necessity, therefore, older people approaching retirement, or already retired, must act collectively as engaged citizens to assert their rights and interests, challenge the inequalities and failings of particular state provisions, and reject negative assumptions about their social status, particularly where these are presented in the media with an aim of influencing public attitudes towards older people. On this reading, the fundamental, *democratic* need of an ageing population can be posed as the requirement for its members to be accepted as an integral part of civic society and not as a dependent or 'needy' group of old people, who have moved out of social and economic activity, and are therefore a burden on the public purse.

This is not to underestimate the reality that ageing brings with it a greater incidence of healthcare and other support needs to sustain active living and mitigate against physical and cognitive decline and social isolation. Such needs translate into practical matters, including pensions and income, housing and community, social and health care and isolation and loneliness. Consequently it is vital for social justice and cohesion that care and support for senior citizens is efficient, effective and designed with the benefit of the best available research in the relevant fields. All of these facets are subject to scrutiny through democratic processes involving civic engagement in campaigns to defend or extend provision in the face of growing social and economic inequality. Arguably the growing move towards a rights-based approach to age and ageing (European Union Agency for Fundamental Rights, 2018) should drive such civic activity. This report offers powerful arguments in support of a more positive approach to ageing populations, and advocates a move away from dependency and deficit models of ageing.

However, achieving this aim is hampered by a partial and inadequate conceptual approach, which tends to view the ageing population as a static formation of 'older people' mainly defined by their retirement from the workforce, and presumed to be dependent on those still economically active. In this view, popular discourse typically presents older people as needy and a major source of demand for health and social care services, with little acknowledgment of their ongoing and positive contributions to society. Some contemporary presentations, particularly in the UK, introduce additional misleading and pejorative views. In particular the claim that the current older generation, the post-World War Two 'baby boomers' (born 1945–65), are not only needy but actually very well-off in terms of accrued wealth, making them a legitimate target of resentment for the currently less well-off younger generations, and therefore constituting a problem of 'intergenerational fairness' for government to solve. This problem can also take form in a popular discourse, which suggests that 'older people' have voted in opposition to the interests of younger people and somehow damaged their future prospects. This narrative can be seen in relation to the recent UK referendum on membership of the European Union. A detailed analysis of the findings of opinion polls is outwith the scope of this chapter; however, there are obvious dangers for democracy if the legitimate votes of a section of the electorate are challenged simply on the grounds of a perceived 'conservatism' based on age. The narrative is that the only way to support the young is to penalise the old and that this is fair because the old are well-off and support conservative policies.

If pressed to extremes this formulation of older people as a 'subaltern' class in society has potentially grim prospects for the old (Sutherland, 2016) and in any case its socio-economic premises and political manifestations are highly contestable (Macnicol, 2015). It is worth noting that what is happening here is the creation of an identity for a whole social group based on a shared characteristic – in this case, age. The labelling and negative attitudes entailed in this procedure of identifying 'baby boomers' can be experienced as demeaning and possibly discriminatory, depending on the circumstances. In practice this position can be termed *ageism*, and should be considered in line with other unacceptable formations such as racism and sexism. Age is in fact a protected characteristic in UK equality legislation, along with race and gender.

In this troublesome representation of the baby boomers, it becomes politically expedient to suggest that such 'well-off' older people should make additional contributions to meet the costs of their care. This is deemed to be 'fair' in relation to younger people, who are now struggling to secure the income needed to obtain mortgages and therefore cannot be expected to carry the burden of paying for care for the elderly. Such attempts at a hegemonic presentation of 'the old' notwithstanding, public perceptions of these matters have been surveyed and analysed showing a more nuanced view; alternative views on the nature and fairness of intergenerational wealth transfers have been described (Gál, Vanhuysse and Vargha, 2018); and proposals for longer working lives suggested as a partial solution to the fiscal pressures of an ageing population (Thomson, 2018). Consequently it behoves politicians to tread carefully in these contested matters. The 'grey vote' is, after all, worth courting and the consequences of upsetting grey voters can be severe. It is also a potent factor in the ongoing debate over Scottish independence (Dalzell, 2018).

Information literacy and the lifecourse: towards information-literate ageing

The discussion above calls for an account of information-literate ageing as it might relate to development over the lifecourse of individuals, including civic participation and engaged citizenship. Some obvious practical needs of members of an ageing population clearly have an important informational component – for example: health and social care information; digital inclusion; finance and consumer rights advice; advocacy; challenging media stereotypes and prejudice. Arguably the better and more widely informed civic society as a whole becomes about ageing, the greater the likelihood of developing effective strategies for a successful old age based on intergenerational cohesion as opposed to division.

However in order to explore this territory it is helpful to have an account of information literacy as a field of research, development and practice. Information literacy can be described concisely as:

> . . . the adoption of appropriate information behaviour to obtain, through whatever channel or medium, information well fitted to information needs, leading to wise and ethical use of information in society
>
> (Johnston and Webber, 2003)

The description involves: (i) a narrow conception in terms of the techniques individuals use to access sources, formulate searches and select relevant information, irrespective of whether the information is in in digital or other forms; and (ii) the holistic aspect of the description referring to 'wise and ethical use of information in society'. Both senses of the term are relevant to an understanding of information-literate ageing in relation to the civic role of citizens in an ageing population. This description posits the research field of information behaviour (Wilson, 2010) as the frame for personal and collaborative information activity, recognising information in all its forms and underlining the complexity of information literacy whilst also highlighting the importance of information literacy to society, the workplace and the economy.

In order to advance the discussion it is necessary to personalise the process of information-literate ageing and locate it in a changing information culture and society. The notional information-literate person of Figure 11.1 is therefore positioned in relation to a number of dynamic facets of information society and culture. Over a person's lifecourse her/his experience and understanding of information will change, evolve and be influenced by alterations in each of the five aspects identified in Figure 11.1 and by interactions between them. All of the five will be relevant to ageing in some degree, but the *personal goals/life stage area* and the *local and national culture and society area* seem most relevant to ageing as discussed above, although *technical changes* will intersect them (for further explanations of this model see Webber and Johnston, 2013; 2017).

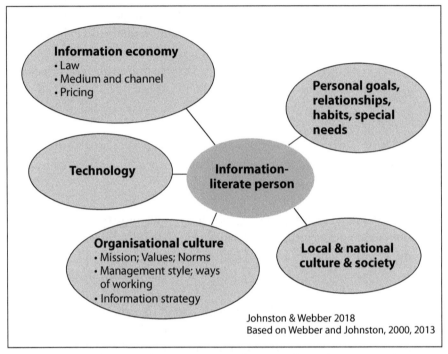

Figure 11.1 *The information-literate person in a changing information culture and society* (Johnston and Webber, 2018, based on Webber and Johnson, 2000; 2013)

The main facets of a changing information culture and society represented by the five 'bubbles' in the diagram of this model can each be detailed by applying features of the account of an ageing society given above. For example, *personal goals* is an obvious reference point of discussion as a person's appreciation of information and forms of information literacy conditioned by ageing and different life stages. If they live in a culture and society, which assumes a very significant difference between pre- and post-retirement, then the nature of information and its ease of access will be impacted. If so, people will need to reassess the information-literacy component of their lives and take steps to develop new approaches linked to their daily experience of retirement and any civic activities they choose to join.

With regards to *local and national culture and society*, the demographic categories, socio-economic composition, cultural assumptions and population trends for a given nation provide a basic framing of the likely information experience of ageing throughout a given person's lifecourse. Equally it is possible to analyse individual experience in terms of socio-economic characteristics across the cohorts of a given population, and on that basis derive some sense of the degree of capacity for democratic participation of different classes of citizens in a given age cohort. In short, it is not simply when an individual was born that counts, but the nature of the historical moment and socio-economic geography of their birthplace, community and subsequent life opportunities and experiences that illuminate their lifecourse. Inequalities at birth are likely to persist over the lifecourse and feature in later life experiences.

Turning to the *technology* bubble, the timing of the appearance of information and computer technologies (ICTs) in relation to individual experience, and the cohorts of a population, would be an obvious way to review thinking about information literacy over time. The contrast between young and older cohorts in relation to digital technology is a current subject of concern, resulting in proposals for positive action to enhance older peoples' capabilities with digital technology; particularly so as more services and state systems move online, leading to concerns that older people might be disadvantaged unless action for digital inclusion is taken (West, 2015). Allied to this technological strand is the evidence of differences and variations in media usage between age groups (Ofcom, 2018), which deserves more attention than space permits.

However, the driving force for information-literate living and ageing resides in a person's situational awareness of the information dimensions of his/her life in different contexts (class position, gender, race, sexual orientation, education, workplace, retirement status, etc.) and their capacity to manage transitions between one stage of life and another. This is not just a matter of acquiring information and digital skills in response to specific need; it is much more about intellectual development over the lifecourse, allied to civic awareness, community engagement, and commitment to democratic participation throughout working life and into retirement. Clearly collective as well as individual experiences of information encompassed by this account of information literacy is relevant. In both cases, personal and collective reflection on information experiences, as well as exposure to formal information literacy programmes, will be important.

Thus the model in Figure 11.1 suggests a schema to identify the blend of individual and collective information engagements, which provide the basis for civic activity. Information literacy in a changing demographic context is needed by individuals to navigate involvement with state agencies providing age-related services, such as pensions and healthcare (West, 2015). However, information is also essential to participative, campaigning activity in civic society. This includes individuals and groups within small communities, and other forms of organised activity: for example, seniors' forums; lunch clubs; men's sheds; community councils; housing associations; political parties; trade unions; and various issue-based campaigns, all with a slant towards older age groups.

A key need is to obtain the knowledge to inform people of their rights and opportunities and back up arguments and demands for improvements. Organised and active sources of age-related information include charities; academic researchers; think tanks; local authorities; health authorities; central government; campaign groups; libraries; international agencies and the media. There is no shortage of information; however, the awareness and will to obtain and use information can be in short supply, and the resources to support systematic access and use inadequate to the task.

In addition to the familiar institutional modes of information capture, storage and communication mentioned above, ethnographic approaches can be adapted to illuminate and develop information-literate civic participation. One example is Information Grounds theory (Fisher and Naumer, 2006). This approach provides a powerful means of exploring the information worlds of small groups in contexts, which are not primarily defined as information organisations. For example, Pettigrew (1999) illuminates a podiatry clinic, predominantly used by seniors, as a grounds or place where information is exchanged, although the setting is not designated for that purpose. The Information Grounds approach has been used in other settings (Fisher, Durrance and Hinton, 2005; Fisher, Landry and Naumer, 2007) and offers a promising tool for investigation of age-specific contexts which sit outside formal education and workplaces.

In this ethnographic sense of information-literate lives, it is vital to acknowledge that all sources of information – people, written, digital, etc. – and all modes of engagement – purposive, contingent, episodic – must be included in the discussion of 'everyday-life' settings (Savolainen, 2008) as they might apply to older age experiences. This is an essential way of conceiving, researching and developing the information experiences, and in turn the information literacy, of retired people. For example, the daily life of seniors can be conceived as an information experience in the broadest sense, with involvement in areas such as charity work constituting a specific context comprising a variety of information practices, which may not conform to more formalised information services in workplaces or educational establishments. In everyday settings embodied and enacted information, blended with external information – print, online – are valuable. Looking at the information literacy of older people through such societal lenses would also illuminate our understanding of information in a changing society more generally as conceived by, for example, Buckland (2017).

The preceding account of information-literate ageing and civic participation offers potential directions of travel for academics, practitioners and policy makers. The following case study illustrates some of the characteristics and dynamics involved in practice.

Informed civic participation: a case study

The following account offers some examples and insights into the forms of information literacy described in the preceding section: in particular, the notion of information literacy as a complex behaviour and the importance of ethnographic approaches to illuminating practice in particular contexts. The case also exemplifies the need to appreciate and organise activity across several information spaces – academic, professional and personal – in order to produce sophisticated information products such as detailed reports. This is significant as a corrective to more simplistic ideas of information processes based in search/find modelling of the process. Such a view assumes that civic information is accessed via portals provided by the state and that skills training will facilitate successful access. Such a 'skills and portals' mindset does not fit well to the complexity of the situation described, which includes older people generating their own information, and shows how that source can be incorporated with material from academic and professional services, to inform government thinking on a key issue in the experience of ageing.

In essence the case study illuminates an exercise in participative democracy using concepts from information literacy and suggests that this is a productive approach. Participative democracy in relation to age and ageing can be enhanced by creating collaborative groupings of older citizens, elected politicians and 'domain' experts to develop thinking about issues like isolation and loneliness. This form of participative democracy does not come cheap and would require reframing with associated costs of new forms and processes; however, the gains in terms of engagement should be worth the effort.

In 2018 the Scottish Government carried out a public consultation on the issue of isolation and loneliness, which though wide ranging, acknowledged the fact that older people are a particularly relevant population (Scottish Government, 2018). I was involved in preparing an invited submission in my role as Chair of the Scottish Seniors Alliance (SSA), a third-sector charity, which seeks to represent older people's interests to the Scottish Government and other interested parties. To an extent this example builds on and develops my earlier paper on the older people's movement in Scotland (Johnston, 2016), which sets out a much broader account of the civic scene and democratic trends in modern Scotland as they relate to age, ageing and older people's issues.

The SSA is a volunteer organisation with strictly limited information and research capacity, given resource constraints, so we are obliged to be agile in leveraging our contacts and calling on the resources and experiences of members. I suspect this precarious situation is not unusual for similar voluntary organisations despite their being an important part of civic society, so this case may resonate with others. The following brief description of the processes involved and reflection on the experience is offered as a worked example to illustrate the view of information literacy set out above in relation to the theme of civic participation. In this example information is viewed as a shared common resource sourced from a variety of organisations and people, shared via SSA Newsletters, openly discussed at meetings and finally distilled as a substantial report submitted to Scottish Government.

The Scottish Government public consultation was managed both online and via print materials, so SSA's initial response was to advertise it to members in local Forums through our Newsletter to generate discussion and encourage individuals to respond. The Forums are at base local groupings of older people and display a variety of ways of working, depending on the needs and capabilities of their members. For example, some Forums are mainly focused on social and caring activities, bringing older people together for lunch clubs, discussion and educational activities. Others combine such activities with regular engagement with local politicians such as councillors, Members of Parliament and Members of the Scottish Parliament. The Scottish Seniors Alliance operates as an umbrella organisation to share information and experience amongst Forums and act as a focal point for communications with the Scottish Government and other relevant national bodies.

The invited collective submission to the public consultation described here took the form of a written report and its production involved discussion amongst the Board of the charity; discussion with academic contacts; consultation with a specialist organisation, the Institute for Research and Innovation in Social Services (IRISS); and a focused discussion of the topic and the consultation brief at a meeting of the SSA Assembly, which is comprised of representatives of local Forums.

Whilst there is not scope in this chapter to elaborate the specifics of SSA's activity and the content of our report, a number of points relevant to the premise of this chapter and the theme of this book can be made:

1 Academic contacts specialising in ageing provided a reliable shortcut to selected review articles and gave useful advice on current academic approaches.
2 IRISS provided additional position papers and reviews, as well as valuable discussion with staff with information expertise.
3 Board meetings allowed us to refine our positions through discussion.
4 The focused Assembly discussion generated a substantial number of points drawn from the everyday experiences of senior citizens and illustrated similarities and differences between different local areas.

These member discussions identified a mix of relevant topics: personal and situational factors; community issues/individual issues; a strong emphasis on what is currently lacking in or being withdrawn from local-authority service provision; and a focus on how individuals in difficult circumstances can be identified and tracked. Interestingly, there was a fair degree of cohesion between many of the points members saw as relevant and the ideas presented in the academic and professional literature, albeit expressed in somewhat different language.

In effect this case illustrates a complex information situation involving civic participation aimed at informing government on an issue relevant to older people. The SSA model of civic participation has shown itself to be successful over several decades. It is a model of a democratically accountable, volunteer-managed, organisation, constituted through relations between local Forums, Assembly and Board meetings and Newsletters, the whole managed by a small, voluntary, implementation team. This structure works by allowing views and information in a variety of forms to be shared, discussed and distilled into various outputs, such as the report to the Scottish Government described here, without the pressure to conform to particular professional or political standpoints. Equally, SSA voluntary activity can, to an extent, be supported by specialist information and advice from a variety of sources, albeit subject to resource constraints. In addition there is a significant level of interaction, discussion, information sharing and learning generated by this mode of participation in the business of democracy, which might not occur otherwise.

Arguably the local Forums can be seen as: (i) small communities of action and learning – an adult education/community-development perspective; and (ii) small information worlds – an information-sharing and mutual-support perspective. They are valuable community resources and vary in their activities, depending on local circumstances. Equally Forums make a contribution to civic action in their communities and society overall. However, austerity-hit municipalities are starving them of funds to meet the cost of room hires and administrative support, and Forums are also hit by reductions in the numbers of community education/community development support workers available to provide practical help.

This is the downside of local level civic participative activity – whilst the official rhetoric is always supportive, the resources to back the rhetoric are often inadequate for the tasks. Inevitably these constraints reduce the amount of democratic capital which can be called upon by groups in civic society. Equally, there are structural difficulties in relations between various levels of state power and local community organisations. Writing in an Australian context Taylor and Donoghue expressed this well:

> While Governments promote concepts such as 'Ageing in Place, and
> Healthy Ageing' the relationship between different levels of government and
> small community organisations that provide services to older people often
> appears to be tenuous and contradictory
>
> (Taylor and Donoghue, 2014, 2)

It seems clear that austerity and underdeveloped government structures notwithstanding, both information literacy and learning are essential to the sustenance, support and full engagement of older people in democratic society. The following section addresses the pedagogical dimension of this aim and offers some tentative suggestions for progress in difficult times.

Lifelong learning and critical pedagogy: a Freirean perspective on dialogue and civic participation

This section is a reflection on the preceding case study and the earlier discussion of ageing and information literacy, aimed at bringing out the pedagogical dimension of civic participation and highlighting its critical potential. This develops the perspective of local Forums, and similar organisations, as small communities of action, learning and information interactions, but highlights their potential for criticality and challenge. Given the importance of these groups, and the threat to their existence posed by austerity, this is an important perspective for our times. The basis of this brief reflection is the work around *critical pedagogy* of the radical educators Paulo Freire (1970; 1974) and Antonia Darder (2011; 2018).

Critical pedagogy can be described by several key features:

1 commitment to developing of critical consciousness of the oppressive social and economic conditions influencing learners and educators
2 collective understandings derived from cycles of dialogic and experiential learning
3 a commitment to challenging and changing the socioeconomic conditions of inequality.

In practice critical pedagogy is often described by several key educational strategies, including 'culture circles', wherein participants share their understandings of reality and their place in society through dialogue, using 'generative themes', i.e. issues of material interest to participants and producing 'codifications' of their thinking, using words, pictures and any media that are appropriate for them. Whilst this might seem similar to many accounts of group learning in a variety of settings, the key difference is in the commitment not just to discussion, but to critical dialogue leading to change of circumstances. As Freire puts it: '. . . reflection and action directed at the structures to be transformed' (Freire, 1974, 126).

From a critical pedagogy perspective, issues of inequality and oppression relevant to an ageing population can be identified in the dependency construct of retirement and old age described above, which structures and controls the position of older people in society. Such oppressive conditions should be exposed and challenged, possibly under the broad heading of ageism, and certainly in relation to specific inequalities in social investment and service provision, for example issues of: poverty; inadequate services; expensive private social care facilities; loss of control and agency; and myths and stereotypes about ageing. Where state policy is ageist or influenced by ageist misinformation, that would be a focus of critique and challenge. The focus would be on people learning to 'read' the power structures they are implicated in and exploring strategies for challenging those structures.

Pedagogical directions could therefore be expressed in terms of understanding and resisting the 'dependency' framing of retirement. In addition the ways of working within small-scale and localised organisations lend themselves to a learning practice derived from Freire's ideas. Dialogue and cycles of activity, including information work, would constitute the reality of such a critical pedagogy in action, and notions of old age, ageing, and particular issues could function as 'generative themes', which could be explored in a variety of local settings. Older people could engage in learning as citizens involved in understanding and changing society and culture, and not simply as 'students' learning subjects or skills. Clearly the ageing experience is intersectional, involving older women, older people with disabilities, lesbian, gay, bisexual and transgender (LGBT) and ethnic communities whose varying needs would have to form part of the activity. It is also essential to recognise that the dominant educational institutions which structure people's social and economic lives also reinforce class divisions and the legacy of these inequalities carry forward into the older learner and activist population.

This brief outline of a Freireian idea of pedagogy seems to fit the working practices of some adult and community educators at least, and also some academics, although Freire's work may not be fully comprehended or applied in every institutional context. However, it is likely that there will be people in those settings with knowledge and commitment, who could be involved in piloting Freirean approaches to working with older people on their issues. The key is to find educators seriously committed to critical pedagogy and are willing to change familiar structures if they inhibit dialogue. Such educators may not be located in the dominant structures of 'learning in later life' (e.g. university lifelong learning departments, U3A). Alternative groupings in education and different pedagogies may need to be sought out locally and drawn into dialogue with older people's formations.

In summary, Freire provides a theory and practice of critical consciousness and pedagogy to characterise 'lifelong learning' as a social, political act, which can give radical shape to democracy, civics and participation. This seems highly relevant to the situations described above.

Neoliberal democracy: from here to where?

In theory democracy remains strong, but in practice is under threat from the 'strong leaders' of world politics; for example: Trump, Putin, Erdogan and even Aung San Suu Kyi shamelessly promote authoritarianism over participation and abuse human rights in the process. The basic forms of elective democracy are under threat from digital manipulations (Anon., 2018) and ideas of open information and freedom of speech are compromised daily by the culture and practice of 'fake news' and the secretive tendencies of state organisations. These are not good times for democracy, civic participation, information literacy and the pedagogical ideas discussed in this chapter and we should be clear that the neoliberal agenda of profit before people is a dominant force in compromising freedom of speech and information, which are central facets of a democratic polity. The assault on democracy is based in the currently dominant neoliberal political economy, which shapes the global economy and drives austerity and inequality at home, although it must be recognised that the authoritarian regimes of Russia and China, for example, hold to different models of political economy. We should not avoid the implications for ageing, information literacy, education and civic participation. In essence, the organic politics of local activism and civic participation considered in this chapter are threatened by authoritarianism and undermined by austerity. Clearly information literacy is a potential victim of authoritarianism and austerity, but arguably information literacy advocates and specialists can take a stand against specific threats to freedom of speech and undermining of the informational aspects of democratic participation.

Neoliberalism is at base a form of political economy characterised by an unshakable belief in unfettered free markets as means of achieving economic, social and political objectives that serve the interests of the rich and powerful at the expense of the majority in society. The topography of neoliberalism is shaped by valuing corporate owned private property over public ownership and employing government policies of privatisation of public resources. In contemporary public policy it is the driving force of austerity. Neoliberalism has been analysed (Mirowski and Plehwe, 2009; Birch, 2017) and critiqued (Harvey, 2007; Streek, 2014; Maclean, 2017). Stepping back from such academic discourses, everyday life is shaped by neoliberalism through our standards of living; culture; class relations; and working conditions. Even those 'baby boomers' who are relatively affluent are subject to the vagaries of neoliberal political economy and stand to see assets such as savings and pensions built up over decades devalued. Given the contested nature of health and social care described above, affluence may not provide a shield against deteriorating services.

I have outlined the impact of neoliberalism on the ageing population in terms of a reframing of the nature of ageing and concepts of retirement, pensions and the place of older people in society. Macnicol elaborates how this process:

> ... has emerged in the context of wider attacks on the welfare rights of all marginalised people in society that are themselves a product of the new economic and political agendas that began to take root in the 1970s and are now in full bloom in the United Kingdom (UK) and United States of America (USA).
>
> (Macnicol, 2015, 1–2)

He goes on to outline the historical context in three main periods:

1   1945 to the oil crisis of 1973, characterised as a period which prized old age and protected the right to retirement
2   1973 to the early 1990s, which saw increasing attacks from the political right on state provision for old-age pensions and even the right to retirement
3   early 1990s to date saw a consensus that the trend to early retirement should be reversed and state pension ages should be raised, with the implication of older people working into their late 60s and early 70s.

The challenge to participatory democracy from neoliberalism is clear. It is not simply a means of securing control over material conditions of life, it is also anti-community, degrades public goods and underpins attacks on gender, age, race, sexual orientation and other characteristics, currently protected in legislation. There is a need for constant effort to assert and secure these rights. In terms of education, neoliberal political economy conditions learning at all levels, including 'informal' situations. Learning is embedded in political economy and if the experience is repressive, then challenging that repression is a key part of learning. This is the critical pedagogy perspective Freire developed in pursuit of democracy and a richer civic life.

Shaping the future: a role for information literacy

Information literacy can also challenge the negative impact of neoliberalism. It should ideally include a blend of investigative journalism; community activism and co-operative rather than corporate forms of working and be organised around people as engaged citizens rather than consumers of state- and corporate-produced 'news' about policies and decisions handed down from 'above'. Key areas for local initiative include housing; community services, thematic groupings, e.g. women's issues, and marginalised groups. All of these aspects will benefit from an engagement with information literacy and the encounters can be shaped using Freirean ideas of critical pedagogy. In the wider information sphere, co-operative, not-for-profit organisations like The Ferret and other fact-checking, services offer models to be adapted and extended as powerful grassroots alternative information and media resources. The Ferret is an investigative journalism platform for Scotland and beyond, which campaign groups can use to get access to professional journalists operating in a co-operative mode. As such resources emerge and grow in importance as challenges to the dominance of the corporate media and political obfuscation, there is clearly scope for collaboration with information literacy specialists and community activists.

Also critiques of neoliberalism from within the library and information profession (Elmborg, 2012 and Lawson, Sanders and Smith, 2015) should be listened to and discussed. The later deserves quotation in relation to the neoliberalisation of the information profession:

> The structures that govern society's understanding of information have been reorganised under a neoliberal worldview to allow information to appear and function as a commodity. This has implications for the professional ethics of library and information labour.
>
> (Lawson, Sanders and Smith, 2015)

Finally, linking up with international organisations like GAPMIL (the Global Alliance for Partnerships on Media and Information Literacy) would be a valuable addition, as would familiarisation with statements such as the Riga Recommendations on Media and Information Literacy (MIL), which calls on all member states to:

> . . . promote awareness and recognition of the relevance of MIL to youth and to ageing populations, and to intergenerational dialogue, by supporting the development and implementation of related initiatives.
>
> (UNESCO, 2016)

Conclusion

I have suggested that a revitalisation of democracy and civic participation, involving information literacy and critical pedagogy, is possible and necessary. The way forward requires an information-literate and critically conscious population, which takes ageing seriously and poses alternatives to the present neoliberal agenda on ageing. This view might define an ideal of the information-literate, engaged senior citizen in the early 21st century. Such a citizen would have, above all else, a purpose, and that makes for positive ageing and a healthy civic society.

Perhaps the following quote from the Scottish Science Advisory Council in response to the UK Government's 'Foresight Report' (HM Government Office for Science, 2016) offers an apt structure for such citizenship:

Increased longevity means that retirees can now typically expect to live for another two or three decades. Maintaining well-being and a good quality of life in the later years is now recognised as involving not only good health and economic security, but also maintaining social connections, keeping mentally and physically stimulated and having a sense of purpose. This can be termed as productive engagement.

(Scottish Science Advisory Council, 2018, 8)

What better purpose to drive this vision than critical civic engagement in a democratic society?

Postscript

At the time of writing this chapter I am 68. In 12 years' time, if I live that long, I will be 80 and joining the oldest of the old. I feel keenly what I write about in this chapter! I also have a growing sense of the inevitable 'unfinishedness' of learning and civic participation, which may be a caring way to describe the cultural horizons of an ageing population.

As to yourself, dear reader, I urge you to check your age and look to the horizon. What sort of world do you want for your later years? How do you aim to achieve it?

References

Anon. (2018) The Cambridge Analytica Files, *The Guardian*, www.theguardian.com/news/series/cambridge-analytica-files.

Birch, K. (2017) *A Research Agenda for Neoliberalism*, Edward Elgar Publishing.

British-Irish Council (2016) *Population-Ageing-Society: policy implications*.

Buckland, M. (2017) *Information and Society*, MIT Press.

Dalzell, C. (2018) *The Demographics of Independence, 2018 Edition: a study of polling on and since the 2014 referendum*, Common Weal Policy.

Darder, A. (2011) Teaching as an Act of Love: reflections on Paulo Freire and his contributions to our lives and our work, *Counterpoints*, **418**, 2011, 179–94, JSTOR.

Darder, A. (2018) *The Student Guide to Freire's 'Pedagogy of the Oppressed'*, Bloomsbury Academic.

Department for Work and Pensions (2017) *State Pension Age Independent Review: final report*, (Cridland Report).

Elmborg, J. (2012) Critical Information Literacy: definitions and challenges. In Wilkinson, C. W. and Bruch, C. (eds) *Transforming Information Literacy Programs:*

intersecting frontiers of self, library culture, and campus community, Association of College & Research Libraries, 75–95.

European Union Agency for Fundamental Rights (2018) *Fundamental Rights Report 2018*, http://fra.europa.eu/en/publication/2018/fundamental-rights-report-2018.

Fisher, K. and Naumer, C. (2006) Information Grounds: theoretical basis and empirical findings on information flow in social settings. In Spink, A. and Cole, C. (eds) *New Directions in Human Information Behaviour*, Springer, 93–111.

Fisher, K., Durrance, J. and Hinton, M. (2005) Information Grounds and the Use of Need-based Services by Immigrants in Queens, New York: a context based, outcome evaluation approach, *Journal of the American Society for Information Science and Technology*, **55** (8), 754–66.

Fisher, K. E., Landry, C. F. and Naumer, C. (2007) Social Spaces, Casual Interactions, Meaningful Exchanges: 'information ground' characteristics based on the college student experience, *Information Research*, **12** (2), paper 291, http://informationr.net/ir/12-2/paper291.html.

Freire, P. (1970 in 2000) *Pedagogy of the Oppressed*, 30th anniversary edn, Continuum.

Freire, P. (1974) *Education for Critical Consciousness*, Bloomsbury Academic.

Gál, R. I., Vanhuysse, P. and Vargha, L. (2018) Pro-elderly Welfare States Within Child-oriented Societies, *Journal of European Public Policy*, **25** (6), 944–8, doi: 10.1080/13501763.2017.1401112.

Harper, S. (2016) *How Population Change Will Transform Our World*, Oxford University Press.

Harvey, D. (2007) *A Brief History of Neoliberalism*, Oxford University Press.

HM Government Office for Science (2016) *Future of an Ageing Population*, (Foresight Report).

Johnston, B. (2016) Ageing and Information: the Scottish older people's movement, *Library and Information Research*, **40** (123), 4–12.

Johnston, B. and Webber, S. (2003) Information Literacy in Higher Education: a review and case study, *Studies in Higher Education*, **28** (3), 335–52.

Lawrence, M. (2016) *Future Proof: Britain in the 2020s*, Institute of Public Policy Research (IPPR).

Lawson, S., Sanders, K. and Smith, L. (2015) Commodification of the Information Profession: a critique of higher education under neoliberalism, *Journal of Librarianship and Scholarly Communication*, **3** (1), eP1182, http://dx.doi.org/10.7710/2162-3309.1182.

Maclean, N. (2017) *Democracy in Chains: the deep history of the radical right's stealth plan for America*, Viking.

Macnicol, J. (2015) *Neoliberalising Old Age*, Cambridge University Press.

Mirowski, P. and Plehwe, D. (2009) *The Road from Mont Pelerin: the making of the neoliberal thought collective*, Cambridge MA 2009.

Ofcom (2018) *Adult's Media Use and Attitudes Report.*

Pettigrew, K. E. (1999) Waiting for Chiropody: contextual results from an ethnographic study of the information behavior among attendees at community clinics, *Information Processing & Management*, **35** (6), 801–17.

Savolainen, R. (2008) *Everyday Information Practices: a social phenomenological perspective*, Scarecrow Press.

Scottish Government (2018) *A Connected Scotland: our strategy for tackling social isolation and loneliness and building stronger social connections*, https://www.gov.scot/publications/connected-scotland-strategy-tackling-social-isolation-loneliness-building-stronger-social-connections/.

Scottish Science Advisory Council (SSAC) (2018) *Reaction to the UK Government Office for Science Foresight Report 'Future of an Ageing Population'.*

Streek, W. (2014) How Will Capitalism End?, *New Left Review*, **87** (May/June), 35–64.

Sutherland, J. (2016) *The War On The Old*, Biteback Publishing.

Taylor, C. and Donoghue, J. (2014) *Towards More Sustainable Community Organisations for Older People*, Working paper 114, Oxford Institute of Population Ageing.

Thomson, P. (2018) *A Silver Lining for the UK Economy? The intergenerational case for supporting longer working lives*, Centre for Ageing Better.

UN Department of Economic and Social Affairs (2017) *The World Population Prospects: the 2017 revision.*

UNESCO (2016) *Riga Recommendations on Media and Information Literacy in a Shifting Media and Information Landscape*, http://www.unesco.org/new/fileadmin/MULTIMEDIA/HQ/CI/CI/pdf/Events/riga_recommendations_on_media_and_information_literacy.pdf.

Webber, S. and Johnston, B. (2000) Conceptions of Information Literacy: new perspectives and implications, *Journal of Information Science*, **26** (6), 381–97.

Webber, S. and Johnston, B. (2013) Transforming Information Literacy for Higher Education in the 21st century: a lifelong learning approach. In Hepworth, M. and Walton, G. (eds) *Developing People's Information Capabilities: fostering information literacy in educational, workplace and community contexts*, Emerald.

Webber, S. and Johnston, B. (2017) Information Literacy: conceptions, context and the formation of a discipline, *Journal of Information Literacy*, **11** (1), 156–83, http://dx.doi.org/10.11645/11.1.2205.

West, S. (2015) *Later Life in a Digital World*, Age UK.

Wilson, T. (2010) Fifty Years of Information Behaviour Research, *Bulletin of the Association for Information Science and Technology*, **36** (3), 27–34, https://doi.org/10.1002/bult.2010.1720360308.

Zimmer, Z. and McDaniel, S. A. (eds) (2013) *Global Ageing in the Twenty-First Century: challenges, opportunities and implications*, Routledge.

Index